THERE WILL BE

WAR

VOLUME IV

THERE WILL BE WAR

WAR

VOLUME IV

CREATED BY
JERRY POURNELLE

ASSOCIATE EDITOR
JOHN F. CARR

CASTALIA HOUSE

There Will Be War Vol. IV

Copyright © 2015 by Jerry Pournelle
All rights reserved

Associate Editor: John F. Carr
Cover Art: Lars Braad Andersen

Published by Castalia House
Switzerland
www.castaliahouse.com

ISBN: 978-952-7303 18-4

The stories and articles were first published and copyrighted as follows:

SIC SEMPER TYRANNIS by Jerry Pournelle was written especially for the 1985 edition. Published by arrangement with the author and the author's agent, Blassingame, McCauley, and Wood. Copyright © 1985 by J.E. Pournelle

MACDONOUGH'S SONG by Rudyard Kipling is in the public domain.

THE CLOAK AND THE STAFF by Gordon R. Dickson was previously published in *Analog* in the August 1980 issue. It is presented by special arrangement with the author. Copyright © 1980 by Conde Nast Publications, Inc.

WINTER SNOW by Eric Vinicoff and Marcia Martin first appeared in the November 1984 *Analog*. Published by special arrangement with the authors. Copyright © 1984 by Davis Publications.

A WAY OUT MAYBE... OR A DEAD END FOR SURE was written especially for this volume by John Brunner. Published by arrangement with the author and his agent, Paul R. Reynolds. Copyright © 1985 by Brunner Fact & Fiction Limited.

A LETTER FROM THE SOVIETS by Alexander Shatravka is in the public domain.

EMERGENCY RATIONS by Theodore R. Cogswell is published by permission of the author. Copyright © 1953 by Greenleaf Publishing Company.

THE PROUD FOOT OF THE CONQUEROR by Reginald Bretnor was published by arrangement with the author. Copyright © 1985 by Reginald Bretnor.

CONTENTS

INTRODUCTION:
SIC SEMPER TYRANNIS

If a nation expects to be ignorant and free, in a state of civilization, it expects what never was and never will be.

—Thomas Jefferson

The Greeks said *tyrannos*, a word that originally meant no more than "master." But free men cannot endure masters, and "Tyrant" soon took on other meanings, until the very name was hateful. When he struck down Abraham Lincoln, John Wilkes Booth shouted *"Sic semper Tyrannis!"*—Thus be it ever with tyrants!—as full and complete justification for his act, and indeed it would have been so had his fellow citizens accepted that Lincoln was no more than a tyrant. Learned authorities, of religion and morality alike, have proclaimed that tyrannicide is not murder.

Booth's act did bring forth real claimants to mastership, men who would be tyrants over part of the land if not all of it, but our institutions were too strong for them. The Constitution and the Union stood and endured. Indeed, the very times were fair for democracy and freedom, here and throughout the world. The tyrannical misrule of Ferdinand of Naples, universally regarded as the worst despot of Europe—his own people called him "King Bomba"—ended in the same decade as our civil war. A Republic was established in France. Greece was freed from the Turks.

Germany received a constitution, as did Austria. Electoral reforms swept through Britain. Civilization and freedom were on the rise–

The dream ended in The Great War of 1914. The history of the twentieth century is the story of the rise and fall of tyrants. Rather more have risen than have fallen. First Russia, then Italy, Germany, Poland, Spain, all fell under the rule of masters.

* New wars began. The Great War was "the war to end war"; its 1938 continuation became "the war to make the world safe for democracy." At enormous cost Italy, part of Germany, and most of western Europe were rescued; but Czechoslovakia, Latvia, Lithuania, Estonia, Bulgaria, Rumania, Poland—for whose independence the war had begun in the first place—and all the Russias were abandoned to Stalin, whose personal power would have been envied by the most despotic of the Roman Emperors.

When Stalin died the world hoped for change. It was not to come. For a few years it looked as if the Soviet Empire would mellow. There was even talk of detente with the West. Now, alas, we find the changes were illusory. Yellow Rain falls on the primitive people of Laos and the hardy mujahideen of Afghanistan. At Sverdlovsk, old Ekaterinberg, city of doom for the Tsar and his family, an explosion in a military laboratory spread anthrax—black death—across the land. Thousands died. Now there is chilling evidence that the Soviet Empire has gone beyond Yellow Rain: are experimenting with gene mechanics and cobra venom to produce new biological terrors.

Despotism spread from continent to continent. Nearly all the peoples of Africa were abandoned to Bhogassa, Nkrumeh, Idi Amin Dada, Kenyatta, and their ilk. Things are no better in Asia. Javanese imperialism rules the former Dutch colonies. Viet Nam, Cambodia, Laos, Burma, China—the list is nearly endless.

Far from a century of liberty, this has become a century of masters, and there is little relief in sight.

Why should this be? One may understand how one man might gain control of the new "nations" in Africa, or other lands with little or no experience in government; but how explain the constant rise and fall of the caudillos in South America? How to explain Hitler and Stalin?

Why should free citizens welcome a master? What is the attraction that tyrants hold?

It is not so difficult to see why nations might turn to a strong leader after a military disaster, or in times of civil war; but that is not the whole of it.

The sad truth is that democracy itself is often unstable. Intellectuals lose faith. Democracy is not flashy. It falls out of fashion. The intelligentsia feel scorned, unappreciated, and turn to new theories.

There are other pressures. Republics stand until the citizens begin to vote themselves largess from the public treasury. When the plunder begins, those plundered feel no loyalty to the nation—and the beneficiaries demand ever more, until few are left unplundered. Eventually everyone plunders everyone, the state serving as little more than an agency for collecting and dispensing largess. The economy falters. Inflation begins. Deficits mount. Something must be done. Strong measures are demanded, but nothing can be agreed to.

In Weimar Germany the price of a postage stamp went to 8 billion marks. In China, Latin America, many of the new African nations, inflation has exceeded 1,000 percent. The middle class is destroyed. The economy collapses. Democratic institutions cannot cope.

Enter the strong man, who will save the state.

For more than two thousand years the decline of democracy has been the precursor of the tyrant, who comes on stage as the nation's protector. Sometimes he will do no more than end the strife: better a single master than hundreds who cannot agree. Julius Caesar was such a one, Francisco Franco another. They promise no more than order. They do not seek to reconstruct the nation, and they do not construct a full fledged totalitarian state. So long as their rule is not opposed, so long as the people are silent, then most are safe.

Nations could do worse than adopt King Log. Even John Stuart Mill said that a degenerate people, unfit to rule themselves, should think themselves fortunate to have a Charlemagne or an Akbar.

There are other masters; masters who will do more than hold fast to the old ways; they will usher in a new era. The theorists proclaim it. Times have changed. Old institutions, devised in simpler times, are outmoded. Modern times demand modern, streamlined, efficient government; government that can sweep away the dead hand of the past, and bring forth the new dawn.

A new friend of the people comes forth. He will end the babble of political parties and factions and class war. He will give meaning to life; will lead a crusade against poverty, squalor, ugliness; will transform the nation into a land beautiful and shining. He will be the Hero, of whom Carlyle said:

> His place is with the stars of heaven. He walks among men; loves men, with inexpressible soft pity—as they cannot love him: but his soul dwells in solitude, in the innermost parts of creation. Thou, O World, how wilt thou secure thyself from this man? He is thy born king, thy conqueror and supreme lawgiver: not all the guineas and cannons under the sky can save thee from him.

Hitler was hailed as a semi-mystical hero who would purify Germany; and Carlyle was quoted to good effect in praising him. Yet, surely, we, in this nation, and in this century, are above such mystical twaddle? Perhaps. Yet...

In 1929, on his fiftieth birthday, Stalin was hailed as: the greatest military leader of all times and nations; Lenin's Perpetuator in Creating the Theory of Construction of Socialism; The Theoretician and Leader of the Fight for Peace and Brotherhood among the Peoples; the Military Genius of Our Time; Mirrored in the Literature of the Peoples of the World; Teacher and Inspired Leader of the World Proletariat; Coryphaeus of World Science; The People's Happiness; Brilliant Thinker and Scholar. The praise for Great Stalin gushed forth, and not merely in the Soviet Union. Western intellectuals seemed equally eager to heap praises on the dictator who was transforming Russia into a modern nation. The era of social engineering was at hand.

By 1938 Stalin had murdered more than 12 million people, nor was this any great secret. The full horror was still hidden, but it was impossible to hide it all. The evidence was there, but Western intellectuals refused to look. Even when Stalin formed a pact with Hitler, giving him access to still more victims, a hard core of intellectuals continued to give him allegiance. Why should they not? They had already accepted the worst.

Alexander Solzhenitsyn describes the horrors of the slave gangs constructing the White Sea Canal; Sidney and Beatrice Webb, Professor Harold Laski, and many others lauded this great "engineering feat." George Bernard Shaw applauded the Soviet "experiments" in penology and reformation of criminals.

In the midst of the Great Purges in the Soviet Union, the American ambassador, Joseph E. Davies, reported that Stalin had "insisted on the liberalization of the constitution" and was "projecting actual secret and universal suffrage." Western intellectuals found democracy tiresome. They wanted to believe that society could be transformed; that the Soviet Union was a model for the future. Had not Lincoln Steffans, "America's philosopher," said it? "I have been over into the future, and it works."

Self-deception never ends.

The truth is that no nation is safe. Tyrants seldom come openly, their hands dripping with blood, their eyes blazing with hate. More often they come as friends of the people; tireless workers for the public good, heroes who will save the nation; who will cut the Gordian knot of parliamentary babble; who will carry out the people's will.

They come with promises. If we will disarm ourselves, they will provide professionals to protect us. If we give over our property they will assure us jobs. Crime will be abolished. Poverty will vanish. Together we will build a nation worthy of the future.

The temptation is large, because we all, at one time or another, have longed to have an end to striving; to create the future and have done with it. Can we not, by one supreme act, solve all human problems? The way will be hard, but after heroic effort the struggle will be over.

War on poverty; war on ignorance; war on illness; war on cancer, mental illness; one supreme act of war, and then eternal triumph. The strife will cease...

We know better, of course. We all know the price of liberty: eternal vigilance. Jefferson said it well: "the tree of liberty is a delicate plant. It must be refreshed from time to time with the blood of patriots and tyrants. It is its natural manure."

Macdonough's Song

by Rudyard Kipling

Editor's Introduction

*Sometimes it is said that man cannot be entrusted with the govern-
ment of himself. Can he, then, be trusted with the government of
others? Or have we found angels in the form of kings to govern him?
Let history answer this question. I know no safe depository of the
ultimate powers of the society but the people themselves; and if we
think them not enlightened enough to exercise their control with a
wholesome discretion, the remedy is not to take it from them, but to
inform their discretion.*

—Thomas Jefferson

The Athenians had a constitution; but on one terrible day they, in
solemn assembly, declared it monstrous that they should not do whatever they willed. By a strange irony of fate, Socrates was chairman of the
assembly of the people on that day; he refused to allow the vote. The
next day, the Athenians abrogated their constitution, and voted to put
their generals to death without trial. Not long after, they condemned
Socrates.

It is the ultimate dilemma: how shall the people be protected from
themselves?

The tyrant comes in many guises, but always with the same promises. "Give me the sword of state, and I will make a beautiful world. Laws are dry and sterile things, a hamper to our great design. Trust me; and I will truly do the will of the people."

Kipling knew the answer to that.

Whether the State can loose and bind
    In Heaven as well as on Earth:
If it be wiser to kill mankind
    Before or after the birth—
These are matters of high concern
    Where State-kept schoolmen are;
But Holy State (we have lived to learn)
    Endeth in Holy War.

Whether The People be led by The Lord,
    Or lured by the loudest throat;
If it be quicker to die by the sword
    Or cheaper to die by the vote—
These are things we have dealt with once,
    (And they will not rise from their grave)
For Holy People, however it runs,
    Endeth in wholly Slave.

What so ever, for any cause,
    Seeketh to take or give
Power above or beyond the Laws,
    Suffer it not to live!
Holy State or Holy King—
    Or Holy People's Will
Have no truck with the senseless thing.
    Order the guns and kill!

Saying—after—me:—

Once there was The People—Terror gave it birth;
Once there was The People and it made a Hell of Earth.
Earth arose and crushed it. Listen, O ye slain!
Once there was The People—it shall never be again!

THE CLOAK AND THE STAFF

by Gordon R. Dickson

Editor's Introduction

For nearly a score of years Gordon Dickson has been creating his "Childe Cycle": a series of novels chronicling the development of man from 1500 A.D. to the far future. *The Final Encyclopedia* (Tor Books, 1984) was the latest in this amazing series.

This isn't all that Gordy has been doing. Slowly and steadily he has been creating a new saga of the Aalaag and The Pilgrim.

The Aalaag are incredibly powerful: physically large, and skilled in technologies nearly beyond the reach of human imagination. In one swift and easy stroke they invaded and conquered Earth. The military forces of humanity were swept away like tin soldiers. The conquest was done almost as soon as it was begun.

The occupation began. Humans were left no means for resistance. All weapons were confiscated, and were useless against the Aalaag in any event. Even metals were restricted or forbidden. The Aalaag victory was complete. The tyrants reigned supreme.

Earth was neither the first nor the last planet to be incorporated into the Aalaag empire. The invaders seemed as skilled in the art of governing as they were in subduing mankind in the first place; and they quickly built a web of government, relying for the most part on their own people. Humans had as little contact with them as possible.

A few humans, though, worked directly for the Aalaag. Despised by their masters as well as their own kind, they suppressed all feelings of defiance. They of all people knew how futile resistance would be…

Descending in the icy, gray November dawn from the crowded bus that had brought the airline passengers over the mountains from Bologna—as frequently happened in wintertime, the airport at Milan, Italy, was fogged in; and the courier ship, like the commercial jets, had been forced to set down in Bologna—Shane Evert caught a glimpse out of the corner of his eye of a small stick-figure, inconspicuously etched on the base of a lamp post.

He did not dare to look at it directly; but the side glance was enough. He flagged a taxi and gave the driver the address of the Aalaag Guard Headquarters for the city.

"*E freddo, Milano,*" said the driver, wheeling the cab through the nearly deserted morning streets.

Shane gave him a monosyllable in a Swiss accent by way of agreement. Milan was indeed cold in November. Cold and hard. To the south, Florence would be still soft and warm, with blue skies and sunlight. The driver was probably hoping to start a conversation and find out what brought his human passenger to an alien HQ, and that was dangerous. Ordinary humans did not love those who worked for the Aalaag. If I say nothing, Shane thought, he may be suspicious. No, on second thought, he'll just think from the Swiss accent that I'm someone who has a relative in trouble in this city and doesn't feel like conversation.

The driver spoke of the summer now past. He regretted the old days when tourists had come through.

To both these statements Shane gave the briefest responses. Then there was silence in the cab except for the noise of travel. Shane leaned his staff at a more comfortable angle against his right leg and left shoulder to better accommodate it to the small passenger compartment of the cab. He smoothed his brown robe over his knees. The image of the stick-figure he had seen still floated in his mind. It was identical with the figure he himself had first marked upon a wall beneath the triple hooks with the dead man on them, in Aalborg, Denmark, over half-a-year ago.

But he had not marked this one on the lamp post. Nor, indeed, had he marked any of the other such figures he had glimpsed about the world during the last eight months. One moment of emotional rebellion had driven him to create an image that was now apparently spawning and multiplying to fill his waking as well as his sleeping hours with recurring nightmares. It did no good to remind himself that no one could possibly connect him with the original graffito. It did no good to know that all these eight months since, he had been an impeccable servant of Lyt Ahn.

Neither fact would be of the slightest help if for some reason Lyt Ahn, or any other Aalaag, should believe there was cause to connect him with any one of the scratched figures.

What insane, egocentric impulse had pushed him to use his own usual pilgrim-sect disguise as the symbol of opposition to the aliens? Any other shape would have done as well. But he had had the alcohol of the Danish bootleg aquavit inside him; and with the memory of the massive Aalaag father and son in the square, watching the death of the man they had condemned and executed—above all, with the memory of their conversation, which he alone of all the humans there could understand—also burning in him, for one brief moment reason had flown out the window of his mind.

So, now his symbol had been taken up and become the symbol of what was obviously an already-existent human underground in opposition to the Aalaag, an underground he had never suspected. The very fact that it existed at all forecast bloody tragedy for any human foolish enough to be related to it. By their own standards, the Aalaag were unsparingly fair. But they considered humans as "cattle"; and a cattle owner did not think in terms of being "fair" to a sick or potentially dangerous bull that had become a farm problem...

"*Eccolo!*" said the cab driver.

Shane looked as bidden and saw the alien HQ. A perfectly reflective force shield covered it like a coating of mercury. It was impossible to tell what kind of structure it had been originally. Anything from an office building to a museum was a possibility. Lyt Ahn, First Captain of Earth, in his HQ overlooking St. Anthony's falls in what had once been the heart of Minneapolis, scorned such an obvious display of defensive strength. The gray concrete walls of his sprawling keep on Nicollet Island had nothing to protect them but the portable weapons within; though these alone were capable of leveling the metropolitan area surrounding in a handful of hours. Shane paid the driver, got out and went in through the main entrance of the Milan HQ.

The Ordinary Guards inside the big double doors and those on the desk were all human. Young for the most part, like Shane himself, but much bigger; for the largest of humans seemed frail and small to the eight-foot Aalaag. These guards wore the usual neat, but drab, black uniforms of servant police. Dwarfed among them, in spite of his five feet eleven inches of height, Shane felt a twinge of perverse comfort at being within these walls and surrounded by these particular fellow humans. Like him, they ate at the aliens' tables; they would be committed to defend him against any non-servant humans who should threaten him. Under the roof of masters who sickened him, he was physically protected and secure.

He stopped at the duty desk and took his key from the leather pouch at his belt, leaving the documents within. The human duty officer there took the key and examined it. It was made of metal—metal which no ordinary Earth native was allowed to own or carry—and the mark of Lyt Ahn was stamped on the square handle.

"Sir," said the officer in Italian, reading the mark. He was suddenly obliging. "Can I be of assistance?"

"I sign in, temporarily," answered Shane in Arabic, for the officer's speech echoed the influence of the throat consonants of that language. "I am the one who delivers messages for the First Captain of Earth,

Lyt Ann. I have some to deliver now to the Commander of these Headquarters."

"Your tongue is skilled," said the officer in Arabic, turning the duty book about and passing Shane a pen.

"Yes," said Shane and signed.

"The Commander here," said the officer, "is Laa Ehon, Captain of the sixth rank. He accepts your messages."

He turned and beckoned over one of the lesser human guards.

"To the outer office of Laa Ehon, with this one bearing messages for the Commander."

The guard saluted and led Shane off. Several flights of stairs up beside an elevator, which Shane would have known better than to use even if the guard had not been with him, brought them to a corridor down which, behind another pair of large, carved doors, they reached what was plainly an outer room of the private offices of the Aalaag Commander in Milan.

The guard saluted and left. There were no other humans in the room. An Aalaag of the twenty-second rank sat at a desk in a far corner of the large, open space, reading what seemed to be reports on the sort of plastic sheets that would take and hold multiple overlays of impressions. In the wall to Shane's left was a window, showing the slight corner shading that betrayed an Aalaag version of one-way glass. The window gave a view of what must be an adjoining office having benches for humans to sit on. This office was empty, however, except for a blonde-haired young woman, dressed in a loose, ankle-length blue robe tied tight around her narrow waist.

There was no place for Shane to sit. But, in close attendance as he customarily was on Lyt Ahn and other Aalaag of low-number rank, he was used to waiting on his feet for hours.

He stood. After perhaps twenty minutes, the Aalaag at the desk noticed him.

"Come," he said, lifting a thumb the size of a tent peg. "Tell me."

He had spoken in Aalaag for most human servants had some understanding of the basic commands in the tongue of their overlords.

But his face altered slightly as Shane answered; for there were few humans like Shane—and Shane both worked and lived with all of those few—who were capable of fluent, accentless response in that language.

"Untarnished sir," said Shane, coming up to the desk and stopping before it. "I have messages from Lyt Ahn directly to the Commander of the Milan Headquarters."

He made no move to produce the message rolls from his pouch; and the Aalaag's massive hand, which had begun to extend itself, palm up, toward him at the word "messages," was withdrawn when Shane pronounced the name of Lyt Ahn.

"You are a valuable beast," said the Aalaag. "Laa Ehon will receive your messages soon."

"Soon" could mean anything from "within minutes" to "within weeks." However, since the messages were from Lyt Ahn, and personal, it was probable that it would be minutes rather than a longer time. Shane went back to his corner.

The door opened and two other Aalaag came in. They were both males in middle life, one of the twelfth, one of the sixth rank. The one of sixth rank could only be Laa Ehon. A Captain of a rank that low-numbered was actually too highly qualified to command a single HQ like this. It was unthinkable that there would be two such here.

The newcomers ignored Shane. No, he thought, as their gaze moved on, they had not merely ignored him. Their eyes had noticed, catalogued, and dismissed him in a glance.

They walked together to the one-way window, and the one who must be Laa Ehon spoke in Aalaag.

"This one?"

They were examining the girl in the blue robe, who sat unaware of their gaze in the other room.

"Yes, untarnished sir. The officer on duty in the square saw this one move away from the wall I told you of just before he noticed the scratching on it." The Captain of the twelfth rank pointed with his thumb at the girl. "He then examined the scratching, saw it was recently made and turned to find this one. For a moment he thought she had been lost among the herd in the square, then he caught sight of her from the back, some distance off and hurrying away. He stunned her and brought her in."

"His rank?"

"Thirty-second, untarnished sir."

"And this one has been questioned?"

"No, sir, I waited to speak to you about procedure."

Laa Ehon stood for a moment, unanswering, gazing at the girl.

"Thirty-second, you said? Did he know this particular beast previous to seeing her in the square?"

"No, sir. But he remembered the color of her apparel. There was no other in that color nearby."

Laa Ehon turned from the window.

"I'd like to talk to him first. Send him to me."

"Sir, he's presently on duty."

"Ah."

Shane understood Laa Ehon's momentary thoughtfulness. As commanding officer, he could easily order the officer in question to be relieved from duty long enough to report to him in person. But the Aalaag nature and custom were such that only the gravest reason would allow him to justify such an order. An Aalaag on duty, regardless of rank, was almost a sacred object.

"Where?" Laa Ehon asked.

"The local airport, untarnished sir."

"I will go and speak to him at his duty post. Captain Otah On, you are ordered to accompany me."

"Yes, untarnished sir."

"Then let us move with minimal loss of time. It is unlikely that this matter has more importance than presently seems, but we must make sure of that."

He turned toward the door with Otah On behind him. Once more his eyes swept Shane. He stopped and looked over at the Aalaag.

"What is this one?" he asked.

"Sir," the Aalaag at the desk was on his feet. "A courier with messages for your hand from Lyt Ann."

Laa Ehon looked back at Shane.

"I will accept your messages in an hour, no more, once I've come back. Do you understand what I have just said to you?"

"I understand, untarnished sir," said Shane.

"Until then, remain dutiful. But be comfortable."

Laa Ehon led the way out of the room, Otah On close behind him. The Aalaag at the desk sat down again and went back to his sheets.

Shane looked once more at the girl beyond the one-way glass. She sat, unaware of what another hour would bring. They would question her with chemicals, of course, first. But after that, their methods would become physical. There was no sadism in the Aalaag character. If any of the aliens had shown evidence of such, his own people would have considered it an unfitting weakness and destroyed him for having it. But it was understood that cattle might be induced to tell whatever they knew if they were subjected to sufficient discomfort. Any Aalaag, of course, was above any such persuasion. Death would come long before any degree of discomfort could change the individual alien's character enough to make him or her say what he or she wished to keep unsaid.

Shane felt his robe clinging to his upper body, wet with a secret sweat. The woman sat almost in profile, her blonde hair down to her shoulders, her surprisingly pale-skinned (for this latitude) face smooth and gentle-looking. She could not be more than barely into her twenties. He wanted to look away from her so that he could stop thinking about what was awaiting her, but—as it had happened to him a year ago with the man on the triple hooks when he had first created the symbol—Shane could not make his head turn. He knew it now for what it was—a madness in him. A madness born of his own hidden revulsion against and private terror of these massive humanoids who had descended to own the Earth. These were the masters he served, who kept him warm and well-fed when most of the rest of humanity was chilled and ate little, who patted him with condescending compliments—as if he was in fact the animal they called him, the clever house pet ready to wag his tail for a kind glance or word. The fear of death was like an ingot of cold iron inside him when he thought of them; and the fear of a long and painful death was like that same ingot with razor edges. But at the same time, there was this madness—this madness that, if he did not control it by some small actions, would explode and bring him to throw his dispatches in some Aalaag face, to fling himself one day like a terrier against a tiger at the throat of his Master, First Captain of Earth, Lyt Ahn.

It was a real thing, that madness. Even the Aalaag knew of its existence in their conquered peoples. There was even a word for it in their own tongue—yowaragh. Yowaragh had caused the man on the hooks a year ago to make a hopeless attempt to defend his wife against what he had thought was an Aalaag brutality. Yowaragh, every day, caused at least one human somewhere in the world to fling a useless stick or stone against some shielded, untouchable conqueror in a situation where escape was impossible and destruction was certain. Yowaragh had knocked at the door of Shane's brain once, a year ago, threatening to break out. It was knocking again.

He could not help but look at her; and he could not bear to look at her—and the only alternative to an end for both of them was to somehow keep it from happening—Laa Ehon's return, the torture of the girl, and the yowaragh that would lead to his own death.

In one hour, Laa Ehon had said, he would be back. Rivulets of perspiration were trickling down Shane's naked sides under the robe. His mind had gone into high gear, racing like an uncontrolled heartbeat. What way out was there? There must be one—if he could think of it. The other side of the coin to what they would do to the girl was built on the same lack of sadism. The Aalaag would destroy property only for some purpose. If there was no purpose, they would not waste a useful beast. They would have no emotional stake in keeping her merely because she had been arrested in the first place. She was too insignificant; they were too pragmatic.

His mind was feverish. He was not sure what he planned, but all his intimate knowledge of the Aalaag in the three years he had lived closely with them was simmering and bubbling in the back of his mind. He went and stood before the Aalaag at the desk.

"Yes?" said the Aalaag after a little while, looking up at him.

"Untarnished sir, the Captain Commander said that he would be back in an hour to accept my messages and until then I should be dutiful but comfortable."

Eyes with gray-black pupils gazed at him on a level with his own.

"You want comfort, is that it?"

"Untarnished sir, if I could sit or lie, it would be appreciated."

"Yes. Very well. The Commander has so ordered. Go find what facilities there are for such activities in the areas of our own cattle. Return in an hour."

"I am grateful to the untarnished sir."

The gray-black pupils were cast into shadow by the jet brows coming together.

"This is a matter of orders. I am not one who allows his beasts to fawn."

"Sir, I obey."

The brows relaxed.

"Better. Go."

He went out. He was moving swiftly now. As when before, in Denmark, he was at last caught up in what he was doing, there was no longer any doubt, any hesitation. He went swiftly down the outside corridor, which was deserted, ears and eyes alert for sign of anyone, but particularly for one of the aliens. As he passed the elevators, he stopped, looked about him.

There was no one watching; and once aboard the elevator, he would be able to go from this floor down to street level or below without being seen. There would be other doors to the outside than the one by which he had come in; and on other levels, sub-main floor levels, he could possibly find them. There would be portals used only by the Aalaag themselves and their most trusted servants, and they would be free to come and go without being noticed.

He punched for the elevator. After a moment it came. The door swung wide. As it opened, he turned away and readied himself to pretend—in case there was an Aalaag aboard—that he was merely passing by. But the elevator compartment was empty.

He stepped inside. The only danger remaining for him now was that some other Aalaag on a floor below would have just punched for this elevator. If it stopped for one of the aliens and the door opened to reveal him inside, he would be trapped—doubly guilty, for being where he should not be and also for being absent from his duty, which at the present was to lie down or otherwise relax. Only Aalaag were permitted to use elevators.

For a moment he thought the one in which he was descending was going to hesitate on the first floor. In the back of his mind, plans flickered like heat lightning on a summer evening. If it did stop, if the door did open and an Aalaag walked in, he planned to throw himself at the alien's throat. Hopefully, the other would kill him out of reflex, and he would escape being held for questioning as to why he was where he was.

But the elevator did not stop. It continued moving downward, and the telltale light illuminating the floor numbers as they passed showed it was approaching the floor just below street level. Shane punched for the cage to stop. It did, the door opened and he stepped into a small, square corridor leading directly to a glass door and a flight of steps beyond, leading upward. He had hit on one of the aliens' ways out of the building.

He left the elevator and went quickly along the corridor to the door. It was locked, of course; but in his pocket he carried the key of Lyt Ahn, or at least the key that all the special human servants of Lyt Ahn were allowed to bear. It would open any ordinary door in a building belonging to the aliens.

He tried the key now, and it worked. The door swung noiselessly open. A second later he was out of it, up the stairs and into the street above.

He went down the street, walking at a pace just short of a run, and turned right at the first crossing, searching for a market area. Four blocks on, he found a large square with many shops. A single Aalaag sat on his riding animal, towering and indifferent to the crowd about him, before a set of pillars upholding a sidewalk arcade at one end of the square. Whether the alien was on duty or simply waiting for something or someone, it was impossible to tell. But for Shane, now, to use a shop on this square would not be wise.

He hurried on. A few streets farther on, he found a smaller collection of shops lining both sides of a blind alley, and one of these was a store for such simple clothing as the Aalaag allowed humans to use nowadays. He stepped inside and a small bell over the door chimed softly.

"Signore?" said a voice.

Shane's eyes adjusted to the interior dimness and saw a counter piled high with folded clothing and with a short, dark-faced man with a knife-blade nose behind it. Remarkably, in these days of alien occupation, the proprietor had a small potbelly under his loose yellow smock.

"I want a full-length robe," Shane said. "Reversible."

"Of course." The proprietor began to come around the counter. "What type?"

"How much is your most expensive garment?"

"Seventy-five new lire or equivalent in trade, signore."

Shane dug into the purse hanging from the rope around his waist and threw on the counter before him metal coins issued by the Aalaag for use as an international currency—the gold and silver rectangles with which his work as an employee of Lyt Ahn was rewarded.

The store owner checked his movement. His eyes moved to the coins, then back to Shane's face with difference. Only humans of great power under the alien authority, or those engaged in the illegal black market, would ordinarily have such coins with which to pay their bills; and it would be seldom that such would come into a small shop like this.

He moved toward the coins. Shane covered them with his hand.

"I'll pick the robe out myself," he said. "Show me your stock."

"But of course, of course, signore." The proprietor went past the coins and out from behind the counter. He opened a door to a back room and invited Shane in. Within, were tables stacked with clothing and cloth. In one corner, under a kerosene lamp, was a tailor's worktable with scraps of cloth, tools, thread, and some pieces of blue or white chalk.

"Here are the robes, on these two tables," he said.

"Good," said Shane harshly. "Go over to the corner there and turn around. I'll pick out what I want."

The man moved swiftly, his shoulders hunched a little. If his visitor was black market, it would be unwise to argue with or irritate him.

Shane located the reversible robes among the others and pawed through them, selecting the largest one he could find that was blue on one side. The other side of it was brown. He pulled it on over his own robe, the blue side out, and drew the drawstring tight at the waist. Stepping across to the worktable, he picked up a fragment of the white chalk. "I'll leave a hundred lire on the counter," he said to the back of the proprietor. "Don't turn around, don't come out until I've been gone for five minutes. You understand?"

"I understand."

Shane turned and went. He glanced at the counter as he passed. He had snatched coins from his purse at random and there was the equivalent of over a hundred and fifty lire in gold and silver on the counter. It would not do to make the incident look any more important to the storeman than was necessary. Shane scooped up fifty lire-equivalent and went out the door, heading back toward the square where he had seen the mounted Aalaag.

He was very conscious of the quick sliding by of time. He could not afford to be missing from the Headquarters more than the hour the officer on duty had allowed him. If the Aalaag had left the square...

But he had not. When Shane, sweating, once more emerged into the square, the massive figure still sat unmoved, as indifferent as ever.

Shane, because of his duties, was allowed to carry one of the Aalaag's perpetual timepieces. It lay in his purse now, but he dared not consult it to see how much time remained. A glimpse of it by the ordinary humans around would identify him as a servant of the aliens and win him the bitter enmity of these others; and that enmity, here and now, could be fatal.

He went quickly through the crowd swarming the square. As he got close to the Aalaag on the riding animal, the adrenaline-born courage inside him almost failed. But a memory of the prisoner back at the Headquarters rose in him, and he pushed himself on.

Deliberately, he made himself blunder directly beneath the heavy head of the riding animal so that it jerked its nose up. Its movement was slight—only an inch or two—but it was enough to draw the attention of the Aalaag. His eyes dropped to see Shane.

Still moving, Shane kept his head down. He had pulled his hair down on his forehead as far as possible to hide his face from the alien's view—but it was not really that he was counting on preserving his anonymity. Few Aalaag could tell one human from another—even after two years of close contact, Lyt Ahn recognized Shane from the other courier-interpreters more by the times on which Shane reported than by any physical individualities.

Shane scuttled past; and the alien, indifferent to something as mere as a single one of the cattle about him, raised his eyes to infinity again, returning to his thoughts. Shane went on for only a few more steps, to the nearest pillar, and stopped. There, hiding his actions with his body from the alien behind him, he pulled the tailor's white chalk from his pouch and with a hand that trembled, sketched on the stone of the pillar the cloaked figure with its staff.

He stepped back—and the sudden, almost inaudible moan of recognition and arrested movement in the crowd behind him drew—as he had known it would—the attention of the Aalaag. Instantly the alien wheeled his animal about, reaching for the same sort of stunning weapon with which the woman prisoner had been captured.

But Shane was already moving. He ran into the crowd, threw himself down so that the bodies about would shield him from the view of the Aalaag, and rolled, frantically pulling off the outer, reversible robe.

Instinctively, defensively, the other humans closed about him, hiding him from the alien, who was now—weapon in one massive hand—searching their numbers to locate him. The reversible robe stuck and bound itself under his armpits, but at last Shane got it off. Leaving it on the ground behind him, still with its blue side out, he scuttled on hands and knees farther off until, at last near the edge of the square, he risked getting to his feet and leaving it as quickly as he could without drawing attention to himself.

Panting, soaked with sweat, leaving behind humans who studiously avoided looking at him and beginning to move now among others who looked at him with entirely normal interest, Shane half-ran toward the Aalaag Headquarters. Subjectively, it seemed as if at least an hour had passed since he had first stepped under the nose of the Aalaag riding animal; but reason told him that the whole business could not have taken more than a few minutes. He stopped at a fountain—bless Italy, he thought, for having fountains—to bathe his face, neck, and underarms. Officially, the Aalaag were indifferent to how their cattle stank; but in practice, they preferred those humans who were physically as much without odor as possible—though it never seemed to occur to them that they were as noisome in human noses as humans were in their own. But for Shane to return smelling strongly from what had theoretically been a rest period might attract interest to the period of time he had spent out of the office.

He let himself in with his key through the same door which had given him egress; and this time he took a stair, rather than the elevator, to the entrance level of the Headquarters. No one saw him emerge on the entrance level. He paused to check his timepiece and saw that he still had some twelve minutes of his hour.

He made use of that time by asking one of the Ordinary Guards where the rest facilities for cattle were, went to it, and retraced his steps from there to the office he had waited in before. Outside the office door, he discovered he had still four minutes left and stood where he was until he could enter at the exact moment on which he had been told to return.

The alien officer at the desk looked up as he came in, glanced at the clock face over the door and returned to his papers silently. Nonetheless, Shane felt the triumph of a minor point scored. Precise obedience was a mark in any human's favor in Aalaag eyes. He went back to the spot on which he had been standing before—and stood again.

It was nearly three-quarters of an hour later that the door opened and Laa Ehon, with Otah On, entered. With a subjected being's acuteness of observation, reinforced by the experience gained in his two years of close contact with aliens, Shane recognized both of the officers at once. They went directly to the one-way glass to stare at the human prisoner beyond, and Shane's heart sank in panic.

It was inconceivable that his actions in the square of an hour before should not have been reported by this time. But it looked as if the two senior officers were about to proceed with the young woman as if nothing had happened. Then Laa Ehon spoke.

"It is indeed the same color," the Headquarters Commander said. "There must be many of the cattle so dressed."

"Very true, untarnished sir," answered Otah On.

Laa Ehon studied the young woman for a moment longer.

"Was she at any time made aware of the specific reason for her being brought here?" he asked.

"Nothing has been told to her, untarnished sir."

"Yes," said Laa Ehon thoughtfully. "Well, then. It is a healthy young beast. There is no need to waste it. Let it go."

"It will be done."

Laa Ehon turned from the one-way glass and his eyes swept over the rest of the room, stopping on Shane. He walked forward to Shane.

"You were the beast with dispatches from Lyt Ahn?"

"Yes, untarnished sir," said Shane. "I have them here for you."

He produced them from his pouch and handed them into the large grasp of the Commander. Laa Ehon took them, unfolded and read them. He passed them to Otah On.

"Execute these."

"Yes, untarnished sir."

Otah On carried the dispatches over to the desk of the duty officer and spoke to him, handing him the papers. The eyes of Laa Ehon fastened on Shane with a glimmer of interest.

"You speak with great purity," said the Commander. "You are one of the First Captain's special group of beasts for speaking and carrying, are you not?"

"I am, untarnished sir."

"How long have you spoken the true language?"

"Two years of this world, untarnished sir."

Laa Ehon stood looking at him, and a trickle of perspiration crept coldly down Shane's spine under his robe.

"You are a beast worth having," said the Commander slowly. "I did not think one such as you could be brought to speak so clearly. How are you valued?"

Shane's breath caught silently in his throat. Existence was barely endurable as one of the favored human group that was the personal property of Earth's ruling alien. The madness he feared would come quickly if instead he should be trapped here, in this building, among the brutes that made up the Interior Guard.

"To the best of my knowledge, untarnished sir–" he dared not hesitate in his answer, "I am valued at half a possession of land–"

Otah On, who had just regained the side of his Commander, raised his black eyebrows at the voicing of this price; but Laa Ehon's face remained thoughtful.

"–and the favor of my master, Lyt Ahn," said Shane.

The thoughtfulness vanished from Laa Ehon's features. Shane's heart was pounding. It was true he had prefaced his answer with *to the best of my knowledge*, but in fact he had never officially been acquainted with the fact that part of his price involved the favor of his owner. What he knew himself to be valued at, half a possession of land— about forty miles square of what the Aalaag called "good country"—was an enormously high price in itself for any single human beast. It was roughly equivalent to what, in pre-Aalaag days, would have been the cost of a top-price, custom-made sports car, gold-plated and set with jewels. But Laa Ehon had looked ready to consider even that, it was not the first time Shane had been aware that he possessed the status of a sort of luxury toy. Only, this time, Shane had mentioned that his price included the favor of Lyt Ahn. "Favor" was a term that went beyond all price. It was a designation meaning that his master was personally interested in keeping him and that the price of any sale could include anything at all—but probably something Lyt Ahn would favor as least as much as what he was giving up. Such "favor," involved in a sale, could constitute in effect a blank check signed by the buyer, cashable at any time in the future for goods or actions by the seller, guaranteed under the unyielding obligation code of the Aalaag.

Shane had never been told he had Lyt Ahn's favor. He had only overheard Lyt Ahn once saying to his Chief of Staff that he must get around to extending his favor over all the beasts of that special group to which Shane belonged. If Laa Ehon should check with Lyt Ahn, and this had never been done, then Shane was doomed as an untrustworthy and lying beast. Even if the favor had been extended, Lyt Ahn might question how Shane had come to know of it.

And then, again, the First Captain, busy as he was with much more weighty affairs of Aalaag government, might simply conclude that he had mentioned it at some time to Shane and since forgotten the fact. Claiming it now was one of the daily gambles necessary to human daily existence in the midst of the aliens.

"Give him his receipt," said Laa Ehon.

Otah On passed Shane a receipt for the dispatches, made out a moment before by the duty officer. Shane put it in his pouch.

"You return directly to Lyt Ann?" Laa Ehon said.

"Yes, untarnished sir."

"My courtesies to the First Captain."

"I will deliver them."

"Then you may go."

Shane turned and left. As the door closed behind him, he drew a deep breath and went quickly to the stairs, then down to the entrance floor and the entrance itself.

"I'm returning to the residence of the First Captain," he told the officer of the Ordinary Guards in charge at the entrance. It was the same man with the Arabic influence noticeable in his spoken Italian. "Will you get me space on the necessary aircraft? I've priority, of course."

"It's already taken care of," said the officer. "You're to travel with one of the Masters on courier duty in a small military craft, leaving in two hours. Shall I order transportation to the airfield?"

"No," said Shane briefly. He did not have to give his reasons for his actions to this uniformed lackey. "I'll get myself there."

He thought he caught a hint of admiration in the officer's steady gaze. But then, if the other ever thought of walking the Milan streets alone, it would be in his regular uniform, which he was never permitted to discard. Someone like this officer would never be able to imagine the freedom of Shane in going about, ostensibly as one of them, among the ordinary humans of the city—nor could he imagine how necessary these few moments of illusory freedom were to Shane.

"Very well," said the officer. "The Master who will carry you is Enech Ajin. The Masters' desk at the air terminal will direct you to him when you get there."

"Thank you," said Shane.

"You are entirely welcome."

They had both picked up inevitably, Shane thought bitterly, the very courtesies and intonations of their owners…

He went out through the heavy, right-hand door of the pair that made up the entrance and down the steps. There were no taxis in sight—of course. No human without need to be there would hang around the alien Headquarters. He turned up the same street he had followed to find the square.

He had gone past no more than two corners when a taxi passed him, cruising slowly. He hailed it.

"To the airport," he said to the driver, looking at the thin, overcoated man behind the wheel as his fingers automatically opened the cab door. He stepped inside—and tripped over something on the floor as he got in.

The door slammed, the cab took off with a rush. He found himself held, pinioned by two men who had risen from crouching positions on the floor of the cab's back seat. They held him helpless and he felt something sharp against his throat.

He looked down and saw a so-called glass knife, actually a dagger made by a sliver of glass held between two bound-together halves of a wooden dagger. The glass formed the cutting edge and could be—as this one had been—sandpapered to razorlike sharpness.

"Lie still!" growled one of the men in Italian.

Shane lay still. He smelled the rank, old stink of dirty clothing from both of the two who held him tightly. The taxi whirled him away through unknown streets to an unguessable destination.

They rode for at least twenty minutes, though how much of this was necessary distance to reach their goal or how much was to mislead Shane in any attempt to estimate the length of the trip, was impossible to guess. At length the taxi turned, bumped over some very uneven pavement, and passed under the shadow of an arch. Then it stopped, and the two men hustled Shane out of the vehicle.

He had just a glimpse of a dark and not-too-clean courtyard surrounded by buildings before he was pushed up two steps, through a door and into a long, narrow corridor thick with ancient paint and cooking odors.

Shane was herded along the corridor, more numb than frightened. Inside him there was a feeling of something like fatalistic acceptance. He had lived for two years with the thought that someday ordinary humans would identify him as one of those who worked for the aliens; and when they did, they would then use him as an object for the bitter fear and hatred they all felt for their conquerors but dared not show directly. In his imagination, he had lived through this scene many times. It was nonetheless hideous now for finally having become real, but it was a situation on which his emotions had worn themselves out. At the end, it was almost a relief to have the days of his masquerade over, to be discovered for what he really was.

The two men stopped suddenly. Shane was shoved through a door on his right, into a room glaringly lit by a single powerful light bulb. The contrast from the shadowed courtyard outside, and the even dimmer hallway, made the sudden light blinding for a second. When his eyes adjusted, he saw that he was standing in front of a round table and that the room was large and high-ceilinged, with paint grimed by time on the walls and a single tall window which, however, had a blackout blind drawn tightly down over it. The cord from the light bulb ran not into the ceiling, but across the face of it, past a capped gas outlet, down the farther wall and to a bicycle generator. A young man with long black hair sat on the bicycle part of the generator and whenever the light from the ceiling bulb began to fade, he would pump energetically on his pedals until it brightened again and held its brightness.

There were several other men standing around the room, and two more at the table together with the only woman to be seen. She was, he recognized, the prisoner he had seen through the one-way glass. Her eyes met his now with the look of a complete stranger, and even in his numbness he felt strange that he should recognize her with such strong emotional identification and she should not know him at all.

"Where's that clothing-store owner?" said one of the men at the table with her, speaking to the room at large in a northern Italian underlaid with London English. He was young—as young in appearance as Shane himself but, unlike Shane, spare and athletic-looking, with a straight nose, strong square jaw, thin mouth and blond hair cut very short.

"Outside, in the supply room," said a voice speaking the same northern Italian but without accent.

"Get him in here then!" said the man with the short hair. The other man beside him at the table said nothing. He was round-bodied and hard-fat, in his forties, wearing a worn leather jacket with a short-stemmed pipe in one corner of the mouth of his round face. He looked entirely Italian.

The door opened and closed behind Shane. A minute later it opened and closed again, and a blindfolded man Shane recognized as the propri-

etor of the store where he had bought the reversible cloak was brought
forward and turned around to face Shane. His blindfold was jerked off.

"Well?" demanded the short-haired young man.

The shopkeeper blinked under the unshaded electric light. His eyes
focused on Shane, then slid away.

"What is it you want, signori?" he asked. His voice was almost a
whisper in the stark room.

"Didn't anyone tell you? Him!" said the short-haired man impatiently. "Look at him? Do you recognize him? Where did you see him
last?"

The store proprietor licked his lips and raised his eyes.

"Earlier today, signore," he said. "He came into my shop and bought
a reversible cloak, blue and brown—"

"This cloak?" The short-haired individual made a gesture. One of
the men standing in the back of the room came forward to shove a
bundled mass of cloth into the hands of the proprietor, who slowly
unfolded it and looked at it.

"This is mine," he said, still faintly. "Yes. This is the one he bought."

"All right, you can go then. Keep the cloak. You two—don't forget
to blindfold him." The short-haired man turned his attention to the
young man slouching on the bicycle seat of the electric generator. "How
about it, Carlo? Is he the one you followed?"

Carlo nodded. He had a toothpick in one corner of his mouth,
and through his numbness Shane watched him with an odd sort of
fascination, for the toothpick seemed to give him a rakish, infallible
look.

"He left the Square of San Marco and went straight back to the aliens'
HQ," Carlo said. "As fast as possible."

"That's it then," said the short-haired man. He looked at Shane.
"Well, do you want to tell us now what the Aalaag had you up to?
Or do we have to wait while Carlo works you over a bit?"

Suddenly Shane was weary to the point of sickness—weary of the
whole matter of human subjects and alien overlords. Unexpected fury
boiled up in him.

"You damn fool!" he shouted at the short-haired man. "I was saving *her*!"

And he pointed at the woman, who stared back at him, her gaze frowning and intent.

"You idiots!" Shane spat. "You stupid morons with your resistance games! Don't you know what they'd have done to her? Don't you know where you'd all be, right now, if I hadn't given them a reason to think it was someone else? How long do you think she could keep from telling them all about you? I'll tell you, because I've seen it—forty minutes is the average!"

They all looked at the woman, reflexively.

"He's lying," she said in a thin voice. "They didn't offer to do a thing to me. They just made me wait a while and then turned me loose for lack of evidence."

"They turned you loose because I gave them enough reason to doubt you were the one who made the mark!" The fury was carrying Shane away like a dark, inexorable tide. "They let you go because you're young and healthy and they don't waste valuable beasts without reason. Lack of evidence! Do you still think you're dealing with humans?"

"All right," said the short-haired man. His voice was hard and flat. "This is all very pretty, but suppose you tell us where you learned our mark."

"Learned it?" Shane laughed, a laugh that was close to a sob of long-throttled rage. "You clown! I invented it. Me—myself! I carved it on a brick wall in Aalborg, two years ago, for the first time. Learn about it! How did you learn about it? How did the Aalaag learn about it? By seeing it marked up in places, of course!"

There was a moment of silence in the room after Shane's voice ceased to ring out.

"He's crazy then," said the hard-fat man with the pipe.

"Crazy," echoed Shane and laughed again.

"Wait a minute," said the woman. She came around and faced him. "Who are you? What do you do with the Aalaag?"

"I'm a translator, a courier," said Shane. "I'm owned by Lyt Ahn—me and about thirty men and women like me."

"Maria–" began the short-haired man.

"Wait, Peter." She held up her hand briefly and went on without taking her eyes off Shane. "All right. You tell us what happened."

"I was delivering special communications to Laa Ehon—you know your local Commander, I suppose."

"We know Laa Ehon," said Peter harshly. "Keep talking."

"I had special communications to deliver. I looked through a one-way mirror and saw you–" he was looking at the woman named Maria. "I knew what they'd do to you. Laa Ehon was talking to one of his officers about you. All that had been spotted was some human wearing a blue robe. There was just a chance that if they had another report of a human in a blue robe making that mark, it would make them doubtful enough so they wouldn't want to waste a healthy young beast like you. So I ducked out and tried giving them that other report. It worked."

"Why did you do it?" She was looking penetratingly at him.

"Just a minute, Maria," said Peter. "Let me ask a few questions. What's your name, you?"

"Shane Everts."

"And you said you heard Laa Ehon talking to one of his officers. How did you happen to be there?"

"I was waiting to deliver my communications."

"And Laa Ehon just discussed it all in front of you—that's what you're trying to tell us?"

"They don't see us, or hear us, unless they want us," said Shane bitterly. "We're furniture—pets."

"So you say," said Peter. "What language did Laa Ehon speak in?"

"Aalaag, of course."

"And you understood him so well that you could tell there was a chance to make them think that the human they wanted was someone else than Maria?"

"I told you." A dull weariness was beginning to take Shane over as the fury died. "I'm a translator. I'm one of Lyt Ahn's special group of human translators."

"No human can really speak or understand the Aalaag tongue," said the man with the pipe, in Basque.

"Most can't," answered Shane, also in Basque. The weariness was beginning to numb him so that he was hardly aware of changing languages. "I tell you I'm one of a very special group belonging to Lyt Ann."

"What was that? What did he say, Georges?" Peter was looking from one to the other.

"He speaks Basque," said Georges, staring at Shane.

"How well?"

"Well…" Georges made an effort. "He speaks it… very well."

Peter turned on Shane. "How many languages do you speak?" he asked.

"How many?" Shane said dully. "I don't know. A hundred and fifty—two hundred, well. A lot of others, some–"

"And you speak Aalaag like an alien."

Shane laughed. "No," he said. "I speak it well—for a human."

"Also, you travel all over the world as a courier–" Peter turned to Maria and Georges. "Are you listening?"

Maria ignored him. "Why did you do it? Why did you try to rescue me?" She held him with her eyes.

There was a new silence.

"Yowaragh," he said dully.

"What?"

"It's their word for it," he said. "The Aalaag word for when a beast suddenly goes crazy and fights back against one of them. It was like that first time in Aalborg, when I snapped and put the pilgrim mark on the wall under the man they'd thrown on the hooks to execute him."

"You don't really expect us to believe you are the one who invented the symbol of resistance to the aliens."

"You can go to hell!" Shane told him in English.

"What did you say?" said Peter quickly.

"You know what I said," Shane told him savagely, still in English and in the exact accent of the London area in which the other had grown up. "I don't care whether you believe me or not. Just give up trying to pretend you can speak Italian."

A small, dark flush came to Peter's cheeks and for a second his eyes glinted. Shane had read him clearly. He was one of those who could learn to speak another language just well enough to delude himself—but he didn't speak it like a native. Shane had touched one of his vulnerabilities.

But then Peter laughed, and both flush and glint were gone. "Caught me, by God! You caught me!" he said in English. "That's really very good! Magnificent!"

And you'll never forgive me for it, thought Shane, watching him.

"Look now, tell me—" Peter seized one of the straight-backed chairs and pushed it forward. "Sit down and let's talk. Tell me, you must have some sort of credentials that let you pass freely through any inspection or check by the ordinary sort of Aalaag?"

"What I carry," said Shane, suddenly wary, "is my credentials. Communications from the First Captain of Earth will pass a courier anywhere."

"Of course!" said Peter. "Now sit down—"

He urged Shane to the chair; and Shane, suddenly conscious of the weariness of his legs, dropped into it. He felt something being put into his hands and, looking, saw that it was a glass tumbler one-third full of a light-brown liquid. He put it to his lips and smelled brandy—not very good brandy. For some reason, this reassured him. If they had been planning to drug him, he thought, they surely would have put the drug in something better than this.

The burn of the liquor on his tongue woke him from that state of mind in which he had been caught ever since he had stepped into the taxi and found himself kidnapped. He recognized suddenly that he had now moved away from the threat involved in his original capture.

These people had been thinking of him originally only as one of the human jackals of the Aalaag. Now they seemed to have become aware of his abilities and advantages; and clearly Peter, at least, was thinking of somehow putting these to use in their resistance movement.

But the situation was still tricky and could go either way. All that was necessary was for him to slip and by word or action imply that he might still be a danger to them and their determination to destroy him could return, redoubled in urgency.

For the moment the important thing was that Peter, who seemed to be the dominant member of their group, appeared to be determined to make use of him. On his part, Shane was finding, now that his first recklessness of despair was over, that he wanted to live. But he did not want to be used. Much more clearly than these people around him, he knew how hopeless their dream of successful resistance to the Aalaag was, and how certain and ugly the end toward which they were headed if they continued.

Let them dig their own graves if they wanted. All he wanted was to get safely out of here and in the future to stay clear of such people. Too late, now that he had answered their questions, he realized how much leverage against himself he had given them in telling them his true name and the nature of his work with the Aalaag. Above all, he thought now, he must keep the secret of Lyt Ann's key. They would sell their souls for something that would unlock most alien doors—doors to warehouses, to armories, to communication and transportation equipment. And the use of the key by them would be a certain way to his association with them being discovered by the Aalaag. He had been making himself far too attractive to them, thought Shane grimly. It was time to take the glamor off.

"I've got thirty minutes, no more," he said, "to get to the airport and meet the Aalaag officer who's flying me back to Lyt Ann's Headquarters. If I'm not there on time, it won't matter how many languages I can speak."

There was silence in the room. He could see them looking at each other—in particular, Peter, Georges, and Maria consulting each other with their gazes.

"Get the car," said Maria, in Italian, when Peter still hesitated. "Get him there on time."

Peter jerked suddenly into movement, as if Maria's words had wakened him from a dream so powerful it had held him prisoner. He turned to Carlo.

"Get the car," he said. "You drive. Maria, you'll go with me and Shane. Georges—"

He spoke just in time to cut short the beginnings of a protest from the man with the pipe.

"—I want you to close this place up. Bury it! We may end up wanting better security on this than we ever have had on anything until now. Then get out of sight yourself. We'll find you. You follow me?"

"All right," said Georges. "Don't take too long to come calling."

"A day or two. That's all. Carlo—" He looked around.

"Carlo's gone for the car," said Maria. "Let's move, Peter. We'll barely make it to the airport as it is."

Shane followed them back through the hall by which he had entered. Crammed in the back seat of the taxi between Maria and Peter, with Carlo driving up front, he had a sudden feeling of ridiculousness, as if they were all engaged in some wild, slapstick movie.

"Tell me," said Peter in English, in a voice that was friendlier than any he had used until now, "just how it happened you made that first mark in—where did you say it was?"

"Denmark," said Shane, answering in English also. "The city of Aalborg. I was delivering messages there, and on my way back from that, I saw two of the aliens, a father and a son, mounted on their riding animals, crossing the square there that has the statue of the Cymri bull—"

It came back to him as he told them. The son, using the haft of his power lance to knock aside a woman who otherwise would have been trampled by his riding animal. The husband of the woman, suddenly mad with yowaragh, attacking the son bare-handed and being easily knocked unconscious. The woman trying to rescue the man and being killed for it—and all of them who were human and in the square at the time being forced to watch under Aalaag law while the man, still unconscious, was thrown onto the sharp points of the triple-punishment hooks on the wall of a building on the edge of the square.

Shane had stood, for the half hour it took the man to die, almost within arm's length of the two Aalaag sitting on their riding animals. He had been trapped into listening as the senior of the two, who could have no suspicion he was within earshot of one of the rare humans who actually understood Aalaag, gently reproved his son for bad judgment in trying to save the woman from being trampled. Because of this, they had been forced to kill not one, but two healthy beasts and also to engage in a ritual of justice—which always had a disturbing effect on the others, no matter how necessary.

Remembering, Shane felt the inner center of his body grow icy with the recalled horror and the near-approach of his own madness. He told how he had gone on to the bar, drunk the bootleg rotgut the bartender had claimed was aquavit, how he had been set upon by the three vagabonds and killed or badly damaged two of them with his staff before the third had run off. He had not intended to tell it all, movement by movement; but somehow, once started, he could not help himself. He told how, once more crossing the now-empty square, on impulse he had scratched the mark of the pilgrim beneath the body on the hooks before returning to the airport.

"I believe you," said Peter.

Shane said nothing. Crowded together as they were, he was conscious of the softness of Maria's thigh pressed against his; and the warmth of her seemed also to press in upon the iciness within him, melting it as if he were someone lost and frozen in a snowstorm who was now getting back life and heat from the living temperature of another human being.

He felt a sudden, desperate longing for her as a woman. Beasts were encouraged by the Aalaag to breed particularly valuable cattle like those special human translator-couriers of Lyt Ahn's; but living continually under the observations of the aliens, as Shane and the others did, cultured a paranoia. They all knew too well the innumerable ways that could bring them to destruction at the hands of their masters; and when their duties were completed, their instinct was to draw apart, to creep separately into their solitary beds and lock their individual doors against each other for fear that close contact with another could put their survival too completely in another's power.

In any case, Shane did not want to breed. He wanted love—if only for a moment; and love was the one thing the highly paid human servants of the First Captain of Earth could not afford. Suddenly the warmth of Maria drew him like a dream of peace...

He jerked himself out of his thoughts. Peter was looking at him curiously. What had the man just been saying—that he believed Shane?

"Get someone to check Aalborg and ask people there what happened. The mark I made might still be there if the Aalaag haven't erased it."

"I don't need to," said Peter. "What you say explains how the mark could spread around the world the way it already has. It would have to take someone who can move around as you can to get it known everywhere as the symbol of resistance. I always thought there must have been someone at the root of the legend."

Shane let the first part of Peter's comment pass without answer. The other man obviously did not understand what Shane had learned in his travels—the speed with which rumor of any kind could travel in a subject population. Shane had been present at the origin of rumors in Paris which he had heard again in this city of Milan less than a week later. Also, Peter seemed to be giving him credit for continuing to spread the mark around, himself; and that, too, was probably a matter on which it was better not to correct the other.

"But I think you ought to face something," Peter said, leaning hard against him for a second as Carlo whipped the taxi around a corner. "It's time to move on from just being a legend, time to set up an organization with practical goals of resistance against the aliens, looking forward to the day when we can kill them all, or drive them off the Earth entirely."

Shane looked sideways at him. It was incredible that this man could be saying such things in all seriousness. But, of course, Peter had not seen what Shane had, up close, of the power of the Aalaag. Mice might as well dream of killing or driving off lions. He was about to say this bluntly when the instinct for survival cautioned him to go cautiously, still. Avoiding a direct answer, he fastened on something else.

"That's the second time you've mentioned a legend," he said. "What legend?"

"You don't know?" There was a note of triumph in Peter's voice. He did not offer to explain.

"There's talk that all the marks are made by one person," said Maria, also in English now. She had only a trace of Italian accent—Venetian. "By someone called simply the Pilgrim, who has the ability to come and go without the Aalaag being able to stop or catch whoever it is."

"And you, all of you, have been helping this Pilgrim, is that it?" said Shane, raising his voice.

"The point is," Peter interrupted, "that it's time the Pilgrim was associated with a solid organization. Don't you think?"

Shane felt a return of the weariness that had deadened him when he had first been abducted by these people. "If you can find your Pilgrim, ask him," he said. "I'm not him, and I've got no opinions."

Peter watched him for a moment. "Whether you're the Pilgrim or not is beside the point," he said. "The point still is, you could help us and we need you. The world needs you. Just from what you've told us, it's plain you could be invaluable just acting as liaison between resistance groups."

Shane laughed grimly. "Not on the best day in the year," he said.

"You aren't even stopping to think about it," Peter said. "What makes you so positive you don't want to do it?"

"I've been trying to tell you ever since you kidnapped me," said Shane. "You're the one who doesn't listen. You don't know the Aalaag. I do. Because you don't know them, you can fool yourself that you've got a chance with this resistance of yours. I know better. They've been taking over worlds like this and turning the native populations into their servants for thousands of years. Did you think this was the first planet they'd tried it on? There's nothing you can come up with by way of attacking them that they haven't seen before and know how to deal with. But even if you could come up with something new, you still couldn't win."

"Why not?" Peter's head leaned close.

"Because they're just what they say they are—born conquerors who could never be dominated or defeated themselves. You can't torture an Aalaag and get information out of him. You can't point a weapon at one of them and force him to back off or surrender. All you can do is kill them—if you're lucky. But they've got so much power, so much military power, that even that'd work only if you killed them all in the same moment. If even one escaped and had warning, you'd have lost."

"Why?"

"Because with any warning at all, any one of them could make himself or herself invulnerable and then take all the time he needed to wipe out whole cities and sections of Earth, one by one, until the other humans who were left served you and anyone else who had been fighting the Aalaag up on a platter, to stop the killing."

"What good would it do just one Aalaag to do all that," Peter said, "if he was the last one on Earth?"

"You don't think all the Aalaag in the universe are here, do you?" said Shane. "Earth, with only one Aalaag left alive on it, would only represent that much new homesteading territory for the surplus Aalaag population elsewhere. In a year or less, you'd have as many Aalaag here as before; and the only result would be the humans who'd died, the slagged areas of Earth, and the fact that the Aalaag would then set up an even stricter control system to make sure no one like you rose against them again."

There was silence in the car. Carlo whipped them around another corner and Shane could see a sign beside the highway announcing that the airport was now only one kilometer distant. The warmth of Maria's body penetrated through him, and he could smell the harsh, clean odor of the all-purpose soap with which she must just this morning have washed her hair.

"Then you won't lift a finger to help us?" said Peter.

"No," said Shane.

Carlo turned the car onto an off-ramp leading up to the airport road.

"Isn't anybody willing to do anything?" burst out Maria suddenly. "Not anybody? Nobody at all?"

An icy, electric shock jarred all through Shane. It was as if a sword had been plunged clear through him, a sword he had been expecting, but a sword to take his life nonetheless. It cut to his instinctive roots, to the ancient racial and sexual reflexes from which yowaragh sprang. The words were nothing, the cry was everything.

He sat for a numb moment.

"All right," he said. "Let me think about it then."

He heard his own voice far off, remote.

"You're never going to get anywhere the way you've been acting so far," he said. "You're doing all the wrong things because you don't understand the Aalaag. I do. Maybe I could tell you what to do—but you'd have to let me tell you, not just try to pick my brains, or it won't work. Would you do it that way? Otherwise it's no use."

"Yes!" Maria said.

There was a slight pause.

"All right," said Peter. Shane turned to stare at him.

"If you don't, it won't work."

"We'll do anything to hit at the Aalaag," said Peter; and this time his answer came immediately.

"All right," said Shane emptily. "I'll still have to think about it. How do I get in touch with you?"

"We can find you if we know what city you're coming into," said Peter. "Can you arrange to put an ad in the local paper before you come—"

"I don't have that much warning," said Shane. "Why don't I go into a shop in the center of a city when I first get there and buy a pilgrim robe—a gray one like the one I'm wearing—and pay for it in a silver or gold Aalaag coin. You can have the shopkeepers warn you if anyone does that. If the description fits me, you watch the local Aalaag HQ and pick me up coming or going."

"All right," said Peter.

"One other thing," Shane said. They were almost to the terminal building of the airport. He looked directly into Peter's eyes. "I've seen the Aalaag questioning humans and I know what I'm talking about. If they suspect me, they'll question me. If they question me, they'll find out everything I know. You have to understand that. If everything else fails, they have drugs that just start you talking and you talk until you die. They don't like to use them because they're not efficient. Someone has to wade through hours of nonsense to get the answers they want. But they use them when they have to. You understand? Anyone they question is going to tell them everything. Not just me—anyone. That's one of the things you're going to have to work with."

"All right," said Peter.

"What it means as far as I'm concerned is that I don't want anyone who doesn't already know about me to know I exist."

He held Peter's eye, glanced meaningfully at Carlo and back to Peter.

"And those who aren't to have something to do with me in the future—if I decide to have anything to do with you in the future—should believe that I get out of this car now and none of you ever see me again."

"I understand," said Peter. He nodded. "Don't worry."

Shane laughed harshly.

"I always worry," he said. "I'd be insane not to. I'm worrying about myself right now. I need my head examined for even thinking about this."

The taxi pulled up to the long concrete walk fronting the airline terminal and stopped. Peter, on the curb side of the car, opened the door beside him and got out to let Shane out. Shane started to follow him, hesitated, and turned back for a second to Maria.

"I will think about it," he said. "I'll do whatever I can, the best I can."

In the relative shadow of the corner of the taxi's back seat, her face was unreadable. She reached out a hand to him. He took and held it for a second. Her fingers were as icy as Milan itself had been this morning.

"I'll think about it," he said again, squeezed her fingers and scrambled out. On the walk, he stood for a second facing the other man.

"If you don't hear from me in six months, forget me," he said.

Peter's lips opened. He appeared about to say something; then the lips closed again.

He nodded.

Shane turned and went swiftly into the terminal. Just inside the entrance doors, he spotted a terminal policeman and swung on him, taking the key from his purse and exposing it for a second in the palm of his hand to the other's gaze.

"This is the key of Lyt Ahn, First Captain of Earth," he said in rapid Italian. "I'm one of his special couriers, and I need transport to the Masters' section of the field, fast. Fast! Emergency! But do it without attracting attention!"

The officer snapped upright, jerked the phone from his belt and spoke into it. There was no more than a thirty-second wait before an electric car came sliding through the crowd on its air cushion. Shane jumped into one of the passenger seats behind the driver, glancing at his watch.

"The hangars for smaller military craft!" he said. He hesitated, then made up his mind. "Use your siren."

The driver cranked up his siren, the crowd parted before him as he swung the car around and drove at it. They slid swiftly across the polished floor, out through a vehicle passway by the entrance to the field itself.

Once on the field, the car lifted higher on its cushion and went swiftly. They swung around two sides of the field and approached the heavily guarded silver hangars housing the military atmosphere ships of the Aalaag. They slowed at the guard gate of the entrance to this area. Shane showed his key and explained his errand to the human Special Guard on duty there.

"We've been warned to expect you," said the Guard. "Hangar Three. The courier ship is piloted by the Master Enech Ajin, who is of the thirty-fifth rank."

Shane nodded and the driver of the car, having heard, moved them off without any further need for orders.

In the hangar, the slim, dumbbell shape of the courier sat dwarfed by the large fighter ships of the Aalaag on either side of her. Yet, as Shane knew, even these seemingly larger ships were themselves small as Aalaag warships went. The true fighting vessels of the Aalaag never touched planetary surface but hung in continual orbit and readiness— as much for reasons of principle as for the fact that there was no air or spaceport on Earth where they could have set down without causing massive damage.

He jumped down from the car as it paused by the open port of the courier vessel and ran up the steps of the port, stepping into the cramped interior. It need not have been so cramped, but even this ship, designed for carrying dispatches, was heavy with armament.

The massive back of an Aalaag showed itself above one of the triple seats at the control panel in the front of the ship. Shane walked up to just behind the seat and stood waiting. This was not only his duty, but all that was necessary, even if the pilot had not heard him come in. This close to the other, he smelled the typical Aalaag body odor plainly; and the pilot was as surely scenting him. After a moment the pilot spoke.

"Take one of the seats farther back, beast." It was the voice of an adult Aalaag female. "I have two other stops to make before I bring you to the area of the First Captain."

Shane went back and sat down. After only a couple of minutes, the courier ship lifted and hovered lightly perhaps ten feet off the floor of the hangar. It slid out into the late daylight of the field, turned and went softly to a blast pad. At the pad it stopped, and Shane let the air out of his lungs and laid his arms in the hollows of the armrests on either side of his chair.

For a second there was neither sound nor movement. Then something like a clap of thunder, a great weight crushing him into the seat so that he could not move for a long moment—then sudden freedom and lightness, so that he felt almost as if he could float out of the chair. Actually, the feeling was exaggerated. He was still within gravity. It was the contrast with the pressure of takeoff that created the illusion of lightness.

He looked at the viewing screen in the back of the seat before him and saw the surface of Earth below, a curving horizon and a general mottling of clouds. Nothing else. The look of no expression on Maria's face as he had left her came so clearly back into his imagination that it was as if her face floated before him in the air this moment. He felt the coldness of her fingers against his fingers, and her voice rang, re-echoing in memory in his ear—

"Isn't anybody willing to do anything? Not anybody? Nobody at all?"

They were all insane. He shivered. He had been wise to play along and pretend to consider their suggestion that he involve himself in their charade of resistance that could only lead to torture and death at Aalaag hands. They had no chance. None. If he had seriously considered joining them, he would have been as insane as they were.

His heart beat heavily. The cold touch of Maria's fingers that lingered in his fingers seemed to spread up his arms and all through him. No, it was no use. It made no difference that they were insane.

He had no choice. Something within him left him no choice, even though he knew what it would mean. He would do it even though he knew it would mean his death in the end. He would seek them out again and go back to them. Join them.

WINTER SNOW

by Eric Vinicoff and Marcia Martin

Editor's Introduction

Two generations of Americans have grown up in the shadow of death. ICBMs and nuclear weapons combine to put the world one half hour from doomsday.

We have grown used to this bizarre situation. Statesmen and politicians have learned to live with it. Indeed, by adopting the doctrine of Mutual Assured Destruction (MAD) we have institutionalized doomsday. Under MAD we strive to make the world safe, not for people and civilizations, but for weapons. We undertake not to defend ourselves, lest we threaten the enemy's rockets.

Common sense would tell us that defenses are useful. It requires considerable intellectual ability to explain why defense and damage limitation are more dangerous than helplessness.

The United States has no great record of success in the field of diplomacy. One of our diplomatic triumphs was the Kellogg-Briand Treaty, which outlawed war even as the storm clouds of World War II were gathering. The Washington Naval Arms Limitation Treaty was another. The United Nations was a third. Yet, despite our previous failures in the world of diplomacy, we are exhorted to entrust our children's safety to Arms Control rather than to our technology. As I write this, we are going once again to Geneva; and all across the nation, learned writers are urging that we once and for all give up "Star Wars"; that we abandon strategic defense.

The Soviet Union has clearly violated the original Ballistic Missile Defense treaty. They have built two large radars; one of them might conceivably be intended for early warning, but the other can only be for battle management. The evidence continues to pile up: the Soviet Union believes in strategic defense, and will install strategic defenses as soon as they are technically available.

Meanwhile, the United States continues to act as if SALT II, the second Strategic Arms Limitation Treaty, were in effect, even though it was rejected by the Senate Armed Services Committee as "not in the national security interest of the United States." Under SALT II we agreed to limit our strategic offensive forces (SOF) to 1200 missiles carrying MIRV (multiple independently targeted reentry vehicles); and pursuant to this non-ratified agreement the United States has not replaced older Minuteman II missiles with already-stockpiled Minuteman III, but proposes to dismantle six perfectly serviceable Poseidon submarines carrying an additional 96 MIRVed submarine-launched missiles. These subs cost $18 billion—which has already been paid.

Since 1979 when SALT II was signed, the Soviet Union has added over 3,850 warheads to their SOF.

The alternative to diplomacy is technology. In his historic speech of March 23, 1983, President Reagan proposed a shift in US policy: that we abandon Mutual Assured Destruction, MAD, and instead begin to implement a new doctrine of assured survival based on defensive systems.

Within minutes of the President's speech there was a howl of protest.

According to Carl Sagan, Richard Garwin (an IBM Fellow) and others, "anything short of an impermeable defense system tends to undermine, not improve, U.S. national security." According to them, if we can't have perfect defenses we're better off with no defenses at all. Perfect defenses are unlikely. Therefore we shouldn't defend ourselves.

The iron logic of MAD has never appealed to the Soviet Union. They have always believed in defensive systems. Their citizens are trained in Civil Defense; the Soviet government has constructed shelters for key officials and a large part of the population; and they have begun to deploy the first elements of a ballistic missile defense system.

Sagan, Garwin, and the Union of Concerned Scientists believe that U.S. deployment of ballistic missile defenses would be destabilizing. They do not believe that we can afford missile defenses, or that the systems would work if we built them; but nevertheless, if we deploy them we invite the Soviets to attack us before the system is in place.

What happens if the Soviets get their system first?

Every so often one of the tiny, ersatz snowflakes sparkled as though reflecting an errant beam of moonlight. But there wasn't any moonlight, only the softened lamp illumination of Premier Kirinski's personal office and, beyond the curtains, the early morning sun raising mists from the stone-strong Kremlin walls.

The snowflakes drifted, seemingly carried by a gentle breeze, around the dark metal ball in the center of the crystal globe. The globe was twelve centimeters across. A slender rod of the same dark metal rose from the globe's base to hold the ball in place. The base was set in a black plastic stand.

The globe was on the corner of Premier Kirinski's desk.

He sat rigidly, his back well away from the chair's padding, and stared at the globe. He had just come from the Central Committee meeting, and he would return to it shortly. But he had chosen to talk to the American President here. (Though of course the committee members would be watching and listening to the conversation.)

The snowflakes were purposeful in their travel, deliberately circling, never touching, the ball or the crystal. They never fell. Unlike the snows of Kiev, where he had been a happy child too many years ago. Or the knife-edged blizzards during the street-to-street fighting in Leningrad, and later in Berlin...

He stabbed a button on the intercom impatiently. "What is delaying the call?"

"My apologies, Premier," Colonel Gurkoff said diffidently. "We have not used the picturephone equipment on the special line except in tests. The technical difficulties will be corrected in a minute or two."

"See that they are, Colonel."

The notes for his discussion with the American President were open in front of him, but his gaze returned to the globe.

His father was a tall presence amid the snowflakes, calling him into the house to finish his chores. *Yes, Father, I have done many chores for my family, my country. The doctors tell me I will be joining you soon, perhaps before the year is out. But I have this last and most important chore to do. Then I can warm myself by the fire and rest.*

The company name, Omutami, was written in fine silver script in the globe's base. The Japanese were very good at devising such clever toys. Many of them had been sent as gifts to influential persons in an effort to secure an import license. Of course the license had not been granted; grain came before toys. But he kept his because it was… clever.

The Nazis killed you, Father. They laid waste to our country and butchered our people, as other invaders did before them. Today we are hemmed in by enemies who would bring the horror upon us yet again if we weren't strong in arms and determination. China. Western Europe. But above all, America.

The battery in the base would keep the snowflakes moving—for how long? He would have to have replacements, purchased from the Japanese company. Much effort to keep a toy working, but few things gave him pleasure now. His body was old, a frail and failing container for his still-strong dedication to his country, party and people.

The Americans are a worse threat than the Nazis. Not as evil, but powerful and willful children. Governed by the whim of the mob. One day they wish to live in peace with us; the next day they hate and fear us. Who can know what they will do next? They corrupt other nations and turn them against us while squandering the world's resources in capitalistic excess. Their atomic weapons are aimed at our cities and military bases. No more! We cannot go on as hostages to the actions of a decadent people!

The intercom buzzed. "The call to President Nivling is ready, Premier."

He sighed and dragged his eyes from the globe to the picturephone. The decades of wishing, the years of hard work; all for this moment. A supreme moment. He would at last be the savior he had dreamed of being ever since the fear-clutched World War II days.

If he were mistaken… But no, the technicians and the military leaders and the party officials were all in agreement. Now was the moment. Any timorousness would let the great opportunity slip through his fingers.

The small screen flickered, then resolved into the head and shoulders of the American President. He was seated in a high-backed chair. No one else was in view, but his eyes revealed that others were present off-camera. With mild surprise the Premier recognized the darkened background as the Pentagon's Situation Room.

"Good morning, Premier," President Nivling said in his very bad Russian. His tone was somber, and he wasn't trying to hide his frown. He was also an old man, but stocky and overweight where the Premier was wiry. He looked like a successful, decadent capitalist—which he was—and foolish, which he definitely was not. An accomplished demagogue, brilliant but not wise, with the morality of a starved wolf. "It is morning for you, isn't it?"

"Yes, it is. You know why I have asked for this conference?"

"I have a pretty good idea."

"Then you know that the matter is very serious. Shall we dispense with preliminaries and discuss it?"

"As you say."

"I am sure your spies have kept you informed as to the progress of our project called Tsarina."

"Of course. Even a few details you weren't kind enough to leak to us." The President paused. "Some of my advisers are puzzled over why you haven't tried to keep it a better secret."

"And you, Mister President, are not?"

"Of course not, Premier. Because by its very nature you couldn't have hidden it even if you had wanted to. Plus you were giving us plenty of time to consider our options."

It was a pleasure to deal with an intelligent opponent. If only that intelligence could be directed to smoothing the way to the necessary future. "Naturally that meant taking some risks. Several of your sabotages delayed us substantially."

The President's brows rose in an exaggerated gesture. "Sabotages?"

"Deny it if you wish. It doesn't matter now. The Tsarina satellites are in orbit and activated—as you must know, since we destroyed your missiles that 'strayed' too close."

The President did not bother with another denial. He waited stoically.

"You had the technology to build the equivalent of Tsarina and maintain parity. But you squabbled over diverting money from your hedonism until it was too late. While we sacrificed to insure our security."

"Not that your citizens had any choice in the matter."

He was bored with such simplistic misconceptions. "You who confuse freedom with anarchy can hardly be expected to see the difference between discipline and oppression. Enough of this. I have called to tell you the realities of the new situation."

The President nodded slightly, as though hearing expected words, but otherwise showed no reaction.

"The particle beams from the Tsarina satellites can destroy missiles and aircraft in flight anywhere in the world, even cruise missiles or jets flying, as you say, down on the deck. You know this is true—you have observed our tests."

"You may be overly enthusiastic about your new ultimate weapon."

"Tsarina is a defense, not a weapon. We are now safe from the strategic nuclear weapons of hostile nations."

"Hopefully your sense of safety will help us reduce the tensions between us. We have never wanted anything from you but peace."

He had to fight down a surge of anger. "We will have peace. We will have peace when no one can ever threaten us with war again. We are not going to sit idly while you develop countermeasures against Tsarina."

Some color left the President's ruddy cheeks. "You have some specific proposals?"

"We have specific demands; let's not mince words. I am telling you this privately so you can put the best possible face on it for your people. You will destroy all of your strategic and tactical nuclear weapons. You will stop all nuclear research, as well as research in certain other areas. You will withdraw your military forces to within your national borders and reduce their number to an acceptable level. A detailed memorandum will be delivered tomorrow by our ambassador. The other nuclear powers will receive similar ultimatums."

"Don't be absurd," the President said. "The United States isn't about to surrender based on a mere threat. If I tried I would be removed from office. I warn you, Premier; if you insist on starting a war, you will get more of a war than you expect."

His eyes wandered briefly to the globe. The snow had been bitterly cold during the scorched-earth retreat to Leningrad. He regained his concentration. "I am not threatening. If you don't destroy your nuclear weapons, we are prepared to do it for you."

"It's not too late to stop this, Premier. Have you really considered that you might be triggering the destruction of the human race?"

"We have given this matter a great deal of serious thought. I hope you will now do the same and avoid senseless slaughter. If you haven't complied with the terms of the memorandum within forty-five days, our naval forces will begin by destroying your missile submarines. Then, if necessary, we will destroy your land-based nuclear weapons. Any retaliation on your part will be crushed and punished."

There was a pause by mutual consent. *Words. Just words such as anyone could say. But because I am who I am, my words are magical spells that can unleash devastation. How can such power lie in two withered old hands? How can I wield it so perfunctorily? If I believed in a god, I would pray for a bloodless victory.*

The President glanced off-camera and seemed to be listening to his unobtrusive earphone. Then he spoke. "Premier, because I know you are an intelligent and honorable man, I had hoped my hard-line advisers were wrong about your purpose. Unfortunately they weren't. So from the highest motives, we are about to kill millions of people. It is my duty to inform you that a state of war now exists between our nations."

He held in a bitter chuckle. "Empty formalities won't change the facts. Time is short. May we please talk sense?"

The President looked even paler. "Yes, time is short. It has almost run out. For over half a century we have lived with the balance of terror. But now you have opted for all or nothing. You win or we win, or maybe everyone loses."

He felt a sharp and totally irrational stab of uncertainty. *It must be a bluff. General Zierten is positive they haven't developed a means of counteracting Tsarina.* "This isn't a debate. We are discussing very real matters."

"I know," the American President agreed. "But your demands are based on incomplete information. Please listen carefully. You will have to act at once on what I tell you."

It has to be a bluff. "Go ahead."

"You were right that our political climate kept us from building our own particle-beam satellites. We realized the danger of that fact several years ago. What you didn't realize—because we did a good job of keeping it secret— was that we were developing a weapons system impervious to your Project Tsarina."

"At the first sign of a disease or chemical attack, we will launch–"

"Nothing so unimaginative, Premier. The idea came from a Department of Energy project to develop an ultra-lightweight power source.

When we realized its potential and evolved our plans, the actual engineering was done in Japan in cooperation with their Secret Service. Aside from being very capable, the Japanese are excellent at maintaining security. Aren't they?"

"It is difficult to discover a weapon that exists only in your wishful thinking."

The President picked up something from his desk and held it so that the Premier could see it.

It was a crystal globe filled with whirling snow. "I see you have a toy like this one on your desk too. Beautiful, isn't it? Almost seductive."

He glanced furtively to reassure himself that his globe was still on the desk, and then tried to hide his confusion. "You want me to believe this is some sort of weapon? You will have to do better than that. It was thoroughly scanned. It is nothing; a glass ball, some iron flakes, a battery and an electromagnet."

"Yes, that is almost exactly what it is. You spent billions of rubles to create a perfect defense against strategic delivery systems. So we used the postal system. Thousands of these toys were mailed all over the Soviet Union. Most of them are as harmless as they look, like mine here. But a few hundred—yours, for instance—are different."

He stared at the globe. The beauty of the swirling snowflakes had turned into a chill, ominous mystery.

The President went on. "The owners of these toys tend to keep them on their desks so they can enjoy them. In a few minutes the immediate vicinity of each special one will disappear. Government centers, military bases, key industrial plants and so on. Slash the head from a highly centralized nation and it dies. Your nation will then be partitioned at the Urals; NATO will occupy the west, China the east."

He felt himself slipping into the mad delusion, the spell woven by the President's words. "How does this miraculous weapon work?"

"Your globe is prettier than mine. Mine doesn't sparkle. But even in the hard vacuum inside the globes there are some air molecules that bump into the snowflakes. The snowflakes in your globe are iron of a unique and valuable sort. Crystalline antimatter iron. Only about an ounce, but $E = MC^2$ is a very long lever. A signal from here relayed through a satellite triggers the detonation."

He vaguely remembered one of the many briefs of scientific re-search proposals that continually crossed his desk. Something about producing antimatter with high-energy particle-accelerator rings and magnetic-containment techniques borrowed from fusion technology. But according to the brief, success was at least a decade away. Could the Americans possibly be that far ahead of his country?

His office door opened and Colonel Gurkoff rushed in. He started to reach for the globe, but the Premier waved him back sharply. In an old and tired voice he said, "If there were time to remove or defuse it, we wouldn't have been warned." *How many more are in Kremlin offices? Four that I know about.* "Aren't I right, President Nivling?"

The President nodded.

He studied the snowflakes. They looked very cold, as cold as death. The blighting frost reached out to fill his mind and soul. "Leave me, Colonel."

"But—"

"Leave me, Colonel!"

Colonel Gurkoff backed out, his face a blank mask.

"Even if this incredible tale were true, why tell us about it? Why not go ahead and set off your bombs?"

The President leaned forward, earnestness showing in his bland face. "Isn't it obvious? We are standing on the brink, but we haven't jumped yet. Some of my advisers wanted a preemptive strike. As it is, I can only delay the signal for a few more minutes. But we can still avoid war."

"How?" He felt himself slipping inexorably toward acceptance of defeat.

"By restoring the balance of terror. You must destroy the Project Tsarina satellites right now. Then we will delay the signal for twelve hours, time enough for you to move all the toys to places where they can be detonated safely."

The fear was plain in the President's expression now. Not fear that what he was doing would fail. Fear that it would succeed too well and he would have to live with the responsibility. His eyes almost pleaded. The Premier had reached and held his high office by reading the truth behind faces. He saw it here.

Father, what have I done to our country? I have brought the horror down on us for the last time. Millions of our citizens will die, and foreigners will rule the survivors. "That is impossible. If I gave such an order based only on what you have told me, I would be arrested for treason and the order ignored. I must have proof to take before the Central Committee. And time."

"Damn it, man, you know I can't give you either!" The fear permeated his voice. "I am not trying to convince you to do anything! I am offering you the only chance I can for you to save your nation!"

He turned to the seldom-used communication console. As the President well knew, he did have the authority to order the immediate destruction of the Tsarina satellites. Of course he would then have to justify his decision to the Central Committee or be executed in disgrace. But that wouldn't be difficult—he would have them witness the safe detonation of the toys at the end of the twelve hours. He couldn't do it.

For all his confidence in his own judgment and his belief that the President was telling the truth, he had no real evidence. *I am a rational man, a practical man. I cannot act on a mere premonition of doom. Not in this ultimate test. If I don't destroy the Tsarina satellites and the President is telling the truth, I have murdered my country. But if I destroy them and he is lying, I have thrown away our victory. I must have verification. Absolute and undeniable.*

He looked into the white current of the globe. For what? The sign he needed? Escape? Simple certainties from which to draw strength?

What he saw there was what he had to do.

A tragic necessity, martyring hundreds of Soviet citizens to the cause of national survival. But every other solution—blocking the signal, removing the toys, decentralizing military forces and so on—failed because of the time limit.

For himself he felt no fear, only relief at having an honorable surcease from guilt.

"Can you detonate one particular globe and not the others?" he asked levelly.

"Yes. But for obvious reasons, we can't give you time to witness and evaluate a demonstration."

"I realize that." *Not even time enough to arrange for a less-important sacrifice.* "Please listen to the call I am about to make." He would have to act quickly, before the Central Committee and the KGB could overcome their shock and interfere. He leaned over the console and activated the direct line to General Kosslov at the Baikonur Space Center. Seconds later the general's blunt features appeared in the tiny screen. A dull, unimaginative but very loyal officer who would slit his own throat if commanded to. "Yes, Premier."

"Copy the recording of my conversation with President Nivling—I am sending it now." He pushed the necessary buttons.

"We have it copied, Premier."

"Good. Now listen carefully, General. The survival of the Union of Soviet Socialist Republics depends on your obedience to the orders I am going to give you."

"I understand, Premier."

"Stand by to activate the destruct mechanism for the Project Tsarina satellites."

Shock ran across the general's face like an ocean wave. "Yes, Premier. But… may I ask why?"

"I am going to leave this line open while I finish my talk with President Nivling. If it goes dead in the next five minutes, it will mean the Kremlin is gone and the Americans have a weapon that will destroy us utterly unless Project Tsarina is ended. You will have three minutes after that in which to activate the destruct mechanism. Then you will inform General Vladisov in Leningrad of your action and transmit the conversation recording to him. Is that clear?"

It took a moment for the entire meaning to penetrate the thick peasant skull. Then: "Yes, Premier."

Vladisov. Yes, he will make a good leader for the difficult time ahead. He is younger, born into this new era of subtlety. He will master his anger, not lash out in retaliation and doom the world. He will be able to make the necessary arrangements with President Nivling.

"We are almost out of time," the President said in an urgent tone. "You must destroy the satellites now."

"Detonate my globe." So easy to say. Just words without real meaning. Everything has become a move on the chessboard, even my own death. "If you can."

There, it was done. Too late now for the KGB to cut the line or shoot him. He had depended on the inertia of their bureaucratic minds to provide the minutes he needed. He wondered if the KGB agents were hunting for the toys, evacuating the Kremlin, or coming to make him change his orders—all equally futile.

The President nodded to someone off-camera. "I see. I have come to know you well, Premier. I have a lot of respect for you. Now you are making me a murderer. Your murderer. Damn us both! We are supposed to be good leaders, not creating idiotic and destructive situations!" He took a long breath. "But if your General Kosslov obeys orders, you will have saved your nation."

"He will." He almost smiled as he imagined the panicked scurrying of the old fools of the Central Committee. *We will pay the price of the failure we wrought together, as it should be. The new leaders will hopefully learn an important lesson from it.*

He picked up the globe and stared at it. Something was wrong. The orbit of the moving snowflakes was descending. The tiny white particles were slowly dropping toward the bottom of the crystal.

Night's darkness was falling with this last snow of winter.

Father was calling to him to come inside, to sit in the warmth by the fire, beyond all cold. To melt the guilt and failure that were jagged ice crystals in his blood. To rest.

The first of the snowflakes touched the crystal—

A Way Out Maybe... Or a Dead End for Sure

by John Brunner

Editor's Introduction

John Brunner is one of Britain's best known science fiction writers. Author of *Stand on Zanzibar, The Sheep Look Up, Shockwave Rider*, he has more than a dozen books in print. I have known him for some twenty years. I don't agree with his politics nor he with mine; but we do have grudging mutual respect for each other's views. I have found John to be intelligent and generally sensible, as well as unfailingly polite.

I don't pretend to be an "impartial" editor. I have strong views about freedom and justice and the need to defend them. The opposition has plenty enough opportunity to present its views of the world, and I feel no obligation to help spread their ideas. We do, however, live on the same planet; and it is well to understand what others are saying.

When last we met, I invited John Brunner to present his views of the defense of the West. I'll reserve my comments for an afterword.

––––––––––––––––

Not only are nuclear weapons the most dangerous weapons ever devised—they are also just about the most useless.

Lord Louis Mountbatten said as much in the last public speech he gave before he was murdered, and he was my country's longest-serving and most distinguished officer. More recently Robert McNamara has defined nuclear weapons as serving no purpose except to frighten other countries out of using them. (Hmm! Don't we normally talk of people being scared "out of their wits," never "into them?")

But long before either man's pronouncement, my late friend Michael Mitchell Howard put it in a nutshell. He wasn't a career soldier, but he rose to be a colonel on Montgomery's staff in North Africa, gaining experience he put to use when acting as Chief Marshal of the protest marches against Britain's Atomic Weapons Research Establishment at Aldermaston in the fifties and sixties.

Michael used to explain why he felt justified in applying his army training to the service of the Peace Movement by saying, "Nuclear weapons have written the factor of infinity into the military equation."

But—you may reply—all of us know that nuclear war would mean the end of civilization, if not of humankind entirely, especially if recent computer simulations of the consequent "nuclear winter" are correct.

All of us know? Really? Then consider U.S. Deputy Undersecretary of Defense T.K. Jones, who is on record as stating: "Everybody's going to make it if there are enough shovels to go around. Dig a hole, cover it with a couple of doors and then throw three feet of dirt on top. It's the dirt that does it."

Apart from knowing a lot of people who live in apartments without access to loose dirt, I can't help wondering how you close those doors behind you...

During the Vietnam War, an American spokesman is alleged to have declared, "It was necessary to destroy the village in order to save it." Our species can tolerate that kind of lunacy in small doses. But when you're talking about destruction on a global scale, it's a very different matter. It is my contention, and it has been the contention of the peace group I've worked with in Britain since its inception in 1958 (CND, the Campaign for Nuclear Disarmament), and indeed the contention of clear-sighted and far-thinking people all over the world for much longer than that—consider Einstein: "The atom bomb has changed everything except our way of thinking!"—that governments both Eastern and Western are behaving as though nuclear, like traditional, weapons could be used to fight and win a war, and that this kind of attitude is insanely dangerous because there could never be a victor, only victims. Yet nuclear war might easily break out tomorrow from any of a dozen flash points in Europe, Central America, Asia or the Middle East.

How did we get into this mess? And what, if anything, can we do to get out of it?

Let me grant straightaway that now that nuclear weapons have been invented, they can never be disinvented and therefore no country can ever be totally secure again. But we could do very much better than we're doing at present. We might as well start by identifying the processes that reinforce our predicament.

Central to the problem is a fundamental misapplication of the term "defense." In my book, defense consists in rendering one's country indigestible to an invader. I speak as one whose earliest childhood memories include being taken by my father, at the age of six, to a light-metalworking shop near our home when the Germans were threatening invasion at any moment. People were improvising pikes from scrap iron and rocket-launchers from domestic drainpipes, and it was taken for granted that were the Germans fool enough to set foot on British soil, they would never have a night's sound sleep until they left. (That's why so many people in Britain sympathized with Vietnam under American attack; we recalled the Blitz.)

Such an attitude to defense may suggest the one adopted by, for instance, the Swedes and, above all, the Swiss, who adhere to a principle of "armed neutrality." (The Swiss government did seriously consider acquiring nuclear weapons but decided not to do so, given that their presence on Swiss territory would inevitably attract a full-scale strike in the event of world war.)

The point is that this definition of defense—in my view, the only one that preserves the traditional meaning of the word rules out *ipso facto* the employment of any weapon that cannot safely be used on one's own territory, let alone one that might entail the extinction of the species. Nuclear bombs are solely for retaliation and revenge...

and by a clever propaganda trick, we have been duped into imagining that policies based on these primitive—indeed barbaric—concepts will prove as efficacious as those we could and should adopt, at far less cost, in order to construct a genuinely *defensive* strategy.

Given that a Hiroshima-sized warhead can wipe out a city of 100,000 people and that the NATO alliance alone now possesses several times as many warheads as there are cities of comparable size, the question arises: What conceivable purpose can they serve?

A cynical answer has to be: They must make a lot of money for people who lack the imagination to understand how radically they reduce the chance of our survival.

And that, sadly—in the West at least—is true.

* * *

There exists a sound strategic precept that was drummed into me— and doubtless into thousands of others—during my service in the Royal Air Force. It states that the most important principle of military planning consists in a *correct assessment* of the other side's intentions.

Do we in NATO have a correct assessment of Soviet intentions? Do the planners in the Pentagon or Whitehall or wherever else? Does the behavior of our governments, or what they authorize for circulation to the press and public, demonstrate that they do? It is easy to cast doubt on that idea. Let us assume what is far from being proven (think of Islamic fundamentalism, for example): that the event most likely to trigger World War III is an attack by the USSR. More often than I care to count, people I have met on visits to America have told me that evidence of the Soviets' hostile intentions can be found in Khrushchev's celebrated exclamation, "We shall bury you!"

Unfortunately, my Russian-speaking friends inform me that what he actually said could more properly be rendered, "We shall be at your graveside!" And this, I submit, is the sort of remark anyone might make who believes that in the long run his system will outdo his rival's. (In Jack London's influential Marxist science-fiction novel, *The Iron Heel*, published ten years before the revolution of 1917, the time span for establishment of a socialist world order is estimated as twelve thousand years…)

Purely as a matter of historical record, be it noted that since they took over from the czars in 1917—and the czars were autocrats like the Somozas in Nicaragua, fighting tooth and nail to retain the serf system, under which peasants were bought and sold along with the land they tilled, against even the relatively minor democratizations proposed by the Duma, a parliament about as representative in the twentieth century as Britain's in the eighteenth—the Soviets have seen their territory invaded by not fewer than fifteen enemy nations. The Germans in the forties carted off their factory equipment wholesale to be worked in Germany by slave labor, much of which was Russian. The buffer states of today—Poland, Czechoslovakia, Hungary, Romania, Bulgaria—were ceded to the USSR under the Yalta Agreement as its sphere of influence in return for its contribution to defeating the Nazis. All those listed, by the way, plus many others, were either conquered by the Germans or allied with them during World War II. For instance, under Admiral Horthy, Hungary was a fascist state, and so was Romania in the days of the Iron Guard. Along with the occupation of the post-Versailles Baltic republics, for which Stalin bargained with Hitler to establish a longer seaboard, the Russo-Finnish War is often cited as evidence for Soviet aggressiveness. Let it not be forgotten, however, that as late as 1944, the Finnish Air Force flew with the swastika as its official insignia and that World War II was ostensibly fought to stop the fascists from taking over any more free and democratic nations.

Of course, very probably data like those do not form part of a regular American History course. A lot of Europeans neglect to take account of just the same facts owing to the impact of contemporary propaganda, especially that concerning Afghanistan. Nowadays it's seldom mentioned that the British invaded that unhappy country several times— most recently in 1919—and in October 1929 turned it into a puppet state by ensuring the murder of a popular rebel leader and installing a general as dictator.

Does that remind you of anything? You say Poland? I was thinking rather of Nicaragua vis-a-vis the USA... not to mention Panama, the Philippines, and recently Grenada.

To quote *The Guardian* (London), 26 Oct 83, when commenting on the last-mentioned invasion:

> *For exactly half of this century so far, a total of 42 years, American troops have been occupying one or another of the countries and islands of Central America and the Caribbean... according to Gordon Connell Smith of Hull University, the historian of the Organisation of American States.*

The article concludes by listing more than twenty American interventions, beginning in 1899.

Confronted with such a record, one can scarcely wonder at the fact that many Europeans take America's endless claims about "Soviet aggression" in the light of the parable about having a mote in one's own eye.

Incidentally, the main reason the Soviets went into Afghanistan in support of its just-deposed pro-Russian government was effectively identical to the grounds on which America invaded Grenada: One-sixth of the population of the territory the Russians inherited from the Czarist Empire is Moslem, and thanks to the way the czars used to treat the Moslems, it took two generations to persuade them they would be better off under socialism—which, in material terms at least, they are. If the Ayatollah Khomeini's revolutionary (sc. reactionary) version of Islam were to take root within their frontiers, there would be a risk of civil war.

Is this not analogous to the way the American government felt about Grenada and still feels about Cuba—that there is a threat to the established order within its own sphere of influence?

I have dwelt on the foregoing matters at such length in support of my belief that the NATO countries have not made a proper assessment of the "other side's" intentions.

As further evidence, let me set alongside that quotation from Khrushchev one that the *Guardian* lately reprinted from the *Jerusalem Post*. The speaker is President Reagan, on the phone to Mr. Tom Dine, executive director of the American-Israel Public Affairs Committee:

You know, I turn back to your ancient prophets in the Old Testament for the signs foretelling Armageddon and I find myself wondering if we're the generation that's going to see that come about. I don't know if you've noted any of these prophecies lately but, believe me, they certainly describe the times we're going through.

Faced with remarks like that, informed circles in Europe, and particularly in Britain, are seriously questioning the wisdom of the course on which we are embarked.

Because, let's face it, neither the eschatological content of Marxism nor a belief in prophecies of Armageddon can constitute the basis for a "defense" policy that genuinely defends what it's claimed to defend.

And no more do nuclear weapons, on which the Western Alliance has relied so long that its entrenched attitudes have become a habit as formidable and threatening to life as is a junkie's dependence on heroin.

Besides, former Pentagon strategic-planner Rear-Admiral Gene La Roque once said, "We fought World War I in Europe, we fought World War II in Europe, and if you dummies let us, we'll fight World War III in Europe!"—which is where I happen to reside.

I'm frightened. And I'm not alone.

Today's world can be summed up by the image of two rival families, each rich, powerful and quarrelsome, in an apartment building shared by many other people, most of them considerably poorer and quite a few of them immigrants who don't speak the same language. One of the rich families lives on the entrance floor and boasts, when visitors call, about the gilt and glass and marble in the foyer. The other rich family—not by any means so well off in objective fact—occupies the top floor and boasts about its splendid view… although now and then their visitors don't arrive on time because the elevators are out of order and the people on the ground floor, saying they don't have any call to use them, refuse to contribute to their maintenance.

Whenever the people on the top floor malign those on the bottom floor, the latter cry, "We'll dynamite the elevator shafts!"

Whenever those at street level slander them, those on the top floor shout, "We'll drop Molotov cocktails down the elevator shafts!"

Caught between the threat of having the walls blown out at ground level and the whole structure being turned into a chimney for a fire storm, a small, concerned group of other occupants pleads and wheedles and begs for a hint of common sense… and is mocked for its pains.

Speaking as an inhabitant of one of the middle floors, that's my honest view of the nuclear-armed world that America and Russia have created—or, strictly, that America has created as the country that came up first with the A bomb, the H bomb, the submarine-launched ballistic missile, MIRVing, the cruise missile… The history of the arms race since 1945 has been that of Russia frantically trying to catch up. About the only things the USSR did first were to launch an orbital satellite and to send a human being into orbit. Check the records of the Apollo-Soyuz linkup for an idea of the desperate expedients to which the Russians were driven in order to achieve those goals.

Nobody except maybe T.K. Jones imagines that a nuclear war can be fought and won. There is exactly one way that it could happen, and that's if one of the nuclear superpowers (I use the word, but do bear in mind that Russia is not a superpower in the American sense: rather, a third-world country with grandiose ambitions… Do you know how far apart emergency telephones are on Russian highways? One hundred and fifty kilometers!)—if one of the nuclear superpowers, anyway, were to throw everything in its arsenal at its adversary, targeted on the means of retaliation, ideally with no warning whatsoever. But even that, according to the latest findings which indicate a subsequent "nuclear winter" during which solar radiation would be cut to five percent of normal, doesn't look like a particularly good bet anymore.

It remains unfortunately true that a nuclear war could be fought and lost not only by the combatants, *but by everybody*.

Despite this knowledge, and despite the fact that every arms race in the whole of history has ended in the war it was allegedly intended to prevent, none of the so-called "multilateral" disarmament negotiations since 1945 have thus far resulted in the abolition of a single weapon. The ultimate hollowness of this "negotiating" approach and the insincerity of those participating were revealed in the claim that the deployment of cruise missiles would "force Russia back to the conference table."

Suppose the boot had been on the other foot, and it had been the Russians who said that about the Americans?

We in the British Campaign for Nuclear Disarmament (which my wife and I joined at its inaugural meeting in 1958) have been arguing for a quarter of a century that there is a way out of this impasse and that Britain is in an ideal position to blaze the trail. I speak as a patriot as distinct from a nationalist; I believe that our way of life is resilient enough to survive no matter what form of political or ideological threat, provided we have a government that adheres to its traditional principles (though our present regime gives cause for considerable doubt on that score), and I not only believe but I know that nuclear war would wipe my country from the slate of history.

There are about a hundred and two foreign military bases in Britain, a figure not exceeded by any of the Warsaw Pact nations on the basis of available evidence, and they now include launch sites for nuclear-tipped missiles over which my government has no control.

These bases make Britain an inevitable target even in a war that serves none of our national interests. The British Medical Association, in a study commissioned by the government but which the government later tried to suppress, concluded that even a one-megaton strike over a center of population would overload our medical resources and that a massive attack would kill up to forty million of our present population. That's what we stand to lose.

It is of course quite true that no place would be totally immune from the consequences of a nuclear war (especially of the nuclear *Fimbulwinter*)—but at least countries where there are no nuclear missiles would stand a better chance than those countries that might be assailed in a preemptive strike, as the Swiss so rightly concluded.

It follows that Britain should therefore become a country where there are no nuclear missiles. Furthermore, it should not be tied to any alliance that is prepared to consider first use of nuclear weapons.

At the same time, Britain should adopt the only sane course for any small and densely populated nation: Establish a citizen militia system combined with a program of shelter-building of the kind that would appear provocative were it undertaken by a nuclear power, and likewise undertake the stockpiling of food and fuel in quantities sufficient to support its population for at least a year—costly, one must admit, but cheap compared with the risk of losing everything.

Some would argue that for a time at least, in the context of this policy, Britain should retain nuclear weapons aboard submarines, provided they were permanently at sea and could thus be reserved for retaliation. (A commitment to "no first use" would obviously be called for.)

I would dispute even this. The proper counter to "nuclear blackmail," as it is sometimes termed, is never found in a threat to use nuclear weapons; such a threat could only make a bad situation worse inasmuch as it might easily provoke the war one was hoping to avoid.

No: The proper counter is public and grand-scale recognition of the fact that nuclear weapons are useless for the defense of any country, no matter how large, no matter where in the world, but most of all for countries as small and populous as Britain, where their limited resources can better be spent on actually increasing the chances of survival.

Faced with the reality of a nation coming to its collective senses and abandoning nuclear weapons for the reasons just outlined, it is not only possible but probable that the world community would respond with a gigantic sigh of relief. We are being bled dry by the cost of the nuclear arms race. Even the United States is in deficit largely because of spending demanded by the military, while the Soviet Union is permanently on the verge of bankruptcy owing to its efforts to keep up with the West. Every third-world country with ambitions is diverting cash and manpower that could be better applied elsewhere—in order to achieve these twentieth-century nuclear status symbols, which, as I trust I have shown, are effectively pointless.

On the one hand, we have been duped into equating defense and revenge; on the other hand, we have failed in that fundamental strategic need to make a correct assessment of the other side's intentions.

Much of this, of course, is due to the bad habit of referring to "the enemy" in a time of peace. There is indeed a worldwide struggle going on between capitalism and communism… but how differently we would view it if we used the more accurate term of "rival," or "competitor"!

In fact, the Soviet Union is not militarily aggressive in the same sense as were the old imperial powers. It doesn't need to be, and on the rare occasions when it tries to be, it makes a dreadful mess of things.

However, in every place and at every time that the vaunted values of the Western way of life are betrayed by greedy, brutal ruling classes and America or Britain or another so-called democratic country allies itself with a dictatorship, another battle in the real World War III is lost and won.

Worse yet: We have corrupted that Western way of life to the point where scarcely anyone admires it anymore—in many cases, not even our own citizens. And much of this corruption is due to the mere existence of nuclear weapons.

I quote Lieutenant Colonel Patrick Lort-Phillips, ex-Brigade of Guards, who resigned his commission to become a Liberal Party spokesman on defense and frequently appeared on CND platforms to argue vehemently for independent nuclear disarmament. Lort-Phillips expressed his reasoning in the following terms:

If, back in the nineteen thirties, anyone had told me the day would arrive when a British government predicated its defence policy on a declared willingness to exterminate cities-ful of women and children, I'd have said, "Maybe those Nazis over there in Germany—but never the British!"

Well, now it is the British and the Americans and the Russians and the French and the Chinese, and very likely the South Africans and the Israelis and the Argentines and the Pakistanis and...

Next year, how many more?

Someone *must* reverse the nuclear arms race before a war breaks out, whether by design or by accident. Being, as I said, a patriot, I'd like it to be Britain that starts the process—but also being cynical, I don't think our present government has the sense to see reason; so, being human too, I don't care who does it, so long as it gets done.

There's one further advantage in the policy proposed by CND. Putting the responsibility for defending our country back on the shoulders of its citizens—instead of leaving everything to computers and a handful of ivory-towered "experts" who calculate with abstracts remote from the reality of blood and death—would do more to restore national pride and confidence than any other course one might imagine. And I honestly believe that the same would hold true in any country that has the guts to admit that nuclear weapons are not defensive but solely adapted to that uncivilized and futile act, revenge.

A recent letter in the *Guardian* pointed out that while dying *for* one's country might still be a noble deed, dying *with* one's country is a different matter. And that is precisely the prospect that now faces all of us.

It was well-said of the draft dodgers during the Vietnam War that they were the people of whom America should be most proud because a free and democratic way of life had taught them that authority must never be obeyed without question. If we survive long enough for future historians to write an account of the twentieth century, I hope they will say of the contemporary Peace Movement that it was made up of people courageous enough to accept the fact that nuclear weapons had made wars unfightable, people who decided that instead of dying with their countries, it made better sense to live for them... and for all mankind.

Partial reference list:

The Guardian, London, 26 Oct 83 ("US Interventions in Other Countries"); 29 Nov 83 ("Reagan's Belief in Armageddon")

New Scientist, London, 3 Nov 83 ("Risk of Nuclear Winter")

The Times Atlas of World History, London, 1978 ("German Invasion of Countries Now Russian Satellites")

Disgrace Abounding by Douglas Reed, London, 1939 ("Fascist Governments in Europe in the 1930s")

World Aircraft, World War II, Part I, London, 1978 ("Finnish Aircraft Wearing the Swastika")

The Modern Encyclopedia & World Atlas, London, n.d., prob. 1937–8 ("British Invasions of Afghanistan")

The Medical Effects of Nuclear War: The Report of the British Medical Association's Board of Science and Education, London, 1983 ("Nuclear War Deaths in the UK")

Editor's Afterword to: A Way Out Maybe... Or a Dead End for Sure

They that can give up essential liberty to obtain a little temporary safety deserve neither liberty nor safety.

—Benjamin Franklin

I asked John Brunner for this contribution because I was interested in his concept of a Swiss militia system. Britain is a small country, perilously near the Soviet Union. Perhaps a case could be made for basing British defense on something other than nuclear weapons.

Consequently, I wasn't surprised by his conclusions; but I am horrified by his assumptions. If this is what the sensible left truly believes, then God help us all.

Begin with this. Brunner dismisses the enslavement of eastern Europe with an airy wave. Poland, Czechoslovakia, Hungary, Romania, Bulgaria, "were ceded to the USSR under the Yalta agreement as its sphere of influence." Ceded? Not by their own actions. They were delivered into the hands of their masters by others. It was no fault of their own, nor were they consulted; indeed, the people of Britain and the United States were not consulted.

If I cede your home to the local bully, are you bound by my decision?

It is no matter, though. "All those listed, by the way, were either conquered by the Germans or allied with them during WWII." Apparently it is an inexcusable crime to have been conquered by the Germans. Will Brunner argue next for the Soviet occupation of France? Moreover, he feels that any nation ever to have had a fascist government deserves to be enslaved by the communists. Can he really believe this? Perhaps it is more likely that he sees no hope for aiding the Poles, Czechs, Slovaks, Balts, Rumanians, Hungarians, Bulgarians, etc. Since he cannot help them, he comforts himself with the myth that they deserve the gulag archipelago. Of course those old enough to participate in government prior to 1940 are either dead or retired now; but Brunner is content that the sins of the fathers be visited on future generations, now and forever.

It is the standard view of the left that the Soviet Union does no more than react to fear of invasion. This analysis of Soviet intentions leaves out too much. Whom do they fear now? In the years following 1945 the United States dismantled the most powerful military force ever assembled on this planet; the result was the conquest of Czechoslovakia and the Berlin Blockade.

The Soviet leadership needs much more than security. Communist officials can never declare permanent peace with the West, because to do so is to repudiate their legitimacy as rulers of the Soviet Union. If the Communist Party is not the vanguard of history—then what is it? What justification has it to be the only political party allowed? Surely not its economic accomplishments.

The fact is that Soviet public opinion is cynically manipulated. Soviet citizens are ceaselessly bombarded with anti-western propaganda designed to prepare them for war. To this day most Soviet citizens seriously believe that the western democracies will invade Russia at the first opportunity. How could they know otherwise? Access to western newspapers and television is officially restricted, and the publications are severely censored to boot.

The left would have us believe that that Soviet "Peace Committees" are genuine; that the Soviets preach peace and brotherhood to their own peoples. The truth is far different. The Soviet Union is one of the most militaristic states in history. One of their largest youth organizations is the Voluntary Society for Cooperation with the Army, Air Force, and Navy. The Pioneers (ages 9–15) and the Komsomol (Communist Youth League) conduct annual summer war games. Military science is a compulsory subject in ninth and tenth grade; nor are these recent phenomena instituted in reaction to President Reagan. All this began in 1979, prior to the invasion of Afghanistan, when "tensions" were supposed to be relaxed.

Arthur Koestler said it in 1946: the legitimacy of the Soviet state is based on the isolation of the Soviet people, who are ceaselessly bombarded with the notion that the USSR is constantly at war with the outside world. Koestler believed the only way to "ease tensions" would be to open the iron curtain: allow Soviet citizens free access to foreign journals, books, films, and newspapers; allow free access of western journalists to Russian territory; abolish restrictions on foreign travelers in Soviet territory; and allow significant numbers of Soviet citizens to travel in the West.

The Helsinki accords were supposed to bring about these free exchanges, to increase the sum of "human rights" enjoyed in the Soviet Union. The agreements were instead a cruel hoax, whose major accomplishment has been to send to jail those few Soviet citizens courageous enough to try to monitor their government's compliance with a treaty it had accepted.

Brunner would, I suppose, reply by saying "you're another," and flippantly refer to the U.S. refusal to allow Khrushchev to visit Disneyland; then invoke the name of Senator McCarthy—as if McCarthy ever sent anyone to a labor camp to be worked to death.

Indeed, it is this assumption of symmetry between the US and USSR that I find so dismaying. The story of the Vietnamese village that had to be destroyed in order to save it is probably apocryphal; at least I can find no primary reference to it. Apocryphal or not, the story caused a stir in the West, and the action was roundly condemned. Have stories of Soviet atrocities in Afghanistan been condemned in Russia? Have they even been published there? Yet we need not strain to find examples of Afghan villages where there was no pretense of "saving" them. They were merely destroyed by bombs and machine guns.

Today's paper brings new horror. The New York Review of Books quotes the Helsinki Watch report on Afghanistan: a tale of two brothers, aged 90 and 95, both blind, who remained in their village when everyone else fled the Soviet coming. The Russians tied dynamite to their backs and blew them up.

The report speaks of "civilians burned alive, dynamited, beheaded; bound men forced to lie down on the road to be crushed by Soviet tanks; grenades thrown into rooms where women and children had been told to wait." All the mechanisms of terror are brought to bear.

The British intervened in Afghan affairs in 1929. How is that relevant to Soviet barbarism in the 1980's? Brunner equates these events. To do that, one must strain hard; one must desperately *want* to make that equation. Why?

James Burnham once described liberalism as a philosophy to console the West while it commits suicide. Is this the rationale for refusing to see the evils of the Soviet system? If they're not so bad; if, really, they're just like us; if there's no fundamental difference between U.S. and USSR, why, then, what's the need for conflict? We are manipulated in any event; at worst, Moscow will pull the strings rather than Washington. Surely that wouldn't be so bad? Is it not better to be red than dead?

Deep inside we know better. Solzhenitsyn has told us; and before him, as early as 1950 Gustav Herling's published accounts of the gulag were accepted by a wide spectrum of critics including Bertrand Russell. There may once have been a time when the sheer horror of the Soviet system was too great to be believed; but there can be no doubt today. Medvedev has estimated the death rates in Soviet labor camps as high as a million a year. Being red does not insure that you will not also be dead.

By refusing to deal with the studied cruelty of the Soviet regime, Brunner robs it of its horrors—and thereby lowers the stakes considerably, for if his strategy fails, not so very much has been lost.

Still: would his strategy work? Brunner asks a legitimate question: what do nuclear weapons contribute to Britain's defense? Wouldn't it be better to scrap them and turn to a militia system modelled after the Swiss? Would not the Soviets then hold their hand? They would have no incentive to use nuclear weapons, yet an invasion would be costly.

Implementing the new defense would not be simple. A "Swiss style" defense would bring great changes in the way the British live. Firearms are rare in Britain; you must have a police permit to own even a .410 shotgun. Under the Swiss militia system the entire populace would have not merely the right, but the obligation, to keep military weapons and ammunition in their homes. There are, however, plenty of precedents. British yeomen were required to learn military arts and keep bows and other weapons throughout Tudor times and after. Let the Britons have weapons, and learn the arts of guerrilla war. Will not England, and Scotland, and Wales become, in Brunner's words, "an indigestible lump" in their Empire?

Perhaps; but there is a large element of wishful thinking in the analysis. Guerrilla wars and passive resistance are seldom effective against a sufficiently determined power. When protestors lie in the path of a British train or tank, the vehicle halts until the protestor is removed. Russian drivers may not be so squeamish. In the days of George I the highlands were held by armed bands no less dedicated to freedom than today's Englishman; but Scotland was pacified all the same. Ruthless measures ruthlessly applied generally succeed. Thich Tri Quang, the Buddhist monk who gathered so many headlines that U.S. analysts seriously believed no government could be formed without his cooperation, was last seen, without his robes, cleaning sewers for the Tonkinese conquerors of Saigon. Afghanistan is a rugged land defended by rugged

people; but it has not proved to be the "Soviet Vietnam." Genocide is
a terribly effective technique of digestion.

Still in all, nuclear weapons are expensive and provocative. There's
little that Britain can do with such weapons; why not discard them?
In 1960 Liddell Hart suggested that Europe abandon nuclear defense
in favor of greatly strengthened conventional forces. Western Europe
has a decided advantage over the Soviet Union in both population and
economic strength. Let the European powers build their armies.

Although popular in Britain, this suggestion was not welcomed by
the French and Germans, who had no desire to have their homes again
become a battleground. Even if Europe could win a conventional
war, could they stand against Soviet tactical nuclear weapons? Despite
Brunner's protests, nuclear weapons can be decisive if one side has them
and the other does not. What would prevent the Soviets from using
them? Something more was needed.

The "something more" was an American commitment; but in an era
of nuclear sufficiency, when both the U.S. and the USSR have enough
thermonuclear firepower to destroy the world a dozen times over, the
American commitment is irrational. Eisenhower's doctrine was simple:
we would meet any Soviet threat to Europe with "massive retaliation at
a time and place of our own choosing." That made sense only in an era
of overwhelming U.S. superiority. It doesn't now, which is why France
insists on its own independent nuclear deterrent.

For thirty years the doctrine of Mutual Assured Deterrence has required us to build weapons of vengeance rather than defense. Even as
I write this, American officers sit ready to launch weapons designed to
kill helpless Soviet civilians, men, women, and children alike. It is a
situation no less repugnant to me than it is to Brunner; but so long as
we are locked to the doctrine of MAD we have no choice.

As accuracies increase and our strategic offensive forces become more
vulnerable, MAD leads us, eventually, to launch on warning as the only
way to protect the force. That is a frightening prospect. Unilateral

disarmament is one path away from that dread end, but that path leads to the gulag. There is a better alternative.

The Strategic Defense Initiative, "Star Wars" if you will, offers a real alternative to MAD. Assured survival will not easily be achieved; but it is feasible, and moves us in the right direction, toward a time when the ICBM, and perhaps all nuclear weapons, become impotent and obsolete without the sacrifice of liberty.

A LETTER FROM THE SOVIET UNION

by Alexander Shatravka

Editor's Introduction

Communism is brutal, but not all those who become Communists begin as brutes. Thousands have joined for the highest of motives. Whittaker Chambers was one of these. He served the Party well, but like many others he found there comes a time when you hear the screams; and then you must choose.

In 1982 Alexander Shatravka was arrested for his activities in the unofficial Group To Establish Trust Between the USSR and USA. Although the petition he circulated was not significantly different from the "official" peace organization's documents, Shatravka was charged with slandering the Soviet nation.

This letter reached the United States in Fall, 1984; as of Spring, 1985, no further word on his condition has been recorded.

Greetings, dear friends:

I want to hope that my letter reaches you, so that you can understand something about my situation in the camp. I consider further silence on my part to be stupid, in that it can only further untie the hands of several officials of the camp. I will begin in order.

I arrived in the camp on Feb. 3, 1984, completely healthy. On Feb. 4, 36 of us were put in a strict regime education division where, with the full permission of the camp administration, we were put under the authority of "prisoner-activists." From the first day, we were beaten by individuals or groups of five. On Feb. 4, I was beaten only because I could not march in step, raising my legs to 30 centimeters (after 19 months of prison). On Feb. 8, I was summoned to camp headquarters to the chief of the punishment detail, Lt. Dulatbaev, where I was beaten. Dulatbaev grabbed me by the ears and beat the back of my head against the wall. My face was blue from bruises. During all of this, he said that he was ready to kill me, cut me up into pieces. He called me a traitor and after this I was put in the punishment isolator where I spent two days and became very ill. From Feb. 13 to 27, I was in the sanitary department with pneumonia and from March 7, I was put under special supervision and expected to report every two hours as one who was inclined to escape. On March 4, we all stood without hats and coats in the strong wind and falling snow for more than two hours by orders of one of the bosses of the division who wanted to know who was guilty of tearing two pages out of the sanitary journal. In February, Pavel Lapko, 21 years old, died of meningitis. He arrived in the division with us healthy.

I have been in the ninth detachment since March 14. The detachment is overcrowded. We sleep three to a bunk. In the camp, there rages a cult of violence, the prisoners are beaten literally for any trifle and particularly for failure to fulfill the work plan, whether this is for sewing production or making nets. Also, in the camp they have begun exercise drills. They demand that after work, the prisoners stand and hold up their left leg extended for several minutes and then their right leg. Those who can't do it are beaten by the prisoner activists. In the division, these prisoners forced me to lean at a steep angle with my head against the wall and with my hands against the wall so that my head pressed against the wall in the bitter cold.

I landed in the 94th brigade for the knitting of big nets of synthetic fiber for vegetables. The norm was six nets in eight hours. We worked from six in the evening until two in the morning. The norm was very high and so the majority of prisoners were forced to knit in their non-working hours, devoting to this another six to eight hours. For failure to fulfill the norm, the foreman several times deprived us of a day's sleep so that in the daytime, we knitted nets. When I and another prisoner mentioned this to the brigade leader of the prisoners, I was summoned to the brigade captain, Dosnatov, who regarded my indignation as anti-Soviet agitation and said that as long as I was in the Soviet Union and not the United States, I would knit nets without any conversation. I several times asked the camp administration to be transferred to any other type of work but each time, I was refused.

On May 31, 1984, I was summoned to the boss of the detachment (I don't know his last name). He locked the door of his office and began to beat me savagely. With blows, he knocked the wind out of me, he kicked me in the groin and then in the skull and continued to beat me for a long time. He gave me to understand that this is the way it would be every day that I did not fulfill the work norm. Leaving him, I was received by the boss of camp. Col. Bakhaev, but he refused my request to be transferred to other work. In despair, not seeing any way out of the situation, I tried to kill myself, stabbing myself in the side. After I was given medical aid, I fell into the hands of the chief of one of the divisions, Dulatbaev, who knowing all of the most vulnerable parts of a man began to beat me. He beat me several times around the neck from which I fell and lost consciousness. He clapped both of his hands on my ears from which began a powerful ringing. He choked me and beat me along the organs of my body, accompanying all this with insults. I was then put for 15 days in the punishment isolator where, despite the filth, parasites, meager food and limited amount of water, I nonetheless was able to recover psychologically. Everything which goes on in the camp resembles one of those films which shows the tortures given by the Gestapo.

On leaving the punishment isolator, I began spitting up bloody phlegm. The doctors diagnosed a worsening of pneumonia. I was given intensive treatment for 14 days during which I received more than 60 injections. Thanks to the doctors, I am now in the sanitary department of the camp. However, my lungs worry me. (There is a very high percentage of prisoners in the camp suffering from tuberculosis.)

And so that is my situation. I consider that to remain silent about this any longer is impossible. I don't receive letters, except from home. How my situation in the camp will be from now on I don't know. They constantly threaten to give me a new sentence when I finish my present sentence.

Alexander Shatravka

Camp 158/3

Zhanatas, Kazakhstan

USSR

Emergency Rations

by Theodore Cogswell

Editor's Introduction

Most military activity is boring. "They also serve, who only stand and wait," said John Milton; a truism that every soldier and sailor knows.

"No man would go to sea who could possibly contrive to go to jail," said Samuel Johnson. "Being in a ship is being in a jail, with the chance of being drowned." The Navy sees things differently. Robert Heinlein said of his choice of Annapolis over West Point, "At sea you may risk being drowned, but until they get you there's enough to eat and a bed to sleep in."

When asked the secret of his great successes in battle, Confederate General Nathan Bedford Forest said "I gets there firstest with the mostest." It's a good formula; alas, all too often the advice is not followed. A small patrol or probe is sent; the enemy hasn't been active in the area for years…

In the early days of World War II the U.S. Navy made use of civilian construction workers (CB's) to build bases and air strips. They weren't supposed to fight, but they often found themselves under fire. Ted Cogswell postulates a time in the far future when civilians are once again called upon to hold against an unexpected attack, and face dangers far greater than boredom and bad cooking.

"The obvious base for offensive operations is this deserted little system here."

Kat Zul, the Supreme Commander of the Royal Zardonian fleet stabbed one tentacle at a point on the star map.

"Once we are established there, the whole Solar flank lies open to us. We can raid here—and here—and here," he indicated sector after sector, "and they will never be able to assemble enough ships in one spot to stop us. What do you think, Sire?"

The Gollen patted his corpulent belly. "There will be good eating. Mind you save the fattest for the royal kitchen." Orange saliva drooled from the corners of both his mouths. "Roasted haunch of human three times a day. How delightful! Remind me to invite you in for dinner some night after you get back."

"Thank you, Sire. I will order reconnaissance patrols out at once. If all is clear, we can begin construction of a base within the month. Once our heavy armament is installed, we will be impregnable. You will eat well then, O Mighty One!"

The Gollen of Zardon burped happily, closed his eye, and dreamed of dinner.

A week later a fast courier came screaming back with news of trouble. The Supreme Commander took one good look at the report, grabbed the photographs that came with it, and rushed in to see the Gollen.

"The system is already occupied, Sire! By humans!"

"Fine, send me a brace of plump ones at once."

"Your forgiveness, Highness, but that is impossible. We can't get at them. They have erected a space station, a heavy Z type with protective screens that can stop anything we throw at them. I have blockading squadrons around it now, but we must act quickly. They got an appeal for help off before we were able to blanket their transmitter."

The Gollen paled to a light mauve. "In that case," he said softly, "I shall have you for dinner. If the humans gain control of that system, *our* whole flank lies open to them!"

"There is yet hope, Sire," said Kat Zul quickly. "The space station is only partially completed and, as far as we can determine, occupied only by a construction crew. None of its defensive armament has been installed yet. Once they drop their screen, we have them. We can fortify the station ourselves, and control of the system will be ours."

The Gollen reached into a silver bowl filled with wiggling guba, selected an especially fat one, and bit off its head with his lower mouth.

"Why should they?" he said with his upper one.

"Should they what?"

"Drop their protective screens. Their power piles can keep them energized for the next hundred years."

"Ah, Highness, but screen generators are tricky things. They require constant attention. When no humans are alive to tend them, they will shut off automatically. And within two months there will be no humans left alive. They will all have starved to death. We captured their supply ship yesterday."

"I don't like it. In the first place, a starved human is an inedible human, and in the second, their relief fleet won't take more than a month to get there. I believe you were talking in terms of two months. You'll have to do better than that, Kat Zul, or you'll be fricassee by evening!"

As the stew pot came nearer, Kat Zul thought faster. He barely beat the deadline.

"In this life, Highness," he said pontifically, "it is either eat or be eaten."

"This is obvious," said the Gollen, "and since for you to eat me would be *lèse majesté*, the second half of your truism is more appropriate to the present occasion. Cook!"

"You don't understand," said Kat Zul in desperation. "In this case we can eat by being ready to be eaten." He retreated around the table. "Listen, please! The robot supply ship we captured was loaded with food. If we wait another two weeks, the humans in the space station will be getting terribly hungry."

"I'm getting mighty hungry right now," said the Gollen. "But I'll listen. Go ahead."

"Among the food on the supply ship we found several hundred cans containing strange clawed creatures in a nutrient solution. They're alive!"

"So?"

"So we'll remove all the food from the ship except those cans. Then we will open them carefully and remove the animals inside. Next we will replace them with ourselves and have the cans resealed."

"What!"

"A stroke of sheer genius, Highness! In each of the cans will be one of my best fighting men. We will put the robot supply ship back on course and chase it to the space station, firing near misses all the way. When they see it coming with us in pursuit, the humans will open their screens enough to let it through. Once they've checked it carefully with their scanners, they'll bring it into the station and unload it at once. They'll be so hungry that the first thing they'll go for will be the food. But when they open the cans, instead of finding little live animals, out will spring my warriors. Ah, Sire, there will be a fine slitting of throats. With the screens shut off, we can arm the station at once, and when the human fleet comes..." He laughed exultantly and clicked his razor-sharp forward mandibles together like castanets.

"As you say, Kat Zul, a stroke of sheer genius," said the Gollen. "Have you selected your personal can yet?"

The fleet commander's olfactory feelers stood straight out. "Me? To tell you the truth, Highness, I hadn't planned on being one of the raiding party. The fact is that I suffer from a touch of claustrophobia and..."

"Would you rather stay for dinner?"

"Well, Sire..."

"Cook!"

"On second thought..."

"Hey, Mac."

"Yeah?"

"What'n the hell's *lobster*?"

"Beats me. Why?"

"Somebody sure fouled up back at base. There's about a thousand cans of it on the supply ship—and nothing else."

"Well, open one and find out. I'm hungry!"

"Who isn't? But they're alive. It says so on the can. They're packed away in some sort of nutrient solution."

"So they're alive. There's a law says you can't take them out and kill them?"

"There's a picture on the can."

"So?"

"They got big claws. Looks like they could take a man's finger off with one good bite. Whatta they mean sending stuff like that out?"

"Look, Pinky, I'm busy. Do what you want but don't bother me. I got to nurse this generator. If it flickers just once, we're done for. Now beat it!"

"Okay. I'll go open one up and see what happens."

There was silence broken only by a chomping of jaws. The eating was good. Kat Zul, the Supreme Commander of the Royal Zardonian fleet, rested motionless at the far end of the table in the place of honor, his belly distended and his eye closed.

At the other end of the table, two hungry mouths opened simultaneously.

"More!"

Pinky beamed cheerfully, picked up the platter on which Kat Zul rested and passed it down to the two hungry electronics men.

"Help yourselves, boys. There's lots more where that came from."

He took another piece himself. "This sure beats chicken.

The way these things are built, there's enough legs for everybody." He pushed his white chef's cap back on his perspiring forehead and surveyed the little group of technicians and construction men happily. This was a red-letter day. Nobody had ever asked for seconds of his cooking before.

"Pinky."

"Yes, Mac?"

"What do they call these things again?"

"Lobsters. They sure don't look like the pictures on the cans, though. Guess the guy that made up the label was one of these here abstraction- ists. You know, those characters that don't paint a thing like it is, but like it would be if it was."

"Yeah," said Mac, "sure." He noticed a bandage on Pinky's right forefinger. "I see ya got nipped after all."

Pinky held his finger up and inspected it with interest. "Sure was a mean cut, almost to the bone it was. And that reminds me, when's one of you mechanical wizards going to fix my can opener for me? For a month I've been after you and all I get is promises."

"Tomorrow, first thing," said Mac.

"Tomorrow, always tomorrow," said Pinky. "Look at that finger. That ain't no bite; it got ripped on the edge of a can. I didn't take no chances on being bitten. I was all set to open the first can when I got to looking at the picture on the label, and the more I looked at it, the less I liked the idea of having something like that running around my galley alive. So ya know what I did?"

"No," said Mac patiently, tearing another leg off the carcass of Kat Zul and munching on it appreciatively.

"Well, you know I mostly cook by intuition…"

A collective groan went up from his listeners. Every time Pinky had an inspiration, it usually involved a handful or so of curry powder.

"But this time I decided to go by the book. The recipe said to boil vigorously for twenty minutes, so I did. Once the kettle got boiling good, I tossed in a dozen, can and all. I figured they would cook as well inside the container as outside, and that way I wouldn't have to worry about their claws. They was alive all right, too. You should have heard them batting around inside those cans for the first couple of minutes."

Mac shivered uncomfortably. "Don't seem human somehow to make critters suffer so. Next time you'd better open the cans and kill them first. If you're scared, call me and I'll come down and do the job for you."

"There's no need for that," said Pinky. "Them things can't feel nothing. They ain't got no nervous systems. It says so in the cookbook."

"If that's what it says," said Mac, "I guess it's so. Just keep dishing them out the way you did tonight and I'll be happy." He loosened his belt, leaned back, and sighed contentedly.

Pinky wasn't listening. He could hardly wait until time came to prepare breakfast. With just a touch of curry...

THE PROUD FOOT OF THE CONQUEROR

by Reginald Bretnor

Editor's Introduction

All power tends to corrupt. Absolute power corrupts absolutely.

—Lord Acton

The ancient Greeks believed that history flowed in cycles. So did government. Monarchy became aristocracy, "rule of the best." Aristocracies became oligarchies of wealth. Democracy rose, became degenerate, and fell, giving place to tyrants, whose descendents became legitimized as monarchs. Through ages of ages these cycles ran.

They did not always run smoothly. Sometimes one stage was prolonged. Another time, one of the stages might be skipped over. Moreover, there were intermediate states, unstable to be sure, but interesting.

One of these was timocracy, defined by Plato as the rule of honor. It generally came about when the soldiers tired of the corruption of an oligarchy and took rule into their own hands. For a time their military virtues prevailed; the state was ruled harshly, but fairly.

The twentieth century has shown that rule by honor does not last. The juntas and caudillos begin with high intentions, but Acton's dictum prevails. Yet even after the inevitable corruption sets in, the ideals of virtue and honor may remain to haunt those who have lost both.

From the Diary of Space-Marshal Sir Francis Mackenzie Latrouche,
United Nations Armed Forces (Canada), Retired.

August 28

It has happened. What we have all hoped for. What we have all feared. What we have been expecting since we ventured out beyond Jupiter, beyond Neptune—ever since the Space Force first came into being. I only wish it had occurred while I was still on active duty, before they forced me out and destroyed Peking, Tientsin, Shanghai—and how many other cities? And how many tens of millions?

As things stand, I suppose I'm fortunate to even have heard about it. Hardesty, my former aide, got in touch from Ottawa, breaking security, which was brave of him. Torkonnen's made it tighter than it ever was before. The world can't hear the greatest story in its history until he gives the word. Space-Marshal V.I. Torkonnen, Hero of the Soviet Empire, Chief of the United Nations General Staff, who killed Bombay, Calcutta, and Peking, is in command now as humanity meets its first alien race, a race from beyond our solar system certainly, and from how much farther out in space and time? Torkonnen, who will never forgive me for sending him that copy of General Burns' *Megamurder*, nor for my inscription in it.

The Fleet first encountered them three weeks ago as they emerged from behind Pluto. Who they are, I do not know—I have not been informed. But their vessels are said to be like little worlds—their size measured in miles. Hardesty didn't say how many there were, but he hinted that communication has been established and that there are a lot of surprises for us all behind Torkonnen's wall of secrecy.

The power and knowledge possessed by beings who can move entire armadas between the stars must be fantastic, and Torkonnen is the last man I'd trust to evaluate them accurately and to influence the critical decisions Earth's leaders may have to make.

Well, we shall see. In the meantime—in this terrible time of waiting—it's hard for me to take an interest in those small things that become so important in one's daily life after retirement. Yesterday Josie, our black Lab, had eleven puppies—five males, six females—and Louise handed me the honor of naming them. Now the only name I can think of is Torkonnen, and I'm damned if I'll call any decent dog after him!

Almost a week has passed, a week of sustained secrecy and silence from UNAF Hqs. However, this morning Hardesty brought me Torkonnen's top-secret report to the Secretary General on our visitors.

It is astounding. We've all wondered what sort of weird aliens the universe might eventually throw our way—wigglies with tentacles, hive minds evolved from insectoids, silicon-based life forms, all the rest. And now, of all improbabilities, they turn out to be men, men very like ourselves, with only minor differences in bone structure and the structure of the eye, at least as far as we can tell—and they are not only men, but *military* men, the very quintessence of military men. Their whole society is military. They are literally *bred* to be military. Their officers are not a class; they are a *race*. So are their noncoms. So are their other ranks. And so are their priest-scientists, themselves a part of the military establishment. We call ourselves men; they call themselves The Conquerors and make no bones about it.

They are extremely methodical, and very patient. They tell us that they remained in the lee of Pluto for months while their drones relayed our media broadcasts to them: audio, video, holo. Their scientists unraveled English with no trouble—it is the nearest thing to a world language—and now they know a great deal about us, about our manners and morals, our diversity of religions and political beliefs, our rivalries and wars. They know a great deal too much in my opinion, considering their own rigid codes of conduct and their absolute uniformity. They seem completely unimpressed by our technology, our weaponry, and they appear to think even less of us as warriors.

How do they define civilization? According to them, the whole goal of man—meaning themselves—is to conquer lesser men, to subdue them so completely that they will remain conquered and continue to serve their conquerors *even after those conquerors have gone their way*. The report doesn't go into detail, but it states that they've shown very convincing evidence that they have done this to many, many worlds. (Can you imagine a web of empire stretched between the stars, an empire without satraps, without prefects, without governors general?)

Typically, Torkonnen sums up by refusing to take their claims seriously. He suggests that very possibly they are bluffing. But even he agrees that we will have to have much more information before we can formulate a policy or reply to any demands they may make. Apparently the first real meeting after contact was at our Saturn Station, in orbit around that mighty planet. They came in a single ship—and it now seems that the original reports were exaggerated; their vessels are huge, but not miles long, perhaps half again as long as the largest twentieth-century giant tanker or aircraft carrier. Eight of their personnel arrived in a shuttle craft, and we now know that, like ourselves, they have antigravity.

The report adds that further information, with photographs and additional details regarding their organization, weapons, etc., will be on its way to the Secretary General as soon as possible. I hope Hardesty can get me a copy of that too.

September 7

Thank God for Hardesty. His personal loyalty has touched me deeply. The report this time is signed by General Casimirski, a very gallant Pole whom I remember well and favorably. He commands the Station, and his description of the deputation sent shivers down my back.

"They are human," he wrote. "But at the same time, they are unhuman. The great differences are in the way they move, in the fact that their faces seem totally expressionless, and even more, in their eyes. Their eyes have pupils like our own, but they have no true whites. It is as though the iris gradually merges with the surrounding eye. Imagine a greenish moss agate, very pale around its outer rim and gradually darkening toward a hard, cold, obsidian pupil. Physically, as men, they are superb, lean as greyhounds, taut as strung bows, yet totally relaxed. Their uniforms are extremely simple, in unobtrusive colors apparently denoting something, their only ornaments insignia of rank worn around their necks and multicolored vertical badges where we would wear our service ribbons. They have no facial hair; their lips are thin, their noses unvaryingly hawklike. They have individuality, but only as Doberman pinschers have individuality. The ones who can speak English, but they speak it slowly, like machines, as though the concepts in their own tongue are so completely alien that every word has to be weighed and sorted.

"Their leader, whom I could tell was older than the others, stared at me for perhaps a minute. Then he introduced himself as General— he hesitated over the word as though it were not precisely accurate— Rhuzar'yi. Then I introduced myself and said, 'General, we welcome you and your people. This is the first time we have had the pleasure of meeting people from another world. Be assured that we shall make the necessary arrangements for you to meet Earth's leaders as soon as possible.'

" 'Your leaders,' he replied, 'are what you call... civilians. We are The Conquerors, please understand. We do not speak with such as these. Our... Commander will speak with your Commander, he who commands your forces, you understand? That is necessary. We must know whether you have—' Again he hesitated, using an alien word; then, reluctantly, he translated it as *honor*. 'We must determine whether you have honor. What we have learned of you tells us that certain men in your history have been capable of honor, but what of your entire...' Again the hesitation. '...your entire army, your command?' "

There had been no exchange of politenesses, no acceptance of preferred hospitality, but they had answered Casimirski's questions openly and fully. They had fourteen ships, each approximately as large as the one that had brought them. "If you wish, you can come back to it with us," the envoy said. "Then you can report to your superiors all we will show you."

Casimirski had of course accepted, taking two of his aides with him. "I was astounded," he reported. "The vessel was *not* a battleship; it seemed completely unarmed. But they showed me that it had many, many small attack craft, each perhaps fifty feet long, like combined vessel/vehicles. But more than anything else, I was reminded of a Mongol *ordo*, for all their women and children were aboard. Everything was disciplined; and at once I saw the great difference between officers, noncommissioned officers, and other ranks. It was physical. The noncoms looked like intelligent but unimaginative prizefighters; the privates hulked like willing tame bears. But the strangest thing was the perfect courtesy between ranks. Subordinates did not always render their equivalent of a salute first; all ranks saluted *one another*. It reminded me of those novels of old Poland by Sienkiewicz: *With Fire and Sword* and *The Deluge* and *Pan Machael*. There was such mutual respect between ranks then."

Casimirski went on to describe the aliens' social structure. There is no social mobility; a man is born a private or a noncom and that is what he remains—and all of them are satisfied, for respect permeates their entire order. Their collective noun for a group of sergeants, for example, is a virtue of sergeants. Ambition is confined to attaining excellence in one's station.

I read the report several times, and it convinced me that they are probably very, very dangerous.

September 22

A long wait, but much has happened. First, Torkonnen's security has been breached. The word is out. No details—just enough to start the media screaming hysterically, spreading every kind of crazy rumor. All sorts of religious fanatics and demagogues have been whipping up fear and frenzy; there have been major riots in India and South America, in Los Angeles and Cairo and Lord only knows where else. The world's national governments, who had not been informed, are raising hell and demanding information, and the screeching in the General Assembly is—if we can believe such an improbability—unprecedented.

So the pressure is really going to hit Torkonnen, not only from the member nations, but also from the Secretary General, Dr. Corua-Fanit, who has always been too close to him for comfort. It will not increase the probability of any sane reaction to the intruders.

Next, I've received two more reports. Just yesterday Hardesty came through on his way back from Geneva and left me copies. These also are from Casimirski. The first simply amplifies his previous one. The second is much more important. The Conquerors' fleet, while it has not entered the solar system proper, has come in closer and is hovering on what—if we discount Pluto—can be considered the system's outer boundary. Casimirski asked them outright if he could visit the fleet, if he could inspect every ship; and the envoy, without hesitation, told him he could. They left immediately, Casimirski taking only a single aide, and it was a strange voyage for there was no conversation. All the envoy and his officers would talk about was business. Though Casimirski and his aide ate with them, at a separate table, in their officers' mess, they talked around them in their harsh, stacatto native tongue—and even then without inflection, without discernible emotion.

When they reached the closely grouped vessels, Casimirski was taken to each of them and found them all identical, all equally disciplined, all with their small assault craft, all with their crowds of women and children, and all definitely not armed. Even more interestingly, they appear to have no provisions for security, none at all. Seemingly, nothing was hidden from him, including the weaponry of their attack craft, which he says is very similar to our own. He, of course, was careful to ask no intrusive questions; and on one occasion, when he started to board an attack craft, he inquired whether he might not be infringing security. The answer was typical of our visitors: The escorting officer said simply, "We are The Conquerors. The strong are always secure."

Of course they showed him records of their conquered planets and their now-subject populations, and he was impressed. "I saw an unending panorama of servility, of heads always bent, of faces on which no shadow of resistance—no, not even of simmering resentment—lives. And when I asked how they managed to so humble those they'd conquered, my escort replied coldly, "That we will not tell you. It is better for you not to know. If you knew, it would affect the decisions your Chief Commander soon will have to make."

It seems that they do not subject each invaded world to the same process, classifying them as—well, there's no other way to put it—*barbarians without honor*, to be subdued utterly, and *primitives with barbaric honor*, who are given a somewhat higher status, rather after the manner of the Romans when they were feeling magnanimous or needed irregular troops.

Casimirski has also seen their priest-scientists, physically almost indistinguishable from the officers, but he has learned nothing much about them except that they serve a religion of conquest, dedicated to a war god who, I gather, makes poor old Mars seem feeble by comparison. What their scientific accomplishments may be, he couldn't guess, except that they obviously have FTL—they'd have to. Also, he suspects that they must be excellent geneticists. Again, he was careful not to be too inquisitive, following the rule of never asking questions he himself would be ordered not to answer or that common sense told him might be sensitive.

Their diet, from what he saw of it, resembles ours: meat and fish, frozen undoubtedly, and hydroponic vegetables, a beverage he could only describe as some sort of sparkling tea, and a variety of alcoholic drinks, taken very ceremoniously and with extreme moderation. If there were beasts aboard, he did not see them, neither pets nor livestock. Nor did he learn anything of their private lives. He was introduced to none of their women—tensely beautiful, austere beings very much in the background, simply and richly robed, their hair generally worn long. He saw the children only at a distance and was astonished at their spontaneous discipline and their expressionless faces when they looked in his direction, small copies of their fathers. He found out, too, that at night, after their evening meal, they sang: long, ominous battle chants, chorales of conquest.

One thing that surprised him, especially in view of their high technology, was that all the officers and noncoms wore edged weapons, swords, dirks, or daggers, and wore them without affectation, as though they were part of themselves.

So, incidentally, did the larger boy-children.

So, of course, in Feudal Japan, had the samurai.

It was not in Casimirski's report, but Hardesty told me they'd turned down Torkonnen's offer to meet with their C-in-C after they learned that he was "only" Chief of Staff. I wonder if that means Corua-Fanit will get Torkonnen promoted. Apparently a Chief of Staff, to their way of thinking, is nothing more than a glorified errand boy. They practically told him that as he did not command troops in the field (if field can be translated into interstellar terms), he simply wasn't fit to speak to.

I'd like to have been there when he got the news.

And now I'd best go downstairs, let Louise show me the pups again, and then have a martini or two with her and try to allay the anxieties any intelligent woman would feel in our threatened world. Yesterday she was worrying about whether I might be recalled to active duty. "Me?" I answered. "With our friend Torkonnen in the driver's seat? Hardly!"

Now, after what I've already told her, I think she's more concerned with the danger to us all. Even as I myself.

September 27

The past days have been anxious ones, with no further word from Hardesty or anybody else. And now, abruptly and without warning, the sword has fallen. I have been proven a poor prophet, a very poor one indeed.

Shortly after five this morning, I received a phone call from the Secretary General's office. Dr. Corua-Fanit wished to speak to me, and would I take the call? Of course I said I would; and a moment later there his voice was, as smooth and insinuating as ever.

"Good morning, Sir Francis."

"Good morning, Doctor."

"I trust you and Madame are both well?"

My God, I thought, *what is the slimy little beast getting at?* "Very well, thank you," I replied.

"Good, good! Sir Francis, we are recalling you to active duty."

"You're *what?*"

"We are recalling you to active duty, of course at the rank you now hold but with even greater responsibilities—oh, yes, very much greater responsibilities. You have, I am sure, heard the news of the arrival of aliens from another system?"

"I've heard a lot of media hysteria. There's been damned little hard information."

"Well, you shall have it—indeed you shall. You will be fully briefed as soon as you arrive. Sir Francis, the world now faces an emergency— the most frightening emergency in all our history. You are needed."

I decided to be frank. "Doctor, I think you'll understand that I'm not anxious to serve under Marshal Torkonnen and that the prospect gives me ample reason to stay retired."

He laughed a little shrilly. "My dear Sir Francis! But you will not be serving *under* him. This I promise you, I myself." His tone changed for the nastier. "In any case, as you are not disabled, the terms of your commission permit us to order you back, do they not?"

I made no reply, remembering that this was the man who, scarcely three years before, had authorized the killing of nearly forty million human beings.

Finally I said, "Very well, Doctor, but I'll have one request, a modest one. I want the officer who was my personal aide, Brigadier Olaf Hardesty, reassigned to me, and I'd like to have his orders issued now."

He thanked me, his voice sounding its insincerity. "Sir Francis, your subspace vehicle will be awaiting you at Ottawa, and your aide will be aboard. I am delighted. I myself will outline your new assignment and your duties."

"Very well, Doctor." We said goodbye.

There was no point in going back to bed, and Louise, who had wakened, was sitting up, looking at me silently.

"No, I suppose you can't turn them down, can you?" she said, almost whispering.

I shook my head. "I wish I could!"

She nodded, leaned toward me, and kissed me. "I'll go downstairs and get Marie up and started fixing breakfast; then I'll send Sergeant Wamick up to help you pack."

Two hours later, Hardesty and I were through the stratosphere.

"Sir Francis," Hardesty said presently, "did the Secretary General tell you what your new job is going to be?"

"He said he'd explain it when I arrived."

Hardesty looked at me a little strangely, a little apprehensively. "Sir," he said, "I—well, I'm sure of this. You're the new C-in-C."

Two hover-limos were waiting for us when we landed, and an Italian colonel, a military aide, took us to them, directing Hardesty to the second, opening the door so I could board the first. I was not surprised to find Corua-Fanit sitting there, a thin, inconsiderable man with sparse black hair and an unhealthy skin, his eyes concealed behind the tinted lenses that are a part of the public image he cultivates—a man to whom circumstances have given great power, in my opinion a weak, cruel, ruthless man. The fact that where matters military are concerned, he is completely under Torkonnen's influence did not help the situation.

As the limo whipped through traffic, I reflected that antigravity and its associated drives had not only reduced the terrific noise level in great cities almost to a whisper, but had been responsible for putting the destiny of the world into Corua-Fanit's hands, for without them, the Space

Force would have remained what it started out to be, a rocket-propelled group of vessels watching out for stray asteroids, giant meteorites and, on the off chance, extraterrestrial visitors.

He smiled at me with his teeth. "I suppose, Sir Francis, that you have been wondering what sort of assignment I have for you?"

"Naturally, sir."

"I'm sure it will please you. We have created a new post, one that our armed forces have never had before, the post of Supreme Commander—Commander-in-Chief. It is a post for which you are ideally fitted, especially under our present extraordinary circumstances. Let me fill you in briefly. When we arrive at my residence, I shall give you the pertinent reports from those officers who have been in closest touch with the—shall we say?—invaders."

Then he proceeded to tell me everything I already knew, including The Conquerors' refusal to negotiate with anyone but a supreme military commander. "They turned down Marshal Torkonnen, not just because he lacked the title, but because they disapproved of his decisive nuclear attack on the rebel powers. They call themselves Conquerors, but they are a strange breed of military, I assure you."

I began to see the light. My controversy with Torkonnen and my retirement had received much publicity. The Conquerors, thorough as they were, would certainly have heard of it. Hence my recall and my new title. What powers it would carry with it remained to be seen.

Corua-Fanit was astute. "I am sure these people will recognize that you are a man of honor." He laughed a shrill little braying laugh. "And the fact that you and they see eye to eye about how war should be waged will be most helpful also."

"Won't they think it odd that the post has so suddenly been created, and that I myself have so suddenly been called to fill it?"

"I think not," he replied. "We've informed them that you were a *de facto* C-in-C prior to your retirement but that it simply is not our custom to use the formal title."

I thought it a pretty thin arrangement but saw no point to saying so. I said, "Doctor, I'm honored. But I can't possibly accept if the whole thing is only a pretense. I will have to have those real powers the title implies—powers of military decision and command—for responsibility, as you yourself said, will inevitably come with it."

"Oh, you will, you will!" he exclaimed, putting his arm around my shoulders, apparently not noticing that I stiffened to avoid shrinking from his touch. "Your orders have already been prepared and signed by me, giving you total authority over our armed forces and also empowering you to act as the world's Ambassador Plenipotentiary. I shall give them to you as soon as we arrive. However— and I trust this will meet with your approval—we do not intend to publish them until your negotiations with the alien commander are completed. We can't afford to let news get out that would lead our already-frightened public to think we prepare for war, which the publicized appointment of a C-in-C certainly would do. So for the time being, the news must be restricted to the few high-level officers directly concerned."

I didn't like it, but still I couldn't quarrel with it. It did make sense.

"And when do you and my alien counterpart want me to leave for our first rendezvous?"

"As soon as possible. Tomorrow morning, if you can. That should give you ample time to go over the reports, and if it doesn't, well, it will take three days to ferry you to Saturn Station and you can take them with you."

"I'll also require a complete report on the present disposition of our major forces. Can Marshal Torkonnen have that ready for me too?"

He frowned. "Torkonnen can't. He's off Earth. He said there was nothing for him to do here in view of your previous—ah, friction. So, with my approval, he left to inspect all our bases and stations." Again he laughed. "He told me he was *not* going to stop off at Saturn Station."

I did not comment.

Then he went on to tell me that according to Casimirski, the aliens were proposing to bring their entire fleet within the solar system. "We're all agreed," he said, "that probably it would be unwise to try to stop them at this stage. But on no account must they be allowed close to Earth, certainly no closer than Saturn Station. Otherwise we could have worldwide panic."

I assured him I'd keep the point in mind.

Finally we arrived at his enormous residence, where I turned down his offer of refreshment and dinner, saying I'd like to set to work immediately and asking for trays to be sent up for Hardesty and me; rather reluctantly, he showed us to our quarters. A few minutes later, the same Italian colonel arrived with a dispatch case containing my orders and the reports. I read the orders in Corua-Fanit's presence and could find no fault with them. I told him so.

As soon as the door closed behind him, we went to work. There was little in the reports we did not know. However, there was much more detail and the addition of about two dozen photos. Apparently the intruders had made no objection to being photographed. I scanned the lot, promising myself I'd study them at length once I was in space, where they could be discussed more freely. But the most interesting report of all I read three times before I said goodnight to Hardesty and went to bed.

It was Torkonnen's *Estimate of Alien Forces and Capabilities.*

September 29

I started the last entry in this journal on the way to Geneva, scribbled a bit more of it after I'd digested Torkonnen's *Estimate,* then finished it after we'd broken free from Earth's gravity and were a long way from Corua-Fanit.

The *Estimate* appalled me, but it is exactly what I'd have expected. I can't, of course, give it in full here, but I shall quote its highlights.

"In my considered professional opinion," Torkonnen wrote, "we should not take the claims of these so-called Conquerors too seriously for several reasons:

1. Their weapons and equipment—which they have not tried to hide from us—are in no way impressive. Their major ships are unarmed,

transports only, and the attack craft they carry are actually inferior to our own vessels of the same class.

2. The fact that their ships are cluttered with women and children indicates a probably nomadic way of life and, consequently, a shortage of serious military resources.

3. They have antigravity and antigravity propulsion. So do we. They have Faster-Than-Light drives, but this does not necessarily indicate scientific superiority. Their priest-scientists are dedicated to the service of a primitive war god, which argues that scientific thinking cannot have penetrated their culture too thoroughly. As, admittedly, they prey on other civilizations, they may very well have obtained FTL by piracy. Furthermore, FTL is of no use within a solar system, only in open space. It gives them no advantage whatsoever.

4. The evidence they have shown us of conquered planets and peoples, while possibly a record of successful suppression, suggests that the conquered probably had no military power or will to resist. Mankind is neither so feeble nor so passive.

Finally, after a detailed survey of comparative weaponry, he gave his conclusions:

5. As I have stated, their attack craft are numerous and adequately armed. However, their armament is in no way superior to that of our own equivalent vessels. *Most important, they have neither ships nor vessels comparable to those of our cruiser class, capable of destroying large asteroids and even minor moons.* In this regard we are superior and, to my mind, decisively so. Their fleet is as vulnerable as Calcutta or Bombay.

I shuddered, not just at his casual mention of those cities, but because he took so much for granted. Our own wars, for example, have shown that savagely primitive beliefs and a high level of science and technology are by no means incompatible. However, when I compared the *Estimate* to the report on fleet dispositions that I had received before leaving, I was to some extent reassured. Signed by General Cordeiro, a Deputy Chief of Staff, it shows every major unit, either deployed or on the way, and each positioned so that if the aliens actually attack,

Earth can be defended—but each far enough away from Saturn Station, where Corua-Fanit suggested The Conquerors place themselves, to offer no suggestion of hostile intent on our part.

Our own ship, *Aconcagua*, and her complement are also reassuring. She corresponds to what, in Nelson's day, would have been called a dispatch boat, very lightly armed, with perhaps a dozen in her crew, all very young, all unaccustomed to having a Space-Marshal aboard and terribly impressed, and all obviously frightened to death by Torkonnen's KGB style of security. They are polite and very pleasant.

October 6

A great deal to report. We arrived at the Station on the twentieth, and of course Casimirski was expecting us. He was delighted to see me, and said so. He had been told of my new post, with strict instructions to keep the news from his personnel except for the very few who would come in contact with the Conquerors' envoy, who naturally had been informed. We had passed the envoy's vessel following in the Station's orbit, and scarcely an hour elapsed before he himself appeared.

Casimirski and I were having a drink together when he was admitted, and I saw instantly that everything I had heard about The Conquerors was true. He had two officers with him and all wore the same uniform, severely cut and golden gray, and at first glance they looked as though they had been hatched from the same egg. Only their neck insignia distinguished them. The envoy's was a studded disk, possibly of platinum, as big as the Order of the Garter and suspended from what looked like a gold-and-black enameled chain. His aides wore smaller ovals, green and rimmed with gold, hanging from narrower plain chains. All three wore rows of vertical metal ornaments, enameled, mysterious in design and color, but of fine craftsmanship; Faberge, I think, could have done no better. But the strangest thing was that although they indeed were men, they were men differently constructed. Their bones seemed not only flatter than our own, but hinged differently, ais if put together by

a different Maker. They did not move as we move. And their eyes—
well, all I can say is that they are alive but not in the same way as ours,
or even as a tiger's or a hawk's.

They are profoundly disquieting.

Casimirski introduced us, and the envoy acknowledged the introduction with only a cursory movement of his right hand, raising it
rigidly, palm upward, to his waist. Then he spoke, and as Casimirski
had described, it was like a machine speaking.

"Our Supreme Commander is ready," he informed me. "He will
speak with you today, you understand? Decisions will be made."

Casimirski was as surprised as I myself. "Where is he?" he asked.

"He is… aboard our ship. He came with us, from our fleet."

We were taken aback.

"You can leave now, yes?" snapped the envoy.

"I shall leave"—I tried to keep my face as expressionless as his—
"when I have refreshed myself and discussed matters with General
Casimirski here. Let us say in one hour."

Giving no evidence of whether or not he was annoyed by this, the
envoy made the strange motion with his right hand again and withdrew.

Precisely an hour later he was back, and in a matter of minutes he
and I and Casimirski, and Casimirski's aide and Hardesty, were in their
shuttle craft and on the way.

Their great ship opened to receive the craft. It settled gently to
its berth. We left it and the envoy led us through seemingly endless
corridors and compartments, all of metal but carpeted in a dark green,
their indirect lighting glowing off walls that alternated between pleasant
light grays and blues to soft yellows. I saw their women and children,
their noncoms and their other ranks, their priest-scientists—and it was
as though none of them saw me. As far as any outward demonstration
was concerned, I simply wasn't there.

Finally an elevator took us vertically at least three hundred feet, and
we emerged into some sort of command center, complete with screens
not too unlike ours, with communications and control consoles, but
all reduced to an utter simplicity we could not have matched.

The room was semicircular, and at the very center of its radius was a crescent console with a single chair behind it. Here one man sat, and I realized immediately that their C-in-C and I now faced each other. I looked at him, and if his officers had seemed to be the quintessence of everything military—well, he was the quintessence of his people. He was tall, taller than any I had yet encountered, and everything about him was accentuated. His face was harder, harsher; his weird moss-agate eyes were colder and more penetrating. A clean white scar zigzagged across his forehead and ended on a cheekbone. His neck insignia was a glowing star hanging from a chain of small golden swords. His service badges swept across his chest.

I looked at him. He looked through me.

The envoy stopped, motioning the others to a halt. "Proceed," he said.

I marched to within two feet of the console. I bowed.

Slowly he stood up and made the same right-hand gesture as the envoy.

I introduced myself; obviously no one else was going to. "I am Space-Marshal Sir Francis Mackenzie Latrouche, Commander in Chief of the Armed Forces of the United Nations on Earth," I said.

"I am Ar'hloyk'ú. I am... Supreme Commander. We are The Conquerors, you... understand?"

His words were recognizable, but his accent could scarcely have been reproduced.

"I shall inform you—yes?—of our demands. Everything then will... depend on you. We have learned much. We understand your wars. Your history is of betrayals, of broken treaties, of war-making against the... defenseless, even women, children, cities. You do not deny this?"

He did not invite me to sit down. He himself showed no sign of doing so. We stood there, staring into each other's eyes, and I could not deny the statement he had made. "What you have said, Supreme Commander, is true—but only partly true. Not all our military men have been men of honor, but many have. I could name you any number whose sense of honor has been inflexible, who would never think of breaking an agreement, who would scorn to wage war against noncombatants."

"This," he said, "we know. We have heard of you and that you were—how do you say?—retired before your last war. Perhaps you, as a man, are capable of honor. Now we must know whether, as Commander-in-Chief, you have power to speak... for all your armed forces? The power to bind them with your word of... *honor?*"

"I have," I said. "I can speak for all the nations, for all mankind."

"That does not interest us. It is whether you can speak for warriors with the honor of a warrior, you understand?"

"I can."

"Then this is what I say to you. We will bring our fleet within your system so that after you... hear our terms, there need be no delay in carrying them out."

I nodded, not letting my face betray my surge of anger at his arrogance.

"We shall do this, and we require your word of honor that we shall neither be interfered with nor attacked."

"You have it," I replied. "However, there will be one condition."

"*Condition?*" He made it sound absolutely unbelievable.

"One condition. The peoples on Earth have no experience of other races. As you know from our media broadcasts, they are already frightened almost to the point of panic. If you bring your fleet too close to Earth, chaos will result. I must request that you come no closer than the vicinity of our Saturn Station, where I met your envoy."

He thought for a moment—at least he stood there staring at me. Finally, "For the time," he said, "we will do this. Then we, you and I, will talk again about our terms... also about the status we will give you."

"And our choice will be?"

His knowledge of English was not quite adequate to putting it concisely, and he had to search for terms to express his exact meaning. At last, however, I gathered that our status, depending on how they rated our capacity for honor, would range from the best, an equivalent of most favored barbarian, to the worst, utter subjugation.

"Your officers have been shown," he declared. "It is not a desirable condition for men with... pride."

"How do you accomplish it?" I asked.

He kept on staring through me. "As we have said, that is the one thing we will not tell you, for your decision then would not be your own... you understand?"

I nodded. Further questioning was useless.

"So, when our fleet arrives, a matter of perhaps five of your days, you and I will meet again. Between us, all will be settled. I have your word... of honor?"

"You have my word of honor," I said.

Again the right-hand gesture. Again I bowed. The conference was at an end. The envoy said, "Come. We shall return."

The trip back to the Station was a silent one. Only after we had arrived and the envoy's ship was on its way did any of us give vent to how we felt. Casimirski swore in Polish for a full minute. "God in Heaven!" he cried. "What arrogant sons of bitches! Insufferable! And yet—sir, I hate to say this. I don't want you, of all people, to think I am a coward, but, sir, I feel that they are a very old culture, incredibly strong, incredibly experienced, and far more dangerous than they look. I don't care if their armament does seem inferior. There's more to them than braggadocio, much more."

"What do you think, Hardesty?"

"I agree, sir. I think we must walk very carefully and maybe even take our lumps, for a time at least, when you and he negotiate. If we have to, of course we'll fight, but we ought to do it only as a last resort."

"That is my view also," I said. "I just hope Corua-Fanit agrees with us when it comes down to the nitty-gritty."

I composed my report to the Secretary General, and Casimirski sent it off directly. With it, I asked for an up-to-the-minute report on the present disposition of our forces and for instructions as to how I was to take over command were military action to prove necessary. Then we waited for the hours to pass while the messages bridged those vast distances.

The answer came during supper. Corua-Fanit approved of how I'd handled things, assured me there had been no changes in dispositions since the Deputy Chief of Staff's last report, and told me that when and if necessary, I could immediately assume command through normal staff channels.

Hardesty isn't happy. He doesn't trust Corua-Fanit. He doesn't trust Torkonnen, even if he is somewhere on the other side of the system. However, he agrees that the course we have followed has been the only possible one and that everything does seem to be in order.

October 14

Yes, everything seemed to be in order. But it was not. On the eleventh, right on schedule, the thirteen alien ships neared Saturn and were in touch with us before we could pick them up visually. They said they'd prefer to hover on antigrav but would go into orbit if we so desired—evincing a degree of consideration that seemed foreign to them. I told them to take their choice but that we would prefer them within easy communicating distance.

And at that point all communication was cut off—all except a flood of signals from vessels of our own, vessels that were supposed to be far, far away. None of the signals were in the clear; we could make nothing of them.

"Christ!" shouted Hardesty. "It sounds like a bloody battle going on!"

"*It is,*" whispered Casimirski.

Half an hour later we found out what had happened. An *Aconcagua*-class ship pulled in, torn almost to ribbons. We winkled out her crew, what was left of it. Torkonnen had put practically all of our main strength hovering behind Saturn—after all, Corua-Fanit, with my un-witting aid, had set the aliens up for him; and they had decelerated almost completely when he struck. There was no way they could have escaped him—

But then, they didn't need to.

They did not move. Around each of their vessels there appeared a faint nimbus, extending out to four or five diameters, and whenever a weapon—whether a missile, a laser, a particle beam, anything—was directed at it, it glowed momentarily and then the weapon was either absorbed or exploded or deflected. Each of those halos was impenetrable.

The C.O. of the *Aconcagua* class sat there having the station medics dress his wounds, gasping out his story. Each of the great ships had opened its maw, and the attack craft had poured forth in swarms— and they too were surrounded by the protective shields. "The bastards must have something combining antigrav and their FTL drives," said the C.O., shaking his head. "They must. How else could they have managed it? How else?"

Of course it didn't matter, not in the least. We could tell by the frantic signals sputtering out that Torkonnen's forces were being swiftly and ruthlessly destroyed, as swiftly and as ruthlessly as he had destroyed those cities.

He had betrayed me. He had tried to betray The Conquerors. He had betrayed Earth and all mankind.

I only hoped that he would be on Earth when I arrived.

Half an hour later, with as many of the Station's people as we could crowd aboard, we were on our way; and we made it in two and a half days, setting down at Geneva Spaceport. We knew The Conquerors would be coming, but we also knew that they'd be in no hurry. They had no need to be.

Ashore, I was immediately surrounded by a gaggle of staff officers and hysterical civilians. I pushed through them to a limo I recognized as Corua-Fanit's, waited for Hardesty to get in with me, and told the driver, "Take me to your leader."

"He's at Armed Forces Headquarters," he said.

"Get there!" ordered Hardesty.

We rode in silence, and it took only a few minutes to reach the old League of Nations building by the lake where I, as C-in-C, would have had my office.

We marched directly, Hardesty and I, to the office of the Chief of Staff, and there we found them both: Corua-Fanit, looking as though he had been suddenly pumped out, then filled with cold, gray dishwater, and Torkonnen, massive and lowering, frightened now but still hostile and defiant. Whether he had returned from space or whether he had even been off Earth, I did not know. Nor did I care.

I said nothing to them. There would have been no point to it. And if they spoke, I did not hear it.

Instead, I drew the pistol I had taken from the Station and shot each of them. I shot them in the forehead, killing each instantly. Then I sent Hardesty to find men to get them out of there, to dispose of them.

I sat down at the desk, began this entry in my journal, and waited for The Conquerors to come down. Hardesty took a chair next to me.

We waited patiently. What else could we do? Now they are here. Through the window I can see the sky filled with their small assault craft, each surrounded by its protective field, the field that renders it invulnerable. They are coming down swiftly. In the distance, they look almost like falling leaves.

Now their first craft has landed, on the lawn across the road and directly in front of Headquarters.

Five of them have marched out of it, and they are striding, in their precise, strangely jointed way, toward us. In moments they will be here. And they are no longer expressionless.

I must say that I do not like the look on their fa–

LEPANTO

by Gilbert Keith Chesterton

Editor's Introduction

Constantinople, the City of the Golden Horn, capital of Byzantium, fell in 1453 to the cannon of the Ottoman Turks; with it fell the last of the Eastern Roman Empire. For the next hundred years all Europe was threatened. Soliman, known to Europe as Suleiman the Magnificent, besieged Vienna in 1529 and came within an ace of taking the city.

In 1571 the Turks struck at the Venetian lion's holdings, and threatened to turn the Mediterranean into a Turkish lake. It was no idle threat. The Turkish fleet of galleys was the largest in the world, and Christendom was hopelessly divided. France had made alliance with the Turks.

One man saw the danger. Pius V prevailed upon the Spanish and the Venetians to join forces in a grand alliance. Philip II of Spain, son of Charles V, sent his fleet under the command of his bastard half brother Don John of Austria. John, at 26, was the most able commander of his time. (He is *not* the fickle "Don John" of Mozart's opera.) The Turkish fleet concentrated at the mouth of the Gulf of Corinth near the fortified town of Lepanto. The Turkish fleet boasted 270 galleys to oppose Don John's 220; but the Christian fleet included six "super galleys," known as galeasses, which were deployed in front of the Christian battle line.

The fleets met in the narrow straits. Ali Pasha, the Turkish commander, had 400 Janissary shock troops aboard his flagship. He steered directly for Don John's flagship *Real*. The ships crashed together and became entangled. Ali called for reinforcements from the galleys in reserve behind his line. Other Christian ships rushed to aid the *Real*.

Twice the Janissaries boarded the *Real* and were swept back by her 300 arquebusiers. Twice again Don John's soldiers boarded the Turkish flagship and reached the mainmast, before Colonna in the Papal flagship came alongside the Turk and raked her decks with musket fire. Don John's third charge carried, and the whole of the Turkish center fled.

The carnage was terrible. Twelve Christian galleys were sunk and one captured, with losses of 15,000 officers and men. Of the Turks, 113 galleys were sunk, and another 117 captured. Tens of thousands of Turks were killed, 8,000 were captured, and 15,000 Christian galley slaves were freed.

The best known casualty of the battle was Miguel Cervantes, whose left hand was carried away by a cannon ball. He survived to write *Don Quixote*.

White founts falling in the courts of the sun,
And the Soldan of Byzantium is smiling as they run;
There is laughter like the fountains in that face of all men feared,
It stirs the forest darkness, the darkness of his beard,
It curls the blood-red crescent, the crescent of his lips,
For the inmost sea of all the earth is shaken with his ships.
They have dared the white republics up the capes of Italy,
They have dashed the Adriatic round the Lion of the Sea,
And the Pope has cast his arms abroad for agony and loss,
And called the kings of Christendom for swords about the Cross,
The cold queen of England is looking in the glass;
The shadow of the Valois is yawning at the Mass;
From evening isles rings faint the Spanish gun,
And the Lord upon the Golden Horn is laughing in the sun.

Dim drums throbbing, in the hills half heard,
Where only on a nameless throne a crownless prince has stirred,
Where, risen from a doubtful seat and half-attainted stall,
The last knight of Europe takes weapons from the wall,
The last lingering troubadour to whom the bird has sung,
That once went singing southward when all the world was young,
In that enormous silence, tiny and unafraid,
Comes up along a winding road the noise of the Crusade.
Strong gongs groaning as the guns boom far,
Don John of Austria is going to the war,
Stiff flags straining in the night-blasts cold
In the gloom black-purple, in the glint old-gold,
Torchlight crimson on the copper kettle-drums,
Then the tuckets, then the trumpets, then the cannon, and he comes.
Don John laughing in the brave beard curled,
Spurning of his stirrups like the thrones of all the world,
Holding his head up for a flag of all the free.
Love-light of Spain—hurrah!
Death-light of Africa!
Don John of Austria
Is riding to the sea.

Mahound is in his paradise above the evening star,
(Don John of Austria is going to the war.)
He moves a mighty turban on the timeless houri's knees,
His turban that is woven of the sunset and the seas.
He shakes the peacock gardens as he rises from his ease,
And he strides among the tree-tops and is taller than the trees,
And his voice through all the garden is a thunder sent to bring
Black Azrael and Ariel and Ammon on the wing.
Giants and the Genii,
Multiplex of wing and eye,
Whose strong obedience broke the sky
When Solomon was king.

They rush in red and purple from the red clouds of the morn,
From temples where the yellow gods shut up their eyes in scorn;
They rise in green robes roaring from the green hells of the sea
Where fallen skies and evil hues and eyeless creatures be;
On them the sea-valves cluster and the grey sea-forests curl,
Splashed with a splendid sickness, the sickness of the pearl;
They swell in sapphire smoke out of the blue cracks of the ground,—
They gather and they wonder and give worship to Mahound.
And he saith, "Break up the mountains where the hermit-folk may hide,
And sift the red and silver sands lest bone of saint abide,
And chase the Giaours flying night and day, not giving rest,
For that which was our trouble comes again out of the west.
We have set the seal of Solomon on all things under sun,
Of knowledge and of sorrow and endurance of things done,
But a noise is in the mountains, in the mountains, and I know
The voice that shook our palaces—four hundred years ago:
It is he that saith not 'Kismet'; it is he that knows not Fate;
It is Richard, it is Raymond, it is Godfrey in the gate!
It is he whose loss is laughter when he counts the wager worth,
Put down your feet upon him, that our peace be on the earth."
For he heard drums groaning and he heard guns jar,
(Don John of Austria is going to the war.)
Sudden and still—hurrah!
Bolt from Iberia!
Don John of Austria
Is gone by Alcalar.

St. Michael's on his Mountain in the sea-roads of the north
(Don John of Austria is girt and going forth.)
Where the grey seas glitter and the sharp tides shift
And the sea folk labour and the red sails lift.
He shakes his lance of iron and he claps his wings of stone;
The noise is gone through Normandy; the noise is gone alone;
The North is full of tangled things and texts and aching eyes.

And dead is all the innocence of anger and surprise,
And Christian killeth Christian in a narrow dusty room,
And Christian dreadeth Christ that hath a newer face of doom,
And Christian hateth Mary that God kissed in Galilee,
But Don John of Austria is riding out to the sea.
Don John calling through the blast and the eclipse
Crying with the trumpet, with the trumpet of his lips,
Trumpet that sayeth ha!
Domino gloria!
Don John of Austria
Is shouting to the ships.

King Philip's in his closet with the Fleece about his neck
(Don John of Austria is armed upon the deck.)
The walls are hung with velvet that is black and soft as sin,
And little dwarfs creep out of it and little dwarfs creep in.
He holds a crystal phial that has colours like the moon,
He touches, and it tingles, and he trembles very soon,
And his face is as a fungus of a leprous white and grey
Like plants in the high houses that are shuttered from the day,
And death is in the phial, and the end of noble work,
But Don John of Austria has fired upon the Turk.
Don John's hunting, and his hounds have bayed—
Booms away past Italy the rumour of his raid.
Gun upon gun, ha! ha!
Gun upon gun, hurrah!
Don John of Austria
Has loosed the cannonade.

The Pope was in his chapel before day or battle broke,
(Don John of Austria is hidden in the smoke.)
The hidden room in a man's house where God sits all the year,
The secret window whence the world looks small and very dear.
He sees as in a mirror on the monstrous twilight sea
The crescent of his cruel ships whose name is mystery;

They fling great shadows foe-wards, making Cross and Castle dark,
They veil the plumed lions on the galleys of St. Mark;
And above the ships are palaces of brown, black-bearded chiefs,
And below the ships are prisons, where with multitudinous griefs,
Christian captives sick and sunless, all a labouring race repines
Like a race in sunken cities, like a nation in the mines.
They are lost like slaves that swat, and in the skies of morning hung
The stairways of the tallest gods when tyranny was young.
They are countless, voiceless, hopeless as those fallen or fleeing on
Before the high Kings' horses in the granite of Babylon.
And many a one grows witless in his quiet room in hell
Where a yellow face looks inward through the lattice of his cell,
And he finds his God forgotten, and he seeks no more a sign—
(But Don John of Austria has burst the battle-line!)
Don John pounding from the slaughter-painted poop,
Purpling all the ocean like a bloody pirate's sloop,
Scarlet running over on the silvers and the golds,
Breaking of the hatches up and bursting of the holds,
Thronging of the thousands up that labour under sea
White for bliss and blind for sun and stunned for liberty.
Vivat Hispania!
Domino Gloria!
Don John of Austria
Has set his people free!

Cervantes on his galley sets the sword back in the sheath
(Don John of Austria rides homeward with a wreath.)
And he sees across a weary land a straggling road in Spain,
Up which a lean and foolish knight forever rides in vain
And he smiles, but not as Sultans smile, and settles back the blade...
(But Don John of Austria rides home from the Crusade.)

A CURE FOR CROUP

by Edward P. Hughes

Editor's Introduction

Edward Hughes lives in Britain. In his masterful future history there have been wars and rumors of war; civilization has fallen, taking much of the ecology with it. Staying alive is a struggle; but the people of the small Irish village of Barley Cross are determined to live normal lives despite the fall. Protected by The O'Meara, Master of the Fist and onetime Sergeant Major of Her Majesty's forces, Barley Cross has been an island of civilized life among the ruins.

The beginning was told in the story "In The Name Of The Father," in Volume II of this series; "A Cure For Croup" continues the tale.

————————

The sound of a tolling bell woke Liam McGrath. He nudged his sleeping wife.

"Hear that racket, Eileen!"

Eileen McGrath stirred in her sleep. She had been up half the night nursing their one-year-old son through an attack of croup, and she was in no mood for conversation.

Liam frowned at the bell's clamor. *That* could only be the village church bell—and Father Con never allowed it to be sounded as a warning.

Eileen opened her eyes. "What time is it?"

Liam reached across her to consult the ancient windup alarm his mother had given them as a wedding present.

"Only five-thirty, by God! D'you think there's something wrong?"

She said drowsily, "Sounds like a death knell to me."

He swung his legs out of bed. Their cottage clung close to the root of Kirkogue Mountain and was a mere cockstride out of the village of Barley Cross. From his bedroom window Liam could see along the village's one and only main street. He peered through the curtains. Figures moved on the distant roadway.

And the bell tolled.

He grabbed his trousers from the chair back and began to dress.

Eileen raised herself on one elbow. "Where are you going?"

He buckled his belt. "I'm off to see what's happened. It may be an emergency."

She sighed. "Don't wake Tommy. I've only just got him off."

Liam nodded. Their son's harsh breathing and racking cough had demanded the village doctor's attention the previous night. Liam could hear stertorous respiration from the next room. He tiptoed downstairs, lifted his jacket from the newel post, and slipped out into the morning light.

Seamus Murray stood at the door of his forge. The smith's face was unduly solemn. He seemed not to notice Liam's presence.

Liam shook his arm. "What's happened, man? What's the bell for?"

Seamus's mouth opened and closed like a fish in a jar. Then the words gushed out. "The O'Meara's dead! They found him at the foot of the stairs when the guard went in to report the 'all clear' this morning. He'd had a heart attack."

Liam stared, his brain refusing to accept the smith's news. Patrick O'Meara, Lord of Barley Cross, Master of the Fist, and focus of village life for as long as Liam could remember, dead? It was like hearing the village clock had vanished.

He said stupidly, "How come they found him so early?"

Seamus Murray shot him a pitying look. "The Master always wanted a report as soon as it grew light enough to see the O'Toole cottage.

We've done it that way for years—though I doubt a lad of your age would appreciate why."

Liam knew why. He had suffered the saga of Barley Cross versus the Rest of Ireland from his elders ever since he had been old enough to pay attention.

He ignored Murray's dig. "So who found him?"

The smith scanned the road. Liam's face appeared to be the last thing he wanted to look at. "Christ, man, how should I know? I don't stand guard at the Fist anymore. Does it matter? We've lost our protector—the man who kept us from death and destruction in the years gone by—and all you want to know is who found him!"

All Barley Cross went to the funeral, that being the villagers' normal procedure. But many a wife shed more than customary tears for the deceased. Patrick O'Meara, the ram of Barra Hill, had left no widow to mourn his passing, but in a very real way he had been a father to the community, and many of the women had particularly fond memories of him.

The O'Meara's henchmen met in the dining hall of the Fist as soon as the obsequies were done.

General Larry Desmond drained a tumbler of poteen with scant regard for its potency. He wiped the back of his hand across his mouth, then set the empty glass on the carpet between his feet. "Well," he said. "We're in a pickle now."

At the other end of the broken-backed settee, Kevin Murphy, the vet, stared gloomily into his own glass. "God dammit!" he muttered. "I loved that bloody man. Why could it not have happened to one of us instead?"

Celia Larkin, MA, schoolmistress and spinster, sipped a cup of herb tea brewed especially for her by Michael, the O'Meara's servant. Neglected runnels in her face powder showed where the tears had flowed. She sniffed. "Maybe it's the Lord's judgment on our presumption. Father Con ranted about it often enough."

Denny Mallon, MD, dwarfed in the great, shiny armchair, sucked at an empty pipe. "Father Con's views on delegated procreation don't necessarily reflect those of our Maker. Think about Judah's advice to Onan in Genesis. And anyway, this is no time to be questioning tenets. But for Patrick O'Meara, Barley Cross would be a futureless dormitory by now. I can't imagine that even Father Con would want that."

General Desmond refilled his glass from the bottle on the floor. "Denny, you are overly pessimistic as usual. A few of us here still have a kick or two left in us. Point is—where are we going to find a man to father the next generation of kids in Barley Cross?"

"That child of the Kellys–" began Celia Larkin.

Kevin Murphy grunted. "Christ, Celia, he's only ten or eleven years old. We're surely not counting on adolescent precocity to–"

General Desmond choked over his drink. "God love us! Let the little fellow grow up first! We're not even sure he's fertile. The Kellys never had any more kids."

Celia Larkin compressed prim lips. "You misunderstand me, gentlemen. It was the father I had in mind. And my idea was for it to be done surgically. Presumably the way Kevin achieves it with his beasts."

Kevin Murphy jerked upright. "Hold on now! I'm no gynecologist. Better ask Denny about that kind of maneuver."

Doctor Denny Mallon lowered his pipe. "The Kelly boy might be a possibility in a year or two—if he is his father's son. But Con Kelly never managed another child. As for artificial insemination, I have no equipment and no skill—nor the wish to employ either. We have discussed this idea before and rejected it. We agreed, if I rightly recall, that women are not cattle. And anyway, to go in now for clinical insemination would explode our carefully nurtured fiction that the husbands of Barley Cross are the fathers of their children. No, my friends, what we need is a new seigneur to exercise his droits."

General Desmond's eyes narrowed in sudden suspicion. He glowered at the doctor. "Just what have you hidden up your sleeve, Denny lad?"

Denny Mallon picked at the charcoaled bowl of his pipe with a black thumbnail. He closed his eyes, as though weighing a doubtful course. Then he shook his head.

"It's not professional ethics to betray a patient's confidence."

"Denny!" squealed Celia Larkin.

"But if you'll each give me your word to preserve–"

"Christ, man! Yes, yes!" interrupted Kevin Murphy.

Denny Mallon swiveled arched eyebrows at the general and the schoolmistress. "You too—both of you?"

"God, man! Give up! Yes!"

"Anything, Denny. Just tell us!"

The doctor tapped his pipe on the heel of his hand. His listeners strained forward to catch his soft-spoken words.

"Eileen McGrath tells me she's missed her menses for the second month in succession. I think she's pregnant with her second child!"

Larry Desmond's breath came out in a low whistle. "Young Liam McGrath?"

Denny Mallon nodded. "Who else?"

Celia Larkin's eyes flashed behind her rimless spectacles. "What exactly does that mean, Denny? You're the expert."

Denny Mallon grimaced. "It could mean that our dear Patrick passed on his fertility to Liam McGrath—for which mercy I would be grateful. Or it could be that our ozone layer is repairing itself since we stopped assaulting it with fluorocarbons. Which is unlikely. Alternatively, It could be that some of our children have developed an immunity to heavy ultraviolet doses. And that would be the best answer of all."

"But you don't know which?"

Denny Mallon shrugged. "Only time will tell. Meantime, I think we should make full use of young McGrath."

Kevin Murphy said, "Will he oblige?"

"Give me a chance to ask him!"

Celia Larkin pounced. "You'll do it, then?"

Denny Mallon grimaced. "Seems like I've got the job."

The general snorted. "Seems like we'll have to get ourselves an interim government."

Kevin Murphy looked doubtful. "D'you think they'll take orders from us?"

"They'll take them from Larry," Celia Larkin pointed out. "He still runs the army. And he can delegate duties to us. It will work 'til we get a new Master."

Denny Mallon got out his pouch and poked his pipe bowl into it. He said casually, "I have to visit the McGraths tomorrow. The McGrath infant is not well, and I have a theory to check. I'll find an opportunity to talk to Liam." He rolled up the pouch and slipped it back into his pocket. "But we've got to offer him everything—Lord of Barley Cross, Master of the Fist, the lot—or it won't work. He must replace Patrick in every way. Anything less would confuse the village."

Kevin Murphy grunted doubtfully. "I'm not sure the village will accept him."

Larry Desmond drained his glass. "I'll guarantee the army's acceptance."

Celia Larkin smiled acidly. "And I the schoolchildren."

The vet said, "But how can we justify his taking the O'Meara's place? He's no more than a boy. They're used to an adult tyrant like we built Pat into."

The general chuckled. "Those in the know won't need any justification other than his fertility."

"But the others? The O'Connors, the Toomeys, the Flanagans—?"

"If Pat had only left a will nominating young Mc-Grath…" Denny Mallon began pensively.

Celia Larkin sniffed disparagingly. "That would be too good to be true."

The doctor fumbled inside his jacket for one of the last ball points in Barley Cross. "Get us a bit of paper, Celia. I'll write one out straightaway that meets the bill."

The following afternoon, Doctor Denny Mallon found Liam Mc-Grath's donkey standing by a peat stack on the main road out of the village. The doctor rested an arm on the animal's rump and waited. Liam appeared from behind the stack, arms piled with clods of turf.

Denny Mallon waved a salute. "God bless the work, Liam. 'Tis a soft day we're having." He shielded his pipe bowl from the drizzle and struck a homemade match.

Liam pitched his peat into the panniers borne by the donkey. "Are you looking for me, Doctor?" His voice was sharp with anxiety. "You're not worried about our Tommy?"

Denny Mallon puffed smoke into the moist air. "I want another look at him, Liam. And maybe take a sputum sample. But nothing to worry about. I want a quiet word with you first."

Liam's face set hard. "About what, Doctor? Is there something wrong with my son? If there is, there's nothing you can't say in front of my wife."

Denny Mallon cocked an eye at the white cottage perched on the toe of the mountain. Up there, presumably, Eileen McGrath went about her wifely duties. The top of Kirkogue was lost in mist. The nearest house in Barley Cross was a drizzle-masked shape. Doctor and youth might have been the only inhabitants of a nebulous, rain-soaked, peaty landscape. Which was the way Denny Mallon had planned it.

He said, "Well now, Liam, I wouldn't be in such a hurry to make such pronouncements meself. What if I was to say I'm here on an errand for General Desmond?"

"Like what?" Liam demanded guardedly. "I'm not old enough to serve at the Fist yet. And if someone wants help with a job, he don't have to get the general to order me to—"

"Now, now," soothed Denny Mallon. "No one is complaining about you, son. And the only person seeking your help is the general himself."

Liam frowned. "What can I do for him?"

Denny Mallon put away his pipe. Homegrown herbs didn't burn well in damp weather. He said, "I believe you had an interview with the O'Meara when you got married?"

Liam McGrath grinned at the memory. On that particular day, he reckoned, he grew up. "The Master told you about it, did he?"

Denny Mallon turned up his jacket collar and dug his hands into his pockets. "Let's say I had his confidence. Did he happen to let you in on a certain secret, about which I would be reluctant to expand any further?"

Liam's grin disappeared. "If you mean, do I know who fathered our Tommy—yes."

"Ah!" Denny Mallon's hobgoblin face creased in what Liam identified as a grin of satisfaction. "But *who* fathered your *second* child?"

Liam goggled at him. "Eileen is going to have another?"

"I'm her doctor, aren't I?"

Liam was abruptly babbling nonsense. He rolled down his shirt sleeves and pulled a scrap of tarpaulin from the top of the peat stack. "Come on, Doctor—let's go! Thanks for the news. Eileen suspected she might..."

Denny Mallon raised a damp hand. "Hold on now, Liam. You've not heard the general's message yet."

Liam pulled the tarpaulin around his shoulders, gripping the donkey's rope. "Make it quick, Doctor. Can't we talk on the way?"

Denny Mallon shrugged. "I'll put it bluntly, son. You're aware of precisely what our recent Master's most important service to the village was. And I've just told you that you've fathered your second child. Well, since your little Tommy will be the only child in Barley Cross with a sibling—"

Liam frowned. "A sibling?"

"A brother or sister."

"Oh!" Liam's mouth made a circle. He said guardedly, "And so?"

"So you are the only male in Barley Cross capable of taking over from the O'Meara. Because you are the only one who has inherited his peculiar talent."

Liam glanced nervously toward the cottage on Kirkogue. "What are you trying to tell me, Doctor?"

Denny Mallon paused, like a man preparing to plunge into icy water. Inwardly he berated Celia Larkin for saddling him with this pest of a job. He said, "Our recent Master has nominated you in his will to be his successor. And since all the kids in Barley Cross are his children, you have as good a claim as any to his title. The general has charged me to invite you to take up your new role immediately."

After what seemed to be several hours' thought, Liam said, "He can't ask me to do that, Doctor!"

Denny Mallon shrugged. "He can, Liam. Haven't I just done it for him?"

"But what would folk in the village say?"

The doctor shrugged again. "You might have to put up with some comment. Even the O'Meara was criticized. You can't expect to please everybody. But you'd have General Desmond and his men behind you."

Liam flicked another glance at the cottage on Kirkogue. "What if I have to—-you know—?"

"That would be your own problem, son."

Liam squared his shoulders. "And if I say 'no'?" Denny Mallon stared impassively from beneath drizzle-bedewed eyebrows. "Then Barley Cross goes down the drain."

Liam grumbled. "It's not fair to expect me to—"

The doctor's face was sphinxlike. "Who told you life is supposed to be fair? Do you imagine Pat O'Meara enjoyed playing a libidinous tyrant? Sometimes there's a need to subordinate personal inclinations to the wishes of the community."

"I'm not sure the community wants me to—"

The wizened, bent figure straightened up. "I'm not just talking about our village. There are bigger communities."

Liam said weakly, "Can I talk to Eileen first?"

"That might be the best idea," agreed the doctor.

Eileen McGrath said, "If you think I'll agree to your taking over from the ram of Barley Cross, you've another think coming, my lad."

"But, Eileen! Didn't you tell me that the O'Meara was a civil man and that it was an honor to be chosen for his *droit du seigneur*?"

"*You* and the O'Meara are two different people," his wife pointed out. "The O'Meara had no wife to object to his shenanigans. And you do!"

"But wouldn't you like to be the First Lady of Barley Cross and live up at the Fist?"

Eileen McGrath's honest face grew sober. "I suppose any girl would say yes to that—although there's a great deal needs doing to that barn of a place before I'd hang my hat in the hall."

"Well, then–"

"There is no 'well, then,'" she affirmed decisively. "One wife is enough for any man, and one wife is all you're going to have."

Liam found Father Con shining brasses in the village church. The priest had aged in the short time since Liam's wedding. He now walked with a stoop, frequently clutching his side.

"Well, Liam," he greeted. "You've come to help me with these dratted brasses, no doubt?"

Liam grinned. He was fond of the old priest. He picked up a rag and a candlestick. "If you like, Father. Actually I called for a bit of advice." He told the priest of the general's proposal.

"'Twould be a fine promotion for you."

"It would be..." Liam hesitated. How aware was Father Con of the reasons for the O'Meara's promiscuity? One had to be discreet.

"But you're bothered about certain aspects of the job?" added the priest.

Liam let out a sigh. "That's about it, Father."

"Hmm." The priest put down the vase he had been polishing and squatted in a pew. "I think we discussed this matter before? And I refused to condemn our recent Master's conduct—much to your dismay?"

Liam nodded. "That's true."

The priest sighed. "Well, Liam, if you decide to take on the O'Meara's job, I might also refuse to condemn *your* conduct. One day you may learn there are higher loyalties than those between husband

and wife." The priest examined the candlestick thoughtfully. "The executioner is not necessarily guilty of murder when he carries out the state's commands. Nor the starving woman of theft when she steals to feed her hungry children. So maybe our recent Master was innocent of adultery when he exercised his seigneurial rights—for surely our fine school would be empty of scholars and our church short of sinners had he not done so." The old man rested his head on the wood of the pew. " 'Tis a problem that's given me little peace these last few years. And I'm no nearer the solution now than I was at the start."

"Perhaps if you appealed to someone higher?" Liam suggested diplomatically.

The priest snorted in derision. " 'Twould be a marvelous day that I hear from a superior, Liam—supposing there are any left. And remember, they too would be only men, with men's limping insight into ethical matters. Sometimes 'tis better to pray and take your answer on trust. Desperate situations demand desperate remedies, lad. And Barley Cross is surely in a desperate situation."

Liam put down the polishing rag. "Are you saying it is okay for me to take the O'Meara's job, Father Con?"

The priest grimaced. "If you didn't want it and I said 'yes,' would you take any more notice than if you did want it and I said 'no'?"

Liam shrugged. Father Con could be pretty vague when he didn't want to come right out with things. He said, "I suppose you are right, Father Con."

"Suppose?" The old man raised his head angrily. "Is that the best you can say? Consider, Liam, who gives me comfort and advice? Do you think you are the only soul in Barley Cross with a problem? On this matter you will have to be guided by your conscience and make your own decision. The days of dogmatic religion are gone. Soon you won't even have this remnant of Mother Church to steer your footsteps."

Liam sidled toward the church door. Father Con with the miseries was a person to avoid. He needed someone more cheerful to talk to. Someone like—Liam clapped his hands. Of course! Eileen's mother.

He muttered, "I'll think about it, Father," slipped out of the porch into the sunshine and was off, running.

Brigit O'Connor was in her kitchen, floury to the elbows over a batch of soda bread. She said, "Mister O'Connor is down at the mill. He'll be making a new blade for Mick Mcguire's waterwheel. Did you want him badly?"

Tom O'Connor, being a joiner by trade, was often called upon to fix bits of Barley Cross's machinery. Liam got on well enough with him, but he would not deny that he had half hoped to find his mother-in-law alone. He said, "No sweat, mam-in-law. I'd just as soon bring my troubles to you."

Dumpy Brigit O'Connor beamed fondly at him. She had always fostered a soft spot for Maureen McGrath's lad.

"Will I be making you a sup of tea," she asked, "while you tell me what's bugging you?"

Liam hoisted himself onto a corner of the table. He swung his legs for a moment, in thought. His mother-in-law might not be as well-informed as Father Con. He said, "Doctor Denny says the O'Meara has left a will naming me as the next Master, and General Desmond has asked me to take over."

"Well now..." Brigit O'Connor hefted, one-handed, a steaming black-iron kettle from the stove top. She poured boiling water into a dented aluminum teapot. "That would be a great step up for you, Liam."

His legs stopped swinging. "You wouldn't mind, mam-in-law?"

She stirred the pot vigorously. "Indeed no! Wouldn't you make as good a Master as the O'Meara after you've had a bit of practice?"

Liam sneaked off the corner from a loaf cooling under a towel. He popped the bread into his mouth. "I wish Eileen felt like that."

His mother-in-law studied him with bright button eyes. "Does she not fancy living up at the Fist?"

"It's not that." Liam hesitated. The Master's actions were not supposed to be discussed, although the deeds were public knowledge. "There's an aspect of the job she's not keen on."

Brigit O'Connor's eyes gleamed—possibly with the memory of a night at the Fist that a bride was supposed to endure with fortitude. "You mean the O'Meara's bedroom antics?"

Liam nodded. Somehow his mother-in-law always understood. "I don't think Eileen is too happy about me doing that sort of thing."

Brigit O'Connor poured out two mugs of herb brew. She pushed one toward Liam. "Well, surely the sexy bits are optional? You don't have to do it, do you?"

He grimaced. "I'm not so sure. Doctor Denny says the village brides will expect it, because it's an honor. And Brege O'Malley gets married in a fortnight, so the question would crop up straightaway."

His mother-in-law lodged her elbows on the table to study him. Liam McGrath was a good lad, nothing prurient about him. But if being Lord of Barley Cross meant he had to take each village bride to bed on her wedding night, then Liam would do it, conscientiously. "I wonder why the Master picked on you," she murmured.

He grinned with embarrassment. "I dunno." He glanced slyly at her. "Eileen is pregnant again."

Brigit O'Connor's eyes opened wide. "Liam! You clever boy!" She darted around the table and hugged him. "I'll have a word with our Eileen for you. Meantime..." She stood back to smile at her reflection in the glass on the sideboard. Mother of the First Lady of Barley Cross! That would shake them. And no harm if some of the dignity rubbed off onto Biddy O'Connor. She said, "Is there any way I can get a glimpse inside the Fist? So I can tell Eileen what it will be like."

Liam said, "I'll have a word with Doctor Denny."

General Desmond ushered Brigit O'Connor through the door at the end of the landing. "It'll be twenty years or so since you saw the inside of this room, won't it, Biddy?" he asked, smiling.

Brigit O'Connor gave the general the gimlet eye. Twenty years ago she had been bright-eyed Brigit Callaghan on the eve of her wedding night. She remembered the bedroom well enough, and the man who had awaited her there. She said, "That's quite enough from you, General Desmond. What passed between me and the O'Meara that night is no business of yours or anyone else's."

General Desmond feigned alarm and backed off.

Brigit O'Connor stared about the room with a grim nostalgia. Same old wooden bed. Same old yellow roses on the wallpaper. Same view of treetops from the window overhung with ivy to render easy clandestine entry and exit. Same worn carpet edged by bare boards. She sighed. For all his tyrant's power, Patrick O'Meara had never looked after himself properly. She gave the general a quick, belligerent glance. "If you want my opinion, Larry Desmond, the place is a pigsty. Typical bachelor's pad. Sure, you wouldn't get me living up here for all the tea in China. And you'll not get our Eileen so easy."

The general's smile faded. "What's to do then, Biddy? Between you and me, it's essential we get young Liam installed up here as Master. And the sooner, the better."

Brigit O'Connor planted knuckles on her hips. "Then you'd best throw out every last stick of furniture and scrap of carpet in the house. Get some women up to scrub the place from top to bottom. Repaint every bit of woodwork. Hang new curtains at every window. Then fill the house with furniture a woman could be proud of."

Larry Desmond rubbed his jaw thoughtfully. "Denny said you'd give me some advice."

She laughed harshly. "It don't take a clarryvoyant to spot a dirty dump. I'm ashamed to think you let the poor divil live and die in this midden."

Larry Desmond studied the carpet. For once his assurance seemed to have deserted him. At length he muttered, "You loved him too, Biddy?"

She sniffed. "Didn't we all? D'you think we'd have put up with his antics for a minute if we hadn't?"

Larry Desmond sighed. "That maybe explains a thing or two. I'll let Denny Mallon know what you recommend. It'll mean mounting a raid for the first time in years, but we'll have to get furniture from somewhere."

The expedition had the village lads hopping with excitement. Reared on stories of the glorious days, they saw the opportunity for an adventure. They pleaded with the general to be let to join in. Straws drawn from a cap decided who got the hard-greased rifles resurrected for the occasion. And the general insisted on personally leading the raid.

Liam watched them march away, slit-eyed with envy. Thirty men, all of them armed, and three horse-drawn carts for the loot.

Eileen came to stand beside him. "And why isn't my bold bucko going with them?"

He grunted bitterly. "General Desmond says he daren't risk me getting killed."

Eileen McGrath pursed her lips. Liam guessed she was perversely pleased with his answer. She said, "But you haven't told him you'll be the next Lord of Barley Cross?"

Liam shrugged. "I don't have to, love. The O'Meara left a will naming me. The general posted it outside the church this morning. As far as he's concerned, I am the next Master."

She said quickly, "Where are they off to?"

He slumped against the door jamb. "There are some fine houses outside Oughterard. They are seeking some furniture for the Fist."

"And who's going to live there when it's all dolled up?" He studied the boggy landscape mutinously. "No one—unless you agree to me being the Master."

Her voice rose. "Liam McGrath—"

He turned his face away. "Forget it, Eileen. If you don't want it, neither do I!"

Their son had another attack of croup the following day. Liam went down to the doctor for a bottle. He seized the opportunity for a quiet chat.

"How long d'you think the raid will take?"

Denny Mallon corked a small sample of his croup mixture and stuck one of his precious labels on the bottle. He handed it to Liam. "Depends on how fast they are at furniture removing. Remember now, tell your Eileen: a teaspoonful only when the little fellow starts to breathe hard."

Liam took the bottle. He said, "I'm afraid they are wasting their time. Eileen won't hear of me being Master."

Denny Mallon got out his pipe and polished the bowl on his sleeve. "Does she know why the general wants you to?"

Liam shrugged. "If she knows, she doesn't care. There's just no way I'll have seigneurial rights with the future brides of Barley Cross."

The doctor grinned. "I'm not sure that I'd agree to it either, in her place. D'you think the Fist might tempt her when we've got it done up?"

Liam rolled his eyes. "She'll be tempted, all right. But no way will she put up with me doing what the Master is supposed to do."

Denny Mallon stared at his pipe. "Maybe she'll have to be let into the secret. I'll be wanting a chat with her soon about the baby. I think we have an allergy on our hands. But I need to make a few more tests before I'm sure."

Liam looked startled. "Can an allergy cause croup?"

The doctor lodged the cold pipe in the corner of his mouth. "Indeed it can, son. But so many other things can too. I'm trying to pin down the hapten or allergen responsible."

"And if you find out, we could do something about it?"

Denny Mallon nodded. "That's the general idea, son."

The raiding party came home the following day. The village turned out en masse to welcome its warriors. General Desmond led the returning column, feet first, on a cart piled high with loot, one leg wrapped in bandages.

Celia Larkin stood beside Denny Mallon. "What's the old fool done now?"

"Got himself shot in the leg, I should imagine." The doctor waved a greeting as the cart bearing the general went past. "I hope he doesn't want the damn thing chopped off."

"They must have been more lively in Oughterard than he expected."

"Maybe those old ones with a kick left are not confined to Barley Cross."

"Don't be snide, Doctor," chided the schoolteacher.

It took the rest of the week to clear out, clean up, and re-furnish the Fist. The village's unofficial ruling caucus met over the weekend in a splendidly furbished dining hall. General Larry Desmond, his crutch on the new carpet at his feet, said, "I've posted a notice in the village proclaiming young McGrath as Master. Everybody is asking when will he take over. She can't ignore that."

Celia Larkin perched primly on a bright, brocaded tuffet.

"That's your trouble, Larry. You never married. You don't understand how a woman feels about a husband's fidelity."

"She can't put young McGrath's fidelity before the future of Barley Cross!"

Kevin Murphy ran a palm caressingly over the pile on the arm of the settee. "I have known animals to refuse to breed."

The general's eyebrows went up. "Are you telling me we've wasted our time? And me with half a dozen slugs in me leg!"

Denny Mallon waved his pipe. "You've done your part well enough, Larry. I think it's now time for diplomacy. Let me have a chat with Eileen McGrath. Maybe I can talk her around to our way of thinking."

The same day, Eileen McGrath got a note from the doctor, asking her to bring the child in for an inoculation. The doctor also made other preparations.

The next day, as she and Liam took Tommy down to the village, Eileen said, "I hope you are not expecting to go all the way out to Killoo farm to visit your parents as well? It's bad enough having to bring the boy out to the doctor."

Liam said, "We can go straight back home if you want. I was hoping we might leave Tommy with your ma while we take a squint at the Fist. I hear they've done marvels with it."

She lifted a corner of the shawl covering her son's face. The infant snored peacefully. She said, "I'd like to see it. My ma thinks I ought to let you accept the Master's job so we can move up there. She says they've made it into a real palace."

He said, "Let's do that, then. We can call at the doctor's afterward."

Brigit O'Connor got to her feet as they entered her living room. She curtsied to Liam. "Come in, me lord. I'll take the little fellow."

Eileen stared, dumbfounded. "Ma—you *bowed* to Liam!"

Her mother puffed out a pouter-pigeon bosom. "And isn't he our new lord? I always bowed to the O'Meara."

"But–" Eileen stared from her husband to her mother. "I haven't agreed!"

Her mother laughed shortly. "My girl, 'tisn't you who appoints our lord and master. We have the O'Meara's word as to who's to follow him."

Tom O'Connor entered from the kitchen, a saw in his hands. He halted, removed his cap, and said, "Good day to ye, sir. Hullo, Eileen, me lady."

His daughter was wide-eyed. "But, Da—!"

Her father said hurriedly, "I'll fill the kettle for a brew." He vanished back into the kitchen.

Eileen stamped her foot. "I don't want to be the First Lady of Barley Cross!"

Her mother shrugged. "You'll be the only person in the village who feels that way."

Later they walked up to the Fist. Villagers stepped out of their path. Men doffed caps or saluted. Women bowed or curtsied. Eileen grew redder and redder. She murmured, "I can't stand much more of this."

Liam gripped her hand. "It isn't far now."

Just past the O'Meara's old water tank, now blooming with bindweed and woodbine, a voice called, " 'Ten*shun!*"

A small Fist guard stiffened.

Sergeant Andy McGrath bellowed, "Present arms!"

Rifles came smartly to the fore. Liam's stepfather came to the salute. Liam, embarrassed, muttered, "Thank you, Sergeant." All those other salutes and curtsies might have been part of an elaborate leg-pull, but no one made Andy McGrath act the fool. Especially while on duty.

General Desmond, limping with his crutch, met them at the entrance of the drive. He sketched a left-handed salute for Liam and addressed Eileen. "Excuse me not bowing, me lady. I'm still in a bit of a state. May I conduct you around your new home?"

"But it's not–" Eileen began. "I haven't…" She let the words trail off. General Desmond was limping ahead of them, running on about the recent raid and how a spry Oughterarder had got him in a shotgun's sights before he could take cover.

They passed through the newly oiled and polished doorway into the great hall. Candles flickered in a shimmering chandelier overhead. Glass gleamed from a glistening oak sideboard. Underfoot the carpet was softer than a field of spring grass.

Michael, the O'Meara's man, appeared. He still wore his grubby flyaway collar and stained green waistcoat, but his hands were spotless. He said, "Can I get you some refreshment, sir? Madame?"

Eileen eyed him, wordless. "Some tea?" Liam suggested. A good stiff jolt from the poteen bottle would have been more to his taste, but Eileen held firm views on alcohol.

"Very good, me lord." Michael turned on his heel.

"Perhaps we could take it in the library?" suggested the general. "This way, me lady."

He opened a door on the left. Liam saw a room lined with more books than he had ever imagined. Denny Mallon got hurriedly to his feet. "Good day, me lord, me lady." He pulled out chairs for them.

"I'll leave ye a moment," said the general, "while I make sure Michael knows where to bring the tay."

They sat down with the doctor. He placed both hands on the baize-covered table. "Well, sir, madame—how d'you like your new home?"

"But, Doctor Denny!" Eileen's face was scarlet. "I haven't agreed to move up here. We only came for a look."

"But sure, it's all been done specially for you and our new Master." Denny Mallon's voice was gentle, persuasive. "And doesn't the whole village want you living up here? It hasn't been the same without a Lord of Barley Cross domiciled at the Fist. So the sooner you move in, the happier we'll all be."

Eileen's expression grew stubborn. "If we move in, you mustn't expect Liam to exercise his droits or whatever when that O'Malley girl gets married next week."

"But, my lady—he may be expected to do just that."

"Expected or no, I'm not having adultery in my house."

Denny Mallon seemed to shrivel even smaller. Perhaps he saw a carefully constructed edifice crumbling despite his bravest efforts. "My lady, could you tolerate it elsewhere? Out of sight?"

Eileen McGrath's mouth set firm. "Indeed I could not, Doctor. And you've no cause to be tempting me so. What's important about these rights of the Master? They're just a tradition we could very well do without."

"But we really can't, my dear." Doctor Denny Mallon was suddenly down on his knees before Eileen McGrath. "I beg of you, my lady. Let your husband inherit his title and duties. For without him, we are doomed. While the O'Meara lived, we could hope. But now he is gone, we have only Liam."

Eileen McGrath whimpered. The sight of Doctor Denny Mallon, a pillar of the community, on his knees before her, pleading, seemed to unnerve her. She grasped his hands and tugged. "Doctor Denny, stop! You mustn't kneel to me. It isn't dignified. Please get up!"

Denny Mallon resisted, head bowed. "My lady Eileen, if I get up without securing your consent to our wishes, all the work of the last twenty-odd years will have been wasted. Will it help persuade you if I get the general, the vet and the schoolmistress to kneel here beside me?"

Eileen McGrath's voice broke in a sob. "Doctor Denny, please get up. It is not fit that you should act like this. The O'Meara wasn't worth it. Everyone knows he was an old lecher with an appetite for virgins."

"Eileen!" Liam was shouting. "You are talking about your real father!"

She paused. Her hand flew to her mouth, her eyes suddenly frightened.

Liam lowered his voice. "Listen to Doctor Denny, love. He's trying to tell you something dreadfully important. Patrick O'Meara was Master here only because he could father children. No one else in Barley Cross—or the whole world so far as we know—was able to do that. And now the doctor thinks I've inherited the man's fertility. So General Desmond has asked me to take over as Master."

Eileen's eyes grew big. "You mean the O'Meara did it out of *duty*?"

"My lady," Denny Mallon interrupted urgently, "let me tell you about two villages. One is a backward place dominated by a medieval-type tyrant and his clique of sycophants. This tyrant's father debauched every bride in the village on her wedding night on the pretext of exercising his *droit du seigneur*. And the tryant himself hopes to pursue the same lustful course despite the protests of good folk like yourself.

"The other village is the only place I know of where babies are suckled, infants play in the street, and children go to school as they used to do the world over. Moreover, it's a place where married couples can hope to have a child of their own to love and cherish. In fact, it's a village with a future to look forward to.

"Both these communities exist because of a fortuitous arrangement of one man's genes and the determination of people to practice self-deception on a heroic scale—because they are aspects of the same place. And it depends on your prejudices which village you choose to inhabit. Because, my dear, you can live in either, depending on what you believe. I, silly old fool that I am, just happen to believe we live in the one with a future."

"Doctor Denny!" Eileen tugged at his wrists, her lips trembling. "Please get up, and say no more. Liam will do it, and I'll try to see things your way."

One hand on the table, Denny Mallon rose awkwardly to his feet. There was no triumph in his face. His eyes were solemn. He said, "Thank you, Eileen McGrath, for finding the courage to make the right decision."

She was dabbing at her eyes. "Hadn't we better be getting down to your house to see about inoculating our Tommy?"

A ghost of a smile flickered at the corners of the doctor's mouth. "Sure that won't be necessary now, my lady. I've ascertained that the little fellow's croup is an allergic reaction to fossil pollen grains blowing off the peat stacks near your cottage. I was going to suggest you move away from there to give him a chance. But now it won't be necessary. Up here at the Fist, far from those stacks, he should be all right."

Eileen McGrath smiled, her eyes inscrutable. "What a wise suggestion, Doctor. It will certainly do for a reason to explain why I changed my mind, if anyone should ask."

Denny Mallon nodded wisely. "It might at that, my lady."

Liam McGrath, Lord of Barley Cross, attended his first meeting with the caucus the following Saturday morning. Neat in his best clothes, he entered the dining hall through his private door.

General Desmond and the vet, Kevin Murphy, sat at each end of the plush new settee, a bottle of poteen and the general's crutch on the floor between them. Celia Larkin, the schoolmistress, perched on a dainty tuffet, sipping tea in silence. An armchair that matched the settee for luxury almost swallowed the shriveled form of Doctor Denny Mallon. And on the other side of the fireplace, an old sagging armchair, arms and back shiny with use, stood empty.

General Desmond cocked a casual thumb in the empty chair's direction. "That used to be the O'Meara's seat. We've kept it specially for you, son, so you'll know your place. Now, about the O'Malley girl's wedding. We've decided you'd better get down there early and show 'em your face…"

Liam slipped obediently into the Master's seat. He nodded, listening carefully to his instructions from the real Masters of Barley Cross. He knew his place.

Comment and Discussion on "Elevation of the U.S. Fleet" by Captain Richard B. Laning, USN (Ret.)

by Kenneth Roy

Editor's Introduction

In August, 1982 Proceedings of the U.S. Naval Institute Captain Richard Laning, USN (Ret) proposed Very Large High Flying aircraft; flying carriers, to be exact. When Kenneth Roy, an Oak Ridge, Tenn. engineer, read that issue of the *Proceedings* he recalled an article he had seen in the May, 1978 issue of *Galaxy* science fiction: my column "A Step Farther Out," which that month was about aircraft powered by laser energy from geostationary satellites

The result was this *Comment*, which proved a bit too far out for the *Proceedings*.

Captain Laning talks about elevating the aircraft carriers of the U.S. fleet to forty thousand feet and flying them at speeds of six hundred knots. It is truly a radical idea and one that holds both great promise and vast quantities of technical, tactical and strategic problems. Any profession that involves the lives of men had better be cautious when considering new and different ideas, for the larger the innovation, the greater the potential debacle.

But to fail to innovate, to cling to the old and familiar in the face of the new and better, is to invite certain disaster. Each military generation faithfully prepares to refight the last war, to a greater or lesser extent. Before World War II, France studied The World War and built accordingly; Germany tried something different...

Very Large High Flying (VLHF) aircraft are not new to aviation thinking, but none have been built. Such an aircraft would look a lot like a flying football field, only larger. It would be a flying wing with jets mounted in or near the trailing edge. Flying at six hundred knots, it could reach anywhere in the world within twenty-four hours. It would probably fly high enough to make use of the jet streams. It would be very fuel-efficient once it reached cruising altitude. With large fuel tanks, it could probably stay aloft for two, maybe three days. Thus we have two major problems with Captain Laning's idea: first, a fleet of such aircraft would use vast amounts of kerosene (otherwise known as jet fuel) and, second, it would not be able to stay on station for any length of time. Such a fleet would have to be very careful about having its line of retreat cut.

But all is not gloom; a paper entitled "Laser Aircraft Propulsion" presented by Kenneth Sun and Dr. Abraham Hertzberg at the Third NASA Conference on Radiation Energy Conversion puts forth a total solution to both problems. The Sun/Hertzberg paper describes plans for a modified Boeing aircraft with a laser-powered turbofan jet engine mounted on the back of the aircraft. This aircraft would take off and land under normal kerosene power but would then switch over to the modified turbofan jet once it reached cruising altitude. The modified turbofan engine has a heat exchanger in the middle, where the combustion chamber normally is located. The heat exchanger is connected to a laser target located on top of the aircraft. There is no reason that this aircraft, or a VLHF aircraft, couldn't fly for months using only laser light.

But there's a catch. The laser light is beamed from a satellite in geosynchronous earth orbit. Sun and Hertzberg used off-the-shelf items when they developed their study in 1977. Their satellite consisted of carbon filament structures covered with not-very-good solar cells that powered very large CO_2 lasers. At the time, Sun and Hertzberg estimated that one and a half square kilometers of satellite would be necessary for each Boeing. Today, or certainly within five to ten years, we could plan on one square kilometer of satellite per VLHF aircraft. One satellite ten by ten kilometers in area could power a fleet of one hundred VLHF aircraft over one-third of the surface of the world for as long as would be necessary. Three such satellites would give the air fleets world coverage, except for the poles. Should something happen to the satellite, or should the fleet need a lot of speed, the fuel tanks should be practically full and the fleet should be able to return home on kerosene.

The satellite at first glance would seem to be the weak point of such a plan, but a power satellite, while a big and stationary target, would have a hundred or so high-energy lasers with which to defend itself. While not in use as an aircraft energy source, excess power could be beamed into ground power grids via ground-mounted solar cells. This would be a good way to deliver energy to very remote areas; build enough such satellites and the energy crisis would be nothing but a memory.

So, the air fleet rolls down the long runway and takes to the air with either a fleet of tankers supplied from an ocean of imported kerosene (or a space power satellite) dedicated to keeping the fleet flying for the duration of the mission. The fleet composition would vary with the mission. A command ship would accompany every mission; it would be very similar to a present-day AWAC, with extensive radar and command facilities. There would certainly be carriers as Captain Laning described. Some carriers would operate manned aircraft of the Tomcat variety, although numbers would be limited, perhaps to two or three per VLHF aircraft. Other carriers would operate Remotely Piloted Aircraft (RPAs) and cruise missiles. The RPAs would be recoverable.

The carriers would have basic maintenance facilities on board, sufficient to check out, arm, fuel and maintain the aircraft, and perhaps to even perform minor repair work.

While all VLHF aircraft would carry air-to-air missiles, some would be dedicated to escort work in order to deal with enemy aircraft that survived the fighters and RPAs. These escorts would also be armed with high-energy chemical laser systems designed to deal with enemy missiles and aircraft, provided that such a weapons system is practical.

Ground-attack VLHF aircraft would be simple bombers. They would carry smart gravity bombs and a handful of bombardiers who would guide each smart bomb to within feet of its target. RPAs would scout out targets and report on damage. Such a bombing mission could take days, with the bombers at high altitude and protected by escorts... slow but thorough, and very, very surgical.

Fleet communications would be by laser light. This would give the enemy nothing to listen to or jam. RPAs would be linked to the fleet via laser and thus would be free of ECM activity. RPAs would be the eyes and hands of the fleet. The antiair capability of these aircraft would be formidable. Not only could they pull incredible G forces, but they could also be used to ram the enemy if all else failed. With RPAs, pilots could be switched around as the situation demanded. A well-defended ground target could be attacked by waves of RPAs, with the same pilots flying each wave, having learned from their previous mistakes.

A fleet of VLHF aircraft could roam the world at will, being able to shift back and forth rapidly from targets thousands of miles apart and yet providing support for ground and naval operations as needed. Supplied with energy from space, the duration of the mission would be limited only by the endurance of the crew.

A cargo fleet of VLHF aircraft would bring new meaning to the term "Rapid Deployment." With an escort of combat VLHF aircraft, the cargo fleet could go anywhere in the world at six hundred knots, laughing at Russian subs and mine fields.

Such an idea is truly radical. It raises many questions: Would it work? Would the Navy or Air Force control it? And so forth. If we started building VLHF aircraft now, there would certainly be cries of anguish from our military professionals. The taxpayer would scream in pain, and Congress would review the project. But above all the racket and noise at home, you might be able to make out the sound of cursing coming from Moscow.

BATTLE AT KAHLKHOPOLIS

by Robert Adams

Editor's Introduction

Robert Adams lives in Florida, where one of his nearest neighbors is
Mrs. Alice Andre Norton. His best known works are the deservedly
popular "Horseclans" novels.

The ancients believed that all civilization moved in cycles. There had
been a Golden Age in the past, and another might come in the future.
Empires rise and fall; civilizations grow and die, and it will ever be thus.

Adams writes of a time centuries after World War III, when civilization is just returning to North America. In the western plains and
beyond dwell the 'Mericans, including the nomadic peoples known
as the Horseclans. To the east are more settled kingdoms, dominated
in part by descendents of Greek speaking Hellene invaders who have
established the rule of the *thoheeks* or dukes.

Before civilization collapsed there had been great advances in genetic
engineering; as a result some families have highly developed telepathic
communications abilities. A very few have extraordinary longevity and
the ability to recover from wounds and disease. These near-immortals
are regarded as gods by the common people.

Adams chronicles the saga of the inevitable conflict between the
nomadic Horseclans and the settled Hellene lands. This tale of the
Horseclans takes place in the early days before the clansmen learned
just how vulnerable the cities were.

With the retreat of the late, unlamented King Zastros' huge army from Karaleenos back into what once had been the Southern Kingdom of the Ehleenoee, the surviving *thoheeksee* of the kingdom set about putting their hereditary lands to order and productivity, filling titles vacated by war, civil war, assassinations, suicides and disease, and in general preparing the southerly territories for the merger with the victorious Confederation of the High Lord, Milos of Morai.

Chief mover and the closest thing to a king that the southern Ehleenoee now owned was *Thoheeks* Grahvos *tohee* Mehseepolis *keh* Eepseelospolis. After taking into consideration all of the varied infamy that had taken place in the former capital, Thrahkohnpolis, Grahvos had declared the new center of the soon-to-be Southern Confederated *Thoheekseeahnee* to be situated at his own principal city of Mehseepolis.

Now that city was become a seething boil of activity—sections of old walls being demolished, the city environs being expanded and new walls going up to enclose them, troops camped far and wide around the city, existing public (and not a few private) buildings becoming beehives with the comings and the goings of Ehleenoee nobility, their retainers and their staffs, as well as the host of attendent functionaries necessary to the operation of this new capital city.

One day, some years after the announcement of the new capital city, two noblemen sought audience with Thoheeks Grahvos and his advisors. One of these two was a gray beard, the other a far younger man, but the shapes and angles of the faces—eyes, noses, chins, cheekbones—clearly denoted kinship between the two, close kinship. The old man was tall, almost six feet, his physique big-boned and no doubt once very powerful, with the scars—at least a couple of which looked to be fairly new—of a proven warrior.

The harried assistant chamberlain knew that he had seen this man, or someone much like him, before, but he could not just then place who or where or when, and the petitioner refused to state his name or rank, saying only that he was a man who had been unjustly treated and was seeking redress of the new government. The only other word he deigned to send in to the *thoheeksee* was cryptic.

"Ask the present lord of Hwailehpolis if he recalls aught of a stallion, a dead man's sword and a bag of gold."

When, on his second or third trip into the meeting room, the assistant remembered to ask this odd question, *Thoheeks* Vikos of Hwailehpolis leaped to his feet and grabbed the assistant's shoulders, hard, demanding, "Where is this man? What would you estimate his age? Is he come alone or did others bring him?"

When the now-trembling functionary had scuttled off to fetch back the oldster, Vikos explained his actions to his curious peers.

"It was after that debacle at Ahrbahkootchee, in the early days of the civil war. I had fought through that black day as an ensign in my late brother's troop of horse, and in the wake of our rout by King Rahndos' war elephants, I and full many another found myself unhorsed and hunted like a wild beast through the swamps of the bottom lands. It was nearing dusk and I was half-wading, half-swimming yet another pool when I heard horsemen crashing through the brush close by to me. Breaking off a long, hollow reed, I went underwater, as I had done right often on that terrifying day, but I knew that if they came at all close, I was done this time, for the water of the pool was clear almost to the bottom, not murky as had been so many others, nor was the spot I had to go down very deep—perhaps three feet, perhaps less.

"Suddenly I became aware that the legs of a big horse were directly beside my body, and not liking the thought of a probing spear pinning me to the bottom to gasp out my life under the water, I resignedly surfaced that I might at least die with air in my lungs.

"I looked up into the eyes of none other than Komees Pahvlos Feelohpóhlehmos himself!

"In a voice that only I could hear, he growled, 'Stay down, damn fool boy!' Then he shouted to the nearing troopers, 'You fools, search that thick brush up there where the stream debouches. This pool is as clear as crystal, nothing in it save fish and crayfish, so I'm giving my stallion a drink of it.'

"Then the *Komees* deliberately set his horse to roiling the sediments of the bottom, clouding the water, while he did the same with the butt of his lance. He dropped a sheathed, jeweled sword upon me, and when I brought my face up to where I could see him, he tossed me a small, heavy bag and said, 'You may well be the last of your House after this day, young Vikos. There is a bit of gold and a good sword. Wait until full dark and then head northwest; what's left of the rebel army is withdrawing south and southeast. If you can make it up to Iron Mountain, you'll be safe. And the next time you choose a war leader, try to choose one with at least a fighting chance to win. God keep you now."

Thoheeks Grahvos nodded. "Yes, it sounds of a piece with all else I know of the man. For all his ferocity and expertise in the waging of war for the three kings he served in his long career, still was he ever noted to be just and, when possible, merciful. Strange, I'd assumed him dead, legally murdered by Zastros, as were the most of his peers. It's good to know that at least this one of the better sort survived the long bloodletting. Who was his overlord anyway? If he'll take the proper oaths, *Komees* Pahvlos the Warlike would make us a good *Thoheeks*, say I."

* * *

"And so," concluded old *Komees* Pahvlos, "when it was become obvious that these usurping scum were determined to not only deny young Ahrahmos here his lawful patrimonies, but to take his very life as well, had they the chance, I knew that stronger measures were required, my lords.

"Could but a single warrior do it alone, it were done already. Old I assuredly am—close to seventy years-old—but I still am tough and the hilt of my good sword has not become a stranger to my hand. But a disciplined, well-armed and well-led force will be necessary to dislodge this foul kakistocracy that presently squats in Ahrahmos' principal city and controls his rightful lands. And due to reverses, I no longer own the wherewithal to hire on fighting men, equip and mount and supply them with the necessaries of warfare."

"But I will wager, Strahteegos *Komees* Pahvlos," said *Thoheeks* Grahvos, "that nothing has robbed you of your old abilities to lead armies, plan winning battles and improvise stunning tactics on the spur of the moment. I had meant to ask you to take oaths to this Council and the Confederation, then assume one of the still-vacant *thoheekseeahnee*, but if you'll indeed take those oaths, I have a better, far more useful task in mind for you now."

Chief Pawl Vawn of Vawn sat at a table in a tent in the camp of *Seentahgmahrtees* Tomos Gonsalos, senior officer of those Confederation forces sent south to aid the *thoheeksee* in securing and maintaining peace. With them at table sat *Ahnteeseentahgmahrtees* of Infantry, Guhsz Hehluh, and *Thoheeks* Portos, figurehead commander of these alien troops deep in the heart of the former Southern Kingdom.

A meal had been eaten while the men talked, and now, while a bottle of a sweet wine circulated, the Horseclans-man asked, "If this Pahvlos is such a slambang Strahteegos and all, how come he didn't tromp you all proper for his king and end it before it even got started?"

"Oh, he did, he did, my good Pawl," said Portos, "in the beginning, years ago. I was a part of that rebel army then, and I know. It required years and the—then-unknown—help of the Witchmen to put Zastros' army back together in a shape fit to once more face *Komees* Pahvlos; and that, finally, we did not have to face him was a great relief to full many a one of us, believe me. By that time all of the ancient royal line was extinct, and *Thoheeks* Fahrkos, who had seized the crown and the capital, had dismissed the royal strahteegoee. Most of the remaining royal troops—the only regular forces the kingdom had had—deserted then, marched away with their officers, so all Fahrkos had when we brought him to bay was his personal war band, such as it was."

"Even so," put in the graying Freefighter officer, Guhsz Hehluh, "before I put me and my Keebai boys under the orders of some white-beard doddard, I'll know a bit more about him. You Kindred and Ehleenoee can do what you want, but if I mislike the sound or the smell of this Count Pahvlos, why, me and mine, we'll just hike back up

156   THERE WILL BE WAR VOL. IV

to Kehnooryos Ahtheenahs and tell High Lord Milos to find us other fights or sell us back our contract."

But within bare days, Guhsz Hehluh was trumpeting the praises of the new Grand Strahteegos, who, with his small entourage, had ridden out and found the Freefighters at drill. After sitting his horse by Hehluh's in the hot sun, swatting at flies and knowledgeably discussing the strengths and weaknesses of pike formations and the proper marshaling of infantry, Pahvlos had actually dismounted and hunkered in the dust of the drill field to sketch with a horny forefinger positions and movements of an intricate maneuver.

To Tomos Gonsalos, Pahvlos remarked, "It's basically a good unit you command here, Colonel. I'd take you and them just as they are now were you not a mite shy of infantry and a mite oversupplied with cavalry. To rectify that situation, I'll be brigading your regiment with two more, all infantry, all veterans too, no grass-green plow-boys.

"I think that both you and your other officers will get along well with Colonel Bizahros, who commands the Eighth Foot, from the outset; but Colonel Ahzprinos, commander of the reorganized Fifth Foot, is another matter entirely. Understand me, Lord Tomos, Ahzprinos is a good warrior, a fine commander in all ways, else I'd not choose him to serve under me. But he also is loud, brash and sometimes overbearing to the point of arrogance. Nonetheless, I can get along with him, and I'll be expecting my subordinates to do so too."

And so in the weeks that followed, the Confederation troops and the two regiments of former Southern Kingdom foot drilled and marched and drilled some more under the critical eye of *Komees* Pahvlos, while all awaited the arrival of the war elephants from the far-western *Thoheekseeahnee*, where they had been bred and trained for centuries, making do in the meantime with the three beasts that had survived King Zastros' disastrous march north.

These three survivors were not the huge, fully war-trained bull elephants now on the march from the west but rather the smaller, more docile cow elephants, mostly utilized for draught purposes. That they were used by *Komees* Pahvlos at all was a testament to the extraordinary control over them exercised by Horseclansman Gil Djohnz, who could demand of the three cows performances of an order that the old strahteegos had never before seen in all his long years of service with elephant-equipped armies. Watching Djohnz and his two Horse-clansmen assistants put the trio of elephants through their paces had reduced native Ehleenoee *feelahksee* to a state of despair and set them to mumbling darkly of sorcery and witchcraft.

The old commander was greatly impressed with Horse-clansmen in general, for never before had it been his pleasure to own such a splendid and versatile mounted force as the squadron of medium-heavy horse under Chief Pawl of Vawn. Southern Kingdom horse traditionally came in three varieties—light horse or lancers, heavy horse, most of whom were noblemen, and irregulars, who frequently were archers and usually recruited from the barbarian mountain tribes and were often undependable, to say the least.

But these northern horsemen were very dependable; moreover, they could fulfill the functions of at least two of the three—they could lay down a heavy and accurate arrow storm, then case their bows and deliver a hard, effective charge against the unit their arrows had weakened and disorganized. Serving in conjunction with such troops, Pahvlos could easily ken just how they and their forefathers had so readily rolled over the armies of Kehnooryos Ehlahs, Karaleenos and assorted far-northern barbarian principalities.

Nor was the reinforced squadron that *Thoheeks* Portos had brought down from the north your normal unit of lancers either. To Pahvlos' way of thinking, they were becoming true heavy horse, and he used them as such, obtaining from Thoheeks Grahvos a half-squadron of old-fashioned light-horse lancers to take over the scouting, flank-guarding and messenger functions of traditional light-horse usage.

To *Thoheeks* Portos' questions regarding the reassignment of function of his squadron, the old strahteegos answered, "My lord *Thoheeks*, to my way of thinking, if you put a man up on a sixteen-hand courser all armored with steel and boiled leather, the man himself protected by a thigh-length hauberk and steel helm and armed with lance and saber and light ax and long shield, then that man is no longer a mere lancer but a medium-heavy horseman at the very least. Your so-called lancers differ from Lord Pawl's force only in that his are equipped with bows rather than lances, carry targes instead of shields."

Although inordinately pleased with all of his cavalry, both native and alien, *Komees* Pahvlos was not quite certain what to make of or do with the most singular pikemen of Lord Guhsz Hehluh. Unless they chanced to be the foot guards of a king or some other high, powerful, wealthy nobleman, or of a walled city, Southern Kingdom pikemen simply were not armored—save for a light helmet of stiffened leather with strips of steel and a thick jack of leather, plus a pair of leather gauntlets that were occasionally reinforced with metal—and only the steadier, more dependable front ranks were provided with a body shield, to be erected before them where they knelt or crouched to angle their pikes. Traditionally, of course, they had died in droves whenever push came to shove; such was and had always been expected.

But not so in the case of the big, mostly fair-skinned, thick-thewed barbarians commanded by Lord Guhsz. Only the cheek-guards and chin-slings of their helmets were of leather, the rest—crown-bowls, segmented nape-guards and bar-nasals—being of good-quality steel. Their burly bodies were guarded to the waists and their bulging arms to the elbow by steel scales sewn and riveted to padded canvas jacks; both their high-cuffed gauntlets and their leathern kilts were thickly sewn with steel mail, and below a steel-plate kneecap, their shins and calves were protected with sets of splint armor riveted inside their boot linings.

Moreover, each and every one of these pikemen carried a slightly out-bowed, rectangular shield a good two feet wide and near twice that in length, and on the command, each man of a formation could raise that shield a bit above his head in such a manner as to over- and underlap those of his fellows and provide a roof that could turn an arrow storm as adroitly as a roof of clay tiles turns a rainstorm.

Nor were these the only differences in the equipage of the alien foot and those of the Southern Kingdom. Aside from his fifteen-foot pike, your average pikeman bore no weapons other than a utility eating knife, while not a one of Lord Guhsz's men but did not also bear a heavy, double-edged sword about a foot and a half in its sharp-pointed blade, one or more shorter dirks or daggers, sometimes even a short-hafted belt-ax of the sort that could be either tool or missle or weapon.

Burdened as they were, the old strahteegos had doubted that these overprotected, overarmed, overequipped pikemen could maintain the needful pace on the march or in a broad-front charge. But that had been before he put them to it; after he had, he knew the—to him, near incredible—facts of the matter. It was at that point that his formerly rock-firm opinions began to undergo a change and he began to wonder just why so many generations of his forebears had callously, needlessly, sacrificed so many pikemen with the excuse, now proven false, that proper armor and secondary weapons would decrease mobility. Colonel Bizahros agreed with him, but Colonel Ahzprinos did not, flatly, unequivocally, and at very great length.

So the *eeahtrosee*, with their bandages and ointments, their saws and other surgical devices, arrived. The artificers were assigned, the quartermasters and the cooks, the smiths, the farriers, the wagoners and the mule skinners. Finally Strahteegos *Komees* Pahvlos, tired of waiting and drilling, announced to the Council that he intended to start on his campaign with only the three cow elephants he already had, wanting to get the business over and done before the autumn rains arrived to complicate things for a field army.

Mainahkhos Klehpteekos and Ahreekhos Krehohpoleeos had risen fast and high from their origins as common troopers in the first, almost-extirpated army of *Thoheeks* Zastros. That both men were savage and completely unprincipled had helped; that they were good war leaders and inordinately lucky had helped even more. During the years of howling chaos in the Southern Kingdom, they and the heterogeneous packs of deserters, banditti, escaped criminals, shanghaied peasants and stray psychopaths they had led had sometimes signed on as a mercenary force to first one then another army of the battling lords.

Sometimes they had given the service for which they had been paid. But more often they had either deserted en masse or turned their coats at a crucial point, especially if the ongoing battle showed signs of being a close one. At length so odious had their reputation become that no lord or city—no matter how desperate—would even consider hiring them on; at that point they followed their basic inclinations, becoming out-and-out warlords, they and their lawless band of ruffians at open war against the world.

When at long last Zastros had made himself High King and, after scouring the length and breadth of the land for soldiers and men of military age, had marched his half million and more north out of the kingdom, on the road to his death in Karaleenos, the two warlords had found themselves in pigs' paradise, able now to prey not only on villages and travelers and isolated estates, but on walled towns and cities as well.

They had behaved in their usual bestial fashion at the intakings of the first few of these urban sites, which were by then all but defense-less despite their walls, what with their once-garrisons now marching north behind the Green Dragon banner of High King Zastros—first raping, plundering, torturing, then killing whole populations until the streets ran with gore, and finally burning everything combustible in the stinking charnel house they had made of the towns.

Then, of a day, a broken nobleman who had joined the bandit army to avoid starving had had words with the two warlords and slowly convinced them of the sagacity of those words. For all that they and their followers were become wealthy beyond their wildest dreams of avarice, each succeeding victory had cost them men—and men of fighting age and strength were become almost as precious as rubies in this land stripped of warrior stock by Zastros' strenuous re-cruitments. Moreover, scattered and fast-moving survivors of those intakings had spread the word of the atrocities far and wide so that all walled enclosures within weeks of marching time were doing everything possible to strengthen their existing defenses and had put aside any pre-vious thoughts of trying to deal with the marauders on a near-peaceful basis.

So although it went hard against the grain, the warlords had begun to rein in their savages, dealing gently—by their personal lights—with the inhabitants of those places that opened the gates without a fight and showed a willingness to treat. Mainahkhos and Ahreekos even took it upon themselves to move against, either recruiting or wiping out, numerous smaller bands of their own ilk then lurking about the countryside. Then they began to recruit from the remaining garrisons of the smaller towns and cities, and slowly their howling pack of human predators metamorphosed into a real, more-or-less organized army.

By the day, three years ago, that they had appeared under the walls of the city of Kahlkhopolis, one-time seat of the *Thoheeksee* of Kahlkhos, the few straggling hundreds of ill-or sketchily armed bandits were become an impressive, very threatening sight indeed.

All classes of infantry marched in their ranks, fully armed and equipped; heavy cavalry rode in that column, with light cavalry on the wings and riding guard on the awesome siege train. Only elephants were lacking, and this deficiency was partly alleviated through the use of old-fashioned, mule-drawn war carts as archery platforms—the stout, armored cart bodies with scythe blades set in the wheel hubs and the big mules all hung with mail having proven almost as effective as elephants at the task of smashing in infantry formations for years before the pachyderms had been adapted to warfare.

The last *thoheeks*, Klawdos, was by then five years dead, a casualty of the civil war, along with all his male kin. His wife and infant son had disappeared shortly after his death, and the city was then being held by a distant cousin of the ancient line, a bastard with little claim to noble blood, even less to military experience. So when he ordered the gates to be closed and the walls to be manned by the pitifully few men he owned, what was left of the city council did the only reasonable thing: They murdered him.

Since then Mainahkhos had been *thoheeks* in all save name, having seen to it that the city councilmen quickly followed their victim into death by one means or another. He had been upon the teetering verge of declaring himself *Thoheeks* Mainahkhos Klehftis of Klehftispolis (as

he and his men had become "respectable," he had adopted the new
surname, and now no man who was undesirous of a messy, agonizing
and brutally protracted demise ever called the warlord Klehpteekos "the
thief"), when he had learned that the son of his legal predecessor still
lived.

He and his fellow warlord had both chanced to be out of the city
when the boy had come nosing about in company with some arrogant
dotard, but the snooping pair had been gone beyond recall when the
would-be *thoheeks* had returned, and he had had the fools who had
allowed their escape flayed alive and rolled in salt for their stupid-
ity. Those cured skins still hung in a prominent place in his hall of
audience—a silent, savage warning to his surviving followers.

As the would-be *thoheeks* sat at meat with his principal officer-
advisors and his longtime partner, Ahreekhos (who had never bothered
to change his surname, still reveling in the cognomen of "Butcher,"
although he was grown now far too fat to do much real fighting of
any nature), the topic of the discussion was that army which they
had received word was even now advancing against them from the
southeast.

In answer to a query from Mainahkhos, the heavy cavalry commander, one Stehrghiahnos—who had been born and reared the heir
to a *vahrohneeskos*, though he had forfeited title and lands and very
nearly life itself through too early a support of the then-rebel *Thoheeks*
Zastros—said cautiously, "My lord, it might be as well to essay a
meeting with these commanders. After all, my lord's claim to this
thoheekseeahn is as good as any; he has been a good lord and owns the
support of the people of the city, at least..."

Ahreekhos nodded agreement. "He's right, you know, Mainahkhos.
From what all my scouts have told me, that army a-coming ain't one
I'd of cared to face three years agone, even when we was at full strength,
much less now. And they got them elephants too, at least three of the
critters, prob'ly more.

"Why not send out Stehrghiahnos, there, and a couple more fellers
and let them palaver with this strahteegos, huh? Ain't nuthin to be

lost by that, is it? Old *Thoheeks* Grahvos and them is making new *thoheeksee* and *komeesee* and such all over the place, and like's just been said, you got you as good a claim to this here city and all as anybody has. Could be, since you say you'll stand a-hint *Thoheeks* Grahvos and them, 't'won't be no battle a-tall."

Mainahkhos shrugged. "Hell, that's right. Ain't a damn thing lost by talking with them bastids... but I want the levy and all raised at the same time too. And send word to old Ratface Billisos to brang up ever swingin' dick he can lay claws to from the western *komeeseeahnee* too, and all the mounts what he can beg, borror or steal too."

Strahteegos *Thoheeks* Pahvlos received Stehrghiahnos of course, but he treated him with the contempt that he felt a renegade nobleman deserved. When he had heard him out, he shrugged and spoke.

"Were the house indeed extinct, there might possibly be a bare modicum of sense in what you have said, but it is not extinct. Here, at this very table, sits the rightful *Thoheeks* of Kahlkhos." He nodded his white head in the direction of young Ahrahmos, who sat stiffly and blank-faced in his dusty, field-browned armor, his plain helm and sheathed sword on the table top before him.

From where he stood (Pahvlos had deliberately proffered no chair or stool), Stehrghiahnos eyed the husky boy critically, then said, "We might avoid a general, assuredly costly battle, you know, my lord *Thoheeks*, by the simple, old-fashioned expedient of arranging a session-in-arms between the present *Thoheeks* of Kahlkhos and this pretender you present here."

"Cow flop!" the old man snorted in scorn, adding, "In addition to being an arrant traitor to your class and your breeding, you seem to possess all the native intelligence of a braying ass. And I warn you, sirrah, if you make the mistake of drawing that blade, I'll see you lose that hand a joint an hour before you leave this camp!

"To begin, *Thoheeks* Ahrahmos here, far from being some pretender, is the rightful overlord of Kahlkhos, *Thoheeks* by birth; as such, he deserves and is being afforded the firm support of every loyal, right-thinking nobleman of this new Confederated *Thoheekseeahnee*... which is precisely why I and my army are here.

"The sort of resolution you've suggested does not apply to this situation. It was considered legal only for cases wherein both contenders owned equal birthright claim or no claim at all. Besides, no gentleman—no true gentleman—of my army is going to go forth to meet a common bandit-chief on terms of equality... and I find it significant of just how far down the ladder you have descended that you would even suggest so dishonorable a course to me and *Thoheeks* Ahrahmos."

Strahteegos *Thoheeks* Pahvlos' original order of battle had been to place the armored pikemen of Hehluh and Bizahros at the center of his line, retaining the unarmored pikemen of Ahzprinos as a reserve, and placing half of the Horseclan's medium-heavy cavalry on each wing to provide enfilading archery against any aggressive movements on the part of the enemy. He did not intend to advance until the opposing force had been bled a bit at trying to break his line.

Reports of probing cavalry patrols, and information gleaned from captives as well as from a few loyalists who had managed to flee the city, had assured the old soldier that, although outnumbered, his was much the better, more reliable army.

The broad, verdant plain surrounding the city was the logical place for any battle. True, it was not all open ground; there were a few copses here and there, a few folds of the landscape, but none large enough or deep enough to allow for ambushes or unpleasant surprises for any save the smallest of units.

A week after the visit of Stehrghiahnos to his camp, the elderly Strahteegos was apprised by a sweating, bleeding galloper that a detachment of his far-ranging lancers had made contact—violent contact—with an estimated two thousand men, mixed horse and foot, who were apparently guarding a long wagon train, a large herd of cattle and a smaller herd of horses and mules. The newcomers were marching west-to-east, in the direction of Kahlkhopolis.

Grinning like a winter wolf, *Thoheeks* Pahvlos dispatched *Thoheeks* Portos and a mounted force consisting of both the heavy and the medium-heavy cavalry. As an afterthought, he reinforced the units of lancers that were ambling about just beyond bowshot of the city walls, lest someone in there get the idea of riding forth to succor the obvious supply train.

A bit after nightfall, *Thoheeks* Portos rode into camp to report few casualties to his own force, most of the foemen dead and the few survivors scattered and running hard. His troopers were bringing in the wagons and the horse herd but had left the scrawny cattle to wander at will.

At dawn a herald was sent to the main gate of the city to summon Stehrghiahnos. When that renegade dismounted before Pahvlos' pavilion, ranged beyond the hitching rail were a number of wooden stakes, each crowned with a livid, blood-streaked head. The sharp features and prominent, out-thrust incisors that had given Ratface Billisos his name were on one of those ghastly heads, and that fact gave Stehrghiahnos the clear, indisputable message that there would no be no reinforcements or resupply, no matter how long his overlord waited.

Pahvlos' words were short and brusque. "Yesterday, Master Stehrghiahnos, my cavalry intercepted and extirpated the western contingent of your chief's bandit band. We captured some two hundred head of horses and mules, considerable amounts of arms and armor and horse gear, and over fifty wagon- and wain-loads of supplies, as well as so many cattle that we had to leave the most of them running loose around the site of the battle.

"You had best advise your chief that he will not now be reinforced or supplied, so he had best come to battle with me as soon as possible, before his force within the city begins to suffer and be weakened by starvation and disease. Not that *Thoheeks* Ahrahmos and I give a damn how many bandits and renegades starve or suffer or waste away of the pox or the bloody flux, but we want no undue suffering to befall the innocent, the noncombatants within the city."

Screened by a long file of mounted lancers who, under orders, were raising as much dust as possible in their slow progress, Gil Djohnz and the elephant Sunshine led the way toward the assigned position. Sunshine, Tulip and Newgrass were armored for the coming battle, but their huge, distinctively shaped bodies had for the nonce been covered with sheets of a dull-colored cloth, while the heavy, cumbersome, wood-and-leather archer boxes had been dismounted and were now being borne in their wake by the teams of archers who would occupy them.

After the third or fourth time he slipped and stumbled on the broken, uneven footing, Gil found himself steadied and lifted easily back onto his feet by the gentle but powerful trunk of Sunshine. "You are silly to try to walk, Man-Gil," the pachyderm mindspoke him. "Your poor little feet will be sore beyond bearing tonight. Those men yonder are astride their horses, so why do you not ride Sunshine?"

Gil sighed. Sunshine was as stubborn as any mule when she so chose to be. "It is still as I have said ere this, sister-mine: High as you are, if I mount you, those watching from the other army will know that at least one elephant is in this area, and it is our plan that they not know such until we are ready to attack them."

"Silly!" Sunshine mindspoke. "Two-legs are surely the very silliest of creatures. Fighting is the silliest of two-leg pastimes, and Sunshine is herself silly for taking part in such silliness; she only does so because she loves you, Gil."

At that same moment, seven huge, tawny felines were but just arrived in position to the rear of the cavalry reserve of the bandit army. They crouched within a tiny copse, their sleek bodies unmoving, their colors blending well with the dead leaves that covered the ground.

One of the prairie cats—for such they were, come south as part of the Horseclans' force—meshed his mind with those of two others to gain sufficient strength for farspeak and beamed out, "We are where

you said we should be. The horses cannot smell us... yet. But I fear
the wind soon may shift..."

Strahteegos *Thoheeks* Pahvlos' well-concocted plan of battle had to
be severely altered. With the bandit army formed up in position, it
became clear that in order to avoid having his center outflanked by the
center of the enemy, he must either stretch his lines of armored pikemen
to suicidal thinness or commit the unarmored pikemen of Ahzprinos;
for the umpteenth time he cursed the old-fashioned, obstinate, obtuse
officer and his failure to emulate the other two pike regiments.

At length the strahteegos made what he felt to be the best of a bad situation. He extended the regiments of Hehluh and Bizahros to a depth
of only six men, but then he ordered the first and second battalions of
Ahzprinos' regiment to form up two men deep immediately behind the
armored regiments.

Of course this left him damnall reserve—one battalion of old-style
pikemen, the headquarters guard of heavy horse and a scattering of
lancers—but it would have to do.

Nor was he formed up any too soon. Out from both wings of the
bandit army came clattering the war carts. Barded to the fetlocks as
they were, there was no way to determine just how heavily or fully the
pairs of big mules were armored; it was only safe to assume that they
were. Three men stood in each jouncing, springless cart, two archers
and a spearman; the man responsible for guiding the pair was mounted
on the near-side mule, fully armored and bearing shield and sword or
ax. The carts kept a good distance from each other lest the steel blades
projecting from each wheel hub become entangled with another set or,
worse, cripple a mule.

Pahvlos saw immediately that there were not enough of the armored
war carts to tempt even such an amateur as the bandit chief to send
them head-on against the massed pikes and hope to get any of them
back. Anyone knew that the cavalry on the wings could easily ride
deadly rings around such slow, cumbersome conveyances, and that left
only a couple of alternative uses for the archaic weapons: an attempt to

drive between wing and center and take the pikemen on the flank, or a series of passes back and forth across the front while raining with darts and arrows the pikemen they assumed to be unarmored and shieldless.

It was the latter. In staggered lines, the war carts were drawn, clattering and bouncing, the length of the formations of pikemen, expending quantities of arrows for precious few casualties. As the first line of war carts reached the end of that first pass and began to wheel about, however, they got an unexpected and very sharp taste of medicine similar to that they had been so lavishly dispensing. Chief Pawl Vawn of Vawn, commanding the left wing, treated the carts and mules to such an arrow storm that some quarter of the carts were unable to return to the raking of the pikelines. Nor did the carts receive any less from the Horseclansmen under Tomos Gonsalos on the right wing.

With it patently clear that the war carts were doing no significant damage to his front, Strahteegos Pahvlos sent *Thoheeks* Portos' heavy lancers out from the rear area and in a wide swing around his own right to deliver a crushing, crashing charge against the units of heavy horse and irregulars making up the left wing of the bandit army. That charge thudded home with a racket that could be heard even within the old warrior's pavilion. The heavy lancers fought bravely for a few minutes after the initial assault, but then a banner went down, and with loud lamentations, they began to disengage piecemeal and withdraw. Sensing victory within grasping distance, the bandits' entire left wing quitted its position to stream out in pursuit.

And no sooner had the cavalry left its assigned flank areas than up out of a brushy gully filed Sunshine, Tulip and Newgrass. Speedily the cloth shroudings were stripped away, the heavy, unwieldy, metal-shod boxes lifted up onto the broad backs and strapped into place. Then the boxes were manned by the archers; Gil Djohnz and the other two were lifted by the elephants to the saddles just behind the domes of the huge heads, and those still gathered about on the ground affixed the last pieces of the pachyderms' armor and uncased the broad and heavy-bladed swords— six feet and more in blade length—each elephant would swing in the initial attack.

All of these preparations were well-rehearsed and so took less than five minutes in the accomplishment. Then the three huge beasts set out abreast at a walk that the trailing and flanking horsemen had some difficulty in matching for speed over the broken ground.

Much of Mainahkhos' "infantry" was no such thing; rather were the most of them a broad cross section of civilian men impressed off streets at sword's point and handed a pike or a spear before being hustled willy-nilly into an aggregation of similar unfortunates, then marched out to add depth to the pikeline. To these, the mere sight of the three behemoths fast bearing down upon them, swinging two-*meetrah* blades and supported by a horde of horsemen, was all that was needful to evoke instant panic.

Pawl, Chief of Clan Vawn, farspoke but a single thought: "Now, cat-brother!"

With bloodcurdling squalls, the seven mighty cats burst out of the tiny copse and sped toward the ranks of the now-mounting cavalry reserve. Broadbeaming hideous mind-pictures of blood and equine death, never ceasing their cacophonies of snarls, growls, squalls and howls, the felines rapidly bore down upon the horses and men.

The harried, wounded commander of the war carts had never before heard of such a thing! Leaving its secure position, the entire four-hundred-yard length of the enemy pikeline was advancing, moving at a brisk walk, pikes still presented—an array of winking steel points that projected well ahead of the marching lines. The miserable infantry simply did not advance against armored war carts! Basically a less-than-imaginative man, the commander did the only thing he could just then think to do—he headed back from whence he and his force had come.

But before the carts could reach their objective, their own infantry had boiled forward, out of formation, to block the way. Deeply contemptuous of footmen at even the best of times, the commander led his survivors in carving a gory path through these up to the moment that a terrified man smote him such a blow with a poleax as to hurl him to the ground just at the proper time and place to be decapitated by the sharp, bloodstreaked, whirling blades projecting from the hub of his own war cart.

Portos and his squadron abruptly turned, raised the "fallen" banner and hacked a good half of their pursuers out of the saddle before said pursuers broke and fled. At that juncture, Portos halted his forces, formed them up and directed them at the nearest protrusion of the roiling, confused mass of men that had formerly been the enemy's center.

But the projection had recoalesced with the main mass by the time the heavy horse reached it, so quick-thinking Portos rode on into the chaos that had lately been the rear areas of the bandit army. After leaving half the squadron to interdict the road leading to the city, the grim officer used the other half to strike the rear and flank of those units still guarding the right wing of the bandit army only bare moments before those units were assaulted all along the front by Chief Pawl Yawn's Horseclansmen.

With the precipitate retreat of the war carts, Strahteegos *Thoheeks* Pahvlos ordered the drums to roll the signal, whereupon the pikemen dropped their shields, lowered their long, heavy pikes to lowguard-present—waist-level—and increased their pace to a trot, though maintaining proper interval and formation up to the very moment that their steel points sank into soft flesh or grated upon armor and bone.

Although the slaughter continued on for some hours more on that bloody field, the charge of the pikemen had ended the Battle of Kahlkhopolis.

THE CONQUEROR OF VECTIS

by Keith Taylor

Editor's Introduction

This story by Australian novelist Keith Taylor is not science fiction. If I have to defend including it in this collection, I'll claim it's fantasy. Mostly, though, it's a whacking good tale of betrayal and revenge.

"Look yonder, lads! A wide, inviting path to Hamo, where the British king sits and shakes every time he looks southward! One of these years we will row up it and plunder his town."

Cerdic laughed loudly and threw out his arm in an extravagant gesture to show the path he'd spoken of. It scarcely needed indicating. One couldn't look to starboard and miss it: an estuary of mirror-bright water, miles long and wide, as Cerdic had said. Nor did any of the chieftain's men have doubts about his eventual plans for the mainland. He'd made the same boast many times of late.

Men laughed in response and threw taunts northward that no Briton could hear. Cerdic was a popular leader. The dourer spirits among his band stayed silent. These were mostly the older, more experienced warriors. They thought that boasting so freely tempted ill luck. Still, that was Cerdic's way. He'd a wide-ranging mind, but one thought that never seemed to enter it was failure. Maybe that was why he almost never did fail.

His three serpent-ships raced on, striped sails full of a powerful breeze that bent the masts a little. He'd been harrying on the Gaulish side of the Narrow Sea and had good pickings. A sudden storm had parted him from his two other ships—from all his other ships, in truth, although two had rejoined him later and two had not. He'd spent time looking for them, to no avail. They might be sunk.

That possibility did nothing to dampen Cerdic's mood. Who could outlive his fate? Either the two ships would come home or they wouldn't. He turned his disconcerting eyes to port and looked on the shore of Vectis, his island by conquest. He grinned and stretched. Life was fine.

"Best we clew up the sails now," said Ulfcetel, the wolf-gray sailing master. He was one of those who had kept his mouth stolidly shut when Cerdic talked of sacking Hamo. The chieftain was not put out. Ulfcetel might be chary of talking, but Cerdic knew he wouldn't find the man backward when it came to doing.

Anent the sails, he nodded. They were as near the wind now as the ships would go. Luckily they were also almost home. Under the long ash oars they moved into an estuary which, while tiny compared with the mainland estuary, was the largest Vectis could show and led nigh to the center of the island. At its head rose Cerdic's fortress of Wiht-gara-byrig. It had been known as Dun Kinmalin until Cerdic had come there with five ships and almost three hundred war-men to carry the palisade and slay the British defenders. The peasants of Vectis had shuddered at the din and learned in the morning that they had a new lord—although he had proved no worse than the old and was at least half British.

The wide-bladed oars flashed wet in sunlight and sank into shadow. The ships moved in file past oak woods, where the acorns had begun to turn brown. Before long they came in sight of Wiht-gara-byrig's palisade and saw two other war-boats drawn up on the shore in front of it, recognizable at once.

"By Frey's prick," Cerdic said. "Withucar is back before us! Yet we returned early ourselves. He must have had great luck."

Cerdic was first to spring ashore, a tall man, large-boned and powerful. The mass of tawny hair sweeping back from his temples and wide forehead was confined by a plain leather band, which also kept his helmet from rubbing him raw. Not that he wore his helmet now. His scale byrnie glittered in the sun, and his plenitude of golden arm-rings, studs, buckles, sword-hilt and scabbard ornamentation far outshone it. The Kentish jewelers were superb craftsmen, and Cerdic believed in adorning himself with the best or nothing.

Men called greetings from the ramparts above the gate, which stood open, but none came forth. Cerdic stood for a moment, looking for Giralda and his children. No sign of them. His frown betrayed astonishment and even slight hurt. Why, he hadn't held Vectis above two years! Were they so used to his coming home from plundering forays that they didn't rush down to the water's edge with embraces, questions about the fighting from Cynric, questions from the girls about the gifts he'd brought them? For a moment the infamous pirate looked his son's age, which was rising five. Then he turned to give a hand with hauling the ships ashore.

"Quiet in the holding," Ulfcetel grunted. "I'll wager they didn't precede us home by much, and there's been heavy drinking done."

Young Lanfrith, just behind him on the rope, said, "There'll be more," and dug in his heels.

The serpent-ships beached, Cerdic led the way toward the gate. He was halfway there when a sound he knew well rang forth hideously: the scream of a mortally stricken man. He bared his sword. Through the open gate he glimpsed savage movement and three figures fiercely beset. A spear flashed and reddened.

Breaking from the fight, one of the three ran for the gate. Despite the plain hooded cloak she wore, Cerdic recognized her by her running. He'd have been in a bad way had he failed to recognize her. With a flaming oath, he began to run himself.

In the background, the two gesiths who had bought her her respite were cut down, overwhelmed by numbers. A warrior darted into view and seized her about the waist. She writhed in his grip and used the sax-knife she held. It opened his arm from shoulder to elbow as if boning a joint of beef. He howled, let her go and commenced bleeding to death.

Her hood had fallen back in the brief struggle. She swung toward the gate again with a swirl of gray mantle and flame-red hair. Her ear splitting yell scared birds off the river.

"Go back, Cerdic! It's a trap!"

The heavy gate thudded shut. From the rampart beside it, spears flew at the chieftain; he sprang nimbly to escape them. Then when he saw bows being drawn, he legged it, dodging, to the shelter of his ship.

"Well, Cerdic," a nasal bass addressed him. "I nearly had you then! Still, I have your woman and brats, and that's near as good. What will you do now?"

"Withucar!" Cerdic said. He comprehended suddenly. Salt-seething rage filled him. "Do? I'll haul you out of my fortress and hack you into twelve pieces!"

The Saxon adventurer laughed like a gander's honk. "Try! Rush this palisade! We'll slaughter you! Even if you get over it, the first thing I'll do will be to throw Giralda's head at you. Then if you begin to get the upper hand within the walls, we can start cutting your children's throats, beginning with the youngest. Tell me though... do you truly think it would come to that?"

Cerdic's men howled and brandished their weapons. The chieftain stood as if carved from heart-of-oak. No. The treacherous cur was right. It wouldn't come to that. Wiht-gara-byrig's defenses were too strong.

Giralda was in there, and the children.

Cerdic mastered himself. The effort it demanded made blood roar hollow in his ears and darkened the sunlight. He said at last, equably:

"That requires thought, doesn't it?"

Withucar chuckled. "Think all you please. I'll still have the best hostages a man could wish. You couldn't think your way past that were you as wise as the One-eyed. Now I'll go take a knotted rope to Giralda's back for warning you."

"Wait!" Cerdic said hoarsely. "Can you be bargained with on that score?"

"Not to thrash her? Come! You will never get her back. Take my word for that. Even if you did, you'd find her the sweeter for it."

Cerdic wanted to roar, "Touch her and I'll kill you!" But he didn't. This was no time for foolishness; he couldn't reach the man, and besides, he intended to kill him no matter what happened. He'd have given an arm to get the remaining hand on the oath-breaker who stood and taunted him.

"What will you take to forget the rope's end?"

"The plunder in your ships!" Withucar laughed.

Cerdic turned to the silent men behind him. "Fetch it up," he said curtly.

A murmur swept them. Young Lanfrith went further. "What?" he yelped. "But, lord—"

Cerdic's lips barely moved. "I wouldn't wish to let that swine see me slay you. Obey me."

Lanfrith shifted his feet, confused. Ulfcetel spoke out. "Lord, I'm not disputing you. But have you thought this may well do no good?"

"And it just may. Whether or no—do you suppose I mean Withucar to keep it long? Or his hostages, or his life? Now we have argued sufficiently." His voice rose to an angry roar. "Move!"

They obeyed, piling their loot before the gate. Cerdic's face was almost black with fury as he watched, less for the plunder than for the rash words he had no notion how to redeem. One idea did occur to him, but even in his wrath he saw it was worthless. Withucar would never agree. Why should he?

They sullenly withdrew to their ships.

"This is the way of it," Cerdic said to his men, his strong voice ringing out. "We are here, and Withucar is there. He holds Giralda, my son and my daughters. May monsters eat his corpse on Nastrand! Well. I could bid him meet me in single fight. He'd laugh. As for ransom, I might sack the world from end to end and pour its treasures before him and he wouldn't part with his hostages. What use is treasure to a dead man? And that he'd shortly be, once he had no threat to hold over my head! Maybe he'd send out the girls, and maybe even Giralda or Cynric with them… one or the other, but not both. Now if there's a man here who knows I'm overlooking something, let him tell me."

Uneasy silence greeted that. At last Lanfrith said, "I'd put a question, lord. Will you accept what Withucar has done?"

Cerdic's broad hand clenched over his sword-pommel. A growl, half anger, half derision, went through the band of warriors. Cerdic said fiercely, "Never!"

"Then it's best we take ourselves to Kent," Ulfcetel advised. "King Oisc will aid you with ships and men. You can return in sufficient strength to retake yon fortress, lord—and maybe to awe Withucar's own men into giving up the lady and the bantlings once they see you are determined. It will be necessary to give them quarter."

"Well," Cerdic said, "it's the soundest rede I've heard today."

His heart was not in it. Gods! How his pride would suffer, to go begging King Oisc for aid to regain the holding he'd let slip through his fingers! Oh, true, it was the logical thing to do. King Oisc had acknowledged Cerdic as his son two years before, when Cerdic had taken the fortress and Vectis-isle for his own. They had cobbled up some story about Oisc and a British princess. It was manure; Cerdic's mother had decidedly not been a princess, and almost the one certain thing about his father was that he hadn't been Oisc. No. Not even that was certain. It just might be so. Yet the story gave Cerdic a pedigree and Oisc a blood tie with this formidable young chieftain.

"Then, lord," said Lanfrith boldly, "we need not fare to Kent! If you mean to do this, it can be done with the men we have! We be three ships' companies. Withucar has only two—less than that, indeed. You left loyal men in the fortress. The Saxon must have taken them by surprise while they sat at meat with his followers, but still, no matter how swift his treachery, he'd have had losses. He made the mistake of leaving a few loyal men alive. I suppose they swore to serve him and then gave the lady Giralda her chance to warn you when the time arrived. Also, they took their scot before they fell. Let Withucar know that you know this, and he's exposed as a bluffer! We can awe his men as we stand."

Cerdic, listening gravely, thought of himself eight years before. He almost smiled.

"Have you more to say?" he asked.

Lanfrith was puzzled. "Why—why, no, lord!"

Cerdic shrugged byrnied shoulders. "Duck him in the river."

The gesiths enthusiastically complied. Later, as the three serpent-ships were racing for Kent with all the swiftness half a hundred strong rowers could give to each, Ulfcetel took the trouble to explain to the youngster.

"You forgot something, lad—or never saw it. Withucar, that bastard, wanted us to enter the fortress. Then he'd ha' taken us by surprise and slain us all. *He couldn't have relied on doing that with two ships' companies only*. It's all he had when the storm parted us from him, true. What of it? The sea's a salt broth of pirates looking for land of their own. He may well have fallen in with some of them. It may even ha' been that which put the thought of treachery into his head. We saw no ships but Withucar's two, but then he wouldn't desire us to see them, and they are easily hidden. The ring-breaker wanted to storm that place far more than you, but he's not one for throwing his men's lives away. You'll learn."

There was also a thing Ulfcetel did not mention, though it had occurred to every man in Cerdic's three ships—and none of them mentioned it either. Touching Cerdic most nearly, never out of his thoughts, it filled him with anguish and murder.

Giralda was in the traitor's hands; his Giralda. She was undoubtedly in his bed as well. He'd be enjoying her there each night while she waited for Cerdic's return, and when Cerdic told the story of what had happened, as he must do in Kent to get the king's aid, every soul on the Isle of Thanet would know. Soon afterward it would be known up and down the Narrow Sea. To a man of Cerdic's colossal pride, this was like a garlic rub after being flayed in dainty patterns. It couldn't be borne. It must be borne. Two visions he saw constantly: Giralda, writhing naked in Withucar's arms, and Giralda, red hair flying loose, red knife slashing, setting her life at stake to warn him of ambush.

"Wotan," he said between his teeth, "give me victory—give me cunning and luck to make it better than hollow victory—and I'll sacrifice a hundred men to you, hanged upon green-growing trees before the summer ends!"

King Oisc of Kent made no difficulty about granting aid. He was Cerdic's putative father, after all. To Cerdic he seemed secretly amused by what had happened, but if so, he'd the tact to conceal it.

"I'd not order men of mine to go on such a venture," he said. "However, any that wish may do so, and they may take ships of mine to fare in. Choose them better than you chose this Withucar."

Cerdic took the advice glumly.

He'd no difficulty in getting men. Besides being glad to go with him and punish an oath-breaker, they all knew Cerdic for the most openhanded of chieftains. He'd give them rich gifts for a service like this. Aye, it would be a merry business, and if Cerdic himself was less merry than usual, well, that was understandable.

Teg and Octha came, late sons of Hengist himself by casual bedmates and thus King Oisc's younger half-brothers. The dreadful Tosti Fenrir's-get came too. He was reputed to be a werewolf, and his behavior lent credibility to the tale. There was also Wecstan, who had been outlawed from among the Elbe Saxons and happened to be Oisc's guest at the time. These were the greatest names, and there were many good if lesser ones besides. When Cerdic sailed west again, he did so with seven ships and four hundred men.

Aboard their ship, Wecstan's cousin Liudehere said, grinning, "The laughter will be heard in Rome if we should find that this traitor has used his respite to plunder Wiht-gara-byrig of all he can carry off and decamped!"

The Saxon outlaw glanced from the gray water hissing along the strakes to the white-and-red sail above him. "Cerdic would hunt him out if he hid under the roots of Yggdrasil. He must know that. Besides, a base like Vectis is what every landless rover dreams of, slavering. I'd be tempted to try for it myself had I more men. I fancy this wolf will yield it with his last breath, and no other way." They came to Vectis by daylight, with no attempt at stealth. Their bright sails could be seen from afar. Ashore, banners of white cloth fluttered in reply. The coast-watchers Withucar had set were giving the alarm. This duty done, they rode or ran to the fortress as fast as they might, while the common folk of the island hugged their children and prayed destruction on every sea-wolf's head.

All save those few who had reason to know how much worse With-ucar would be than Cerdic.

From the ramparts of Wiht-gara-byrig, men watched Cerdic's force leave the ships. Cerdic himself was conspicuous by his beard and helmet. Withucar smiled.

"They have numbers, but ours is the strongpoint," he said to the henchmen nearest him. "Pass the word. Cerdic is to be slain at all costs. With him dead, we can deal with the others. Oisc of Kent will take wergild for him and leave us in peace. But while Cerdic lives, we'll none of us draw a safe breath."

He said it not fearfully but as one who recognizes a fact. Withucar was a big man, as tall as Cerdic, barely a few pounds lighter, and longer of arm. He'd braided his hair for fighting. A grin moved his heavy flaxen mustache as he watched Cerdic come up the shore for a parley.

The Brittano-Jute halted a long spear's cast from the gate. "Well, oath-breaker, you see I've returned!" he thundered. "Now send out my family."

"I will," Withucar answered. "Be sure I will! Whenever you wish! Fragment by fragment. Rush this palisade when it pleases you. Not many will get over it, and none of those who do will survive."

"Do you think so? Then you're a greater fool than I was to trust you! I took Wiht-gara-byrig once, and I'll take it again! The difference is this. Send out my family unharmed and I'll spare such of your men as live by the day's end. Do scathe or harm to any," Cerdic promised, his voice thick with passion, "and I'll slay your men to the last of the lot—aye, and those who die by edge or point will be fortunate."

"Bereavement makes you fluent," the Saxon said, laughing. "You haven't said what you will do for me."

Cerdic laughed as well, unpleasantly. "No! It might mar our friendship if I did! Suppose we settle this between ourselves? I offer you combat. If I'm slain, you pay wergild for me and send my family to Kent. If you're slain, the fortress is mine again and your men depart alive. Believe me, Withucar, you will be making a good bargain either way, compared with what you will receive if you refuse."

Withucar yawned ostentatiously. "You were ever the fine one for bluster. It's the Celtic blood, I reckon. My answer's no, even though you do have me quaking with fear."

Cerdic said with immense dignity, "Come out here with sword and shield. I'll meet you with sword only."

Jaws dropped on both sides. Those who listened were warriors; they knew how vast an advantage this would give and that Withucar was a fighting man little, if any, inferior to Cerdic. There was also his longer reach. But Withucar, who had taken oath to serve Cerdic and then broken it, would not believe that Cerdic was honest. He saw the offer only as a trick to lure him out of the fortress alone. "Do you think me a fool?" he jeered.

Cerdic did not answer that. He said, "Reflect. You have until midday."

Turning abruptly, he went back to the ships.

Withucar found his henchmen looking at him strangely. One opined, "You were mistaken; he'd stand by it. If for no better reason, he's too proud to renege."

"That is fine! As you're so confident, you go out there and meet him!"

The other proved not so ready to be daunted or shamed. "Easy to say, but it solves nothing. It's not me he wants."

Then Withucar was the one silenced.

The serpent-ships' crews carried scaling ladders ashore, Cerdic having fetched them from Kent to save making them in Vectis. He'd also brought a heavy log and numbers of ox hides. With these and farm carts that his men commandeered from nearby steadings on the chalk downs, he had them begin building a wheeled, covered ram. He watched the work impatiently, whetting his sword. He thought of Giralda within Wiht-gara-byrig's palisade, and the knowledge that he was gambling with her life turned his stomach cold. Yet he knew she would not have him act otherwise.

Stuf, one of Cerdic's captains, appeared with a local farmer beside him. The fellow was short, thickset, balding and paunchy, but there was a look of steadiness about him and he did not cringe. Oddly, he lugged a small cauldron from which wafted a rank smell. Cerdic looked inquiringly at Stuf.

"He would speak with you," the captain said. "I told him you have no time for trifles and that I'd drive a spear through him if his errand proved such. He said it was a bargain."

"Did he now?" Interest kindled in Cerdic. "Who are you?"

"My name is Antonius, mighty lord. My forebears were Roman and have held land hereabouts since the days of Trajan. I'd not prevaricate... but when you have heard me, you are likely to think me witless or joking. Thus I ask that you hold your hand and allow me to show the truth of what I say."

"Has it to do with the taking of yon fortress?" Cerdic snapped.

"Yea, lord! Everything to do with it."

"Then I will hear you. However, talk swiftly."

Antonius did; and as he had foreseen, his claims were received as maundering or ill-timed malice. He'd been wise to gain Cerdic's promise of patience beforehand. Yet he spoke on. His air of earnestness and sense swayed them at last.

"By the gods," Stuf chuckled, "you are the least likely sorcerer that ever I saw!"

" 'Tis a little magic, and rustic," Antonius replied.

"So," Cerdic said grimly. "I'll believe for now that you can do it. Tell me this. Why do you risk approaching me? What is it to you who wins this day? For you it will mean no more than a change of masters."

Antonius looked at him directly. "Even that, lord, can be a thing to fear. Say that I have reason to prefer your rule to his. And you are half-British! Say also, if you like, that I hope for reward."

"Reward you shall have according to what you achieve." Cerdic nudged the odoriferous kettle with his foot. "Stuf, take that away. Now, Antonius, let me see you work your wonder. 'Tis almost midday."

The farmer began his preparations. With sticks, earth and pebbles he fashioned a model of the stockade and the ditch around it. With straw and twigs he made small likenesses of the eating-hall within, the barns, byres and pens. He was accustomed to such work; he kept more bees than any other man on the island and made their hives from plaited straw. Also, he had children. When he'd finished, he had a near similitude of Wiht-gara-byrig.

"Yes," he nodded, cocking his head and examining the model. "It will do."

From around his neck he took a pendant of yellow amber, clear as the best ale, an insect frozen forever within. Cerdic had seen wasps and beetles so preserved, but this was a bee and by its size, a queen. Surely that was rare, if not unique.

"Best prepare your men, lord," Antonius said. "Sign me when I may begin."

Cerdic felt suddenly foolish and unsure. The loon, he thought, the earth-smelling country loon. He ought to be fooling peasant wenches with love philtres. And I stand here, I who command ships and warmen, believing him, playing his games—

He'd given his word. He said angrily, "You had best not fail."

The ram stood ready, slung from beams under its roof of soaked ox hides, mounted on cartwheels. Scaling ladders lay on the ground, ready to be carried over the ditch. These sights cheered Cerdic.

"Well, friends," he said, grinning, "with all else, we now have magic on our side! If it comes to nothing, I give you leave to laugh at me forever. With or without it, we are going to burst in yon gate and carry the wall. You know what is to be done. Once we hold the ramparts and have swept them bare, we go no farther. We make the shield-wall and stand. I'll parley with the Saxon, and this time he will listen. All of you know what hostages he holds." Cerdic ceased to smile. "Let one man go farther who has not my leave—let him carry the fighting one step toward the hall—and I'll rip open his breast myself and pull out his heart with my hands! I promise it!"

Tosti Fenrir's-get said shortly, "All this we know."

Cerdic looked at him, wondering. Tosti's half-insane savagery was a byword. Of all men there, he was the most likely to run wild with fighting lust and ignore Cerdic's orders.

"So that you remember." The big Britanno-Jute looked upon his men and sniffed the air. "Well, you have made all the preparations I said. I can smell that."

"I did not." It was Tosti again, of course. " 'Tis foolishness."

"Please your own self." Not even Cerdic was over-quick to respond to provocation from the pale-eyed giant with the wolf skin over his shoulders. "But never complain to me that I did not tell you."

He gestured to Antonius.

The farmer dangled his amber gem above the tiny fortress. A wordless chant came from his lips, humming, droning. He voiced it loud and pitched it low in a curious rhythm, the while moving his pendant along the line of the ramparts in a leftward round, against the sun.

In the great hall, Giralda and her children faced Withucar. Tall for a woman—with sleek, useful muscle gliding under curves of hip and thigh and breast—since her twelfth year, Giralda had been causing men to clench their fists and groan with desire when she walked by. Even the ones with better manners tended to draw their breath in sharply. She carried Orva, her younger girl, on her hip; Orva had just begun to talk, and she slobbered. Fain had her mother's red hair and sufficient years to know that something was wrong. She clung fretfully to Giralda's legs through the stuff of her apple-green gown. The boy, Cynric, stood a pace before them all, clinging to nothing, solid and strong, with his father's tawny hair and his father's steady gray-green eyes; yet all his courage could not make him other than small and helpless.

Beneath her gown, Giralda carried the black bruises of more than one thrashing.

"You had better go to the ramparts," she suggested. " 'Tis midday, and Cerdic will not wait long."

Withucar laughed like a man who knows himself unbeatable. "You think not? He'll wait as long as he can without seeming weak in hopes that I'll yield. He cannot overrun the stockade with all his numbers. Bah! His men will lie dead in the ditch! Some may well burst the gate, but I have archers to shoot them down as they enter; not Saxon archers, my lady, nor Goths, but Danish longbowmen who can skewer a man through his mail. Should they fail me, I have you to bargain with."

"Yes." Giralda looked at him scornfully. "All of us. I judge we are your only hope, you oath-breaker."

The Saxon's face changed. "Be not a greater fool than you were born, woman! I fear Cerdic not. I want him to attack! I've given orders that he must be slain at all costs. If he leads the charge, he will be. He's not immortal. Then I'll hurl back the others and make them swear peace, and you will be mine past any man's power to gainsay."

Giralda replied with one short word. She added, "You betrayed your master for the rule of Vectis and took his wife to your bed because she happened to be here. It's late to pretend you did all this on my account. Nor would I care if you had. The fool under this roof is not I, Withucar."

He seized her savagely by one arm. Tiny Orva squawked. "Had I the time," he snarled. "I'll see to you when this is settled! I grow weary of you, my fine lady. I'm about prepared to give you to my men."

He flung her aside. Cynric ran at him, head lowered, and butted him hard between the legs. He would have hurt him considerably but for the man's byrnie. Withucar knocked Cynric away with a casual backhanded blow.

"Game little cub," he commented with bleak humor.

"Sad it would be if he shouldn't live to grow and become the splendid, rash warrior his father is."

He left the hall.

Giralda shivered. *O my darling boy… if your father prevails, that swine will slay you for spite… and if Withucar should triumph, then still he will slay you lest you grow to avenge your father! And how can we find a way out of that?*

The farmer, Antonius, continued to move his amber jewel and croon above it. Little seemed to happen. One of the thirty Danish longbow-men posted on the platform above the gate slapped his neck, cursing.

Some of the others looked about in irritation. On the far side of the burg, a warrior yelled in pain. A few men swung their arms wildly. In a moment they were all doing it as frenzy came to the ramparts of Wiht-gara-byrig. The air filled with humming and a haze of minute yellow bodies that stung.

"Ha-yaa!" Cerdic yelled. "Follow me, and slay till your arms are weary!"

He ran for the palisade, heavy in his war-gear, feet pounding the earth. Behind him, men lifted scaling ladders and bore them for-ward, baying war-cries. Some put their backs against the covered ram, gripped its sides and strained to start it moving. The wheels rumbled; the axles shrieked. Arrows flew against it, but not in the concentrated or deadly accurate flights Withucar had counted on.

Cerdic mounted the bank of earth beyond which lay the fosse, with two feet of water and ooze at the bottom. Men flung spears at him. Cerdic, anticipating, swept his linden shield above his head and sprang aside. Weapons rattled on the shield's cowhide cover, jarring his arm to the shoulder. One struck into the bank uncomfortably near his foot. He never noticed.

Beside him, his gesiths trod into the water and rammed the bases of scaling ladders into the muck beneath. These were simply long poles with crossbars lashed to them, but high and strong, they were also muscle-crackingly heavy to lift. From the corner of his eye Cerdic glimpsed Tosti—huge, his pale eyes glaring, the white wolf skin flap-ping and spattered with mire—grip one of the ladders and heave it into place by himself. And ascend it.

Cerdic, aided by Lanfrith, manhandled a second ladder into place. Drawing his sword and using his shield for balance, he mounted the rungs. The air about him seethed with bees. He wasn't stung because he'd smeared his uncovered face and arms with the stinking salve Antonius had brewed in his cauldron—as had more than half Cerdic's warriors before the salve ran out. Those so protected were first to the attack, and Tosti with them, although he had refused the salve. He went among the defenders with a fury that would have ignored stinging bees had they been the size of sparrows.

The defenders, too, quickly forgot the insects. A bee sting is nothing compared to a spear. The bees had served their purpose by throwing the defense into confusion until Cerdic's men could gain the ramparts in a dozen places—almost without losses, which had else been great. Antonius ceased his droning. With swift movements of his hands, he flattened his similitude of the burg into rubbish. There was no more for him to do but watch.

Cerdic had reached the palisade's top. Spears assailed him, thudding on his shield, striking his armor. He chopped a spear shaft aside. Bracing his feet on the ladder, he rammed his shield forward, slashed at one man's leg and got his own over the wall. For precarious heartbeats he stood half on the ladder and half on the ramparts while men raged to destroy him.

Cerdic plied his sword with a redness over his brain. He got past a painted shield and smote its bearer low on the side between ribs and hip. The leather sark was slashed through. No blood was drawn, but the man doubled over, winded and sickly helpless. Cerdic bulled forward by main strength, shield battering, sword hewing. In a moment he had both feet on his own ramparts again.

A sword broke on his shield-rim. Cerdic feinted to bring his enemy's shield down, then slashed open the front of his head. Beside him, the fellow he'd winded was struggling to rise, head thrust far forward as he choked after breath. There was green bile in his beard. Cerdic hewed at the exposed neck. This time the man fell dead. Lanfrith came off the ladder, yelling, and others swarmed after.

"Clear the ramparts!" Cerdic roared as he cut his way along them. "Clear the ramparts and hold them!"

His sword flickered, rang, bit. He made remorselessly for the platform above the gate where the Danish bowmen were. Not a few of his warriors lay outside the stockade with arrows in them, and the Danes were now shooting at the ram immediately below. It was spitting distance in literal truth. At that range, with the power of those bows behind them, the arrows went straight through the ram's ox hide roof. Men were dying beneath it.

Cerdic warded his face all he could. The Danes were looking for targets and his shield sprouted arrows. The last man between him and the platform swung an ax two-handedly. It split Cerdic's shield into two; it nigh broke his arm. He staggered. The ax leaped at his thigh. His sword whined over in a red-spattering arc to split knuckles and crack the ax haft. Although his shield was battered to ruin, Cerdic still held the grip and the conical iron boss. He struck with it. The ax-wielder's jawbone snapped, half his teeth were exposed, and he sagged against the steps that led to the platform. Cerdic killed him. A dozen or twenty feet trod over the body.

Then they were too close, and the platform too crowded, for archery. The same applied in a measure to sword work. Most of the Danes had heavy, single-edged fighting knives. So did Cerdic. The instant he got a decent hack at someone with his sword, he left it lodged in the warrior's chine and drew his backup weapon.

There followed a straining, gasping, stamping melee, stinking of sweat and blood, each man for himself. Several were forced over the edge of the platform. Often as not they went gripping an adversary. The rain of arrows having ended, men began swinging the ram again. It boomed against the gate. The impact vibrated in soles and spines where Cerdic fought. His mouth was full of a stocky Dane's red beard. He'd stabbed the man many times and was beginning to think he *couldn't* be killed. But the big frame shuddered and went limp just as the gate burst.

Cerdic broke away from the Dane's death grip. Breathing raggedly, he looked about. The platform above the gate belonged to him. The

gate itself hung open drunkenly and the rammers were within. Elsewhere the last resistance was dying fiercely on the ramparts.

I've won, he thought. *I've done it.*

Not quite yet. Hoarsely, he gave commands. The confusion was
replaced by firm control in moments. His rammers made a shield-wall
in the gateway. Others did likewise along the ramparts, and Cerdic had
some of his men join him on the platform so that a rush might not take
him unaware.

Teg Hengist's son lay dead. Tosti Fenrir's-get swayed on his feet,
dazed by an ax blow on the helm that would have broken another man's
neck. Cerdic did not feel saddened; it was probably all that had kept
the wolf-hearted giant from precipitating a thorough slaughter.

There'll be one anyhow if Giralda or the children are hurt.

Cerdic retrieved his sword. It was notched and had lost its edge.
Blood was jellied darkly on the blade. He himself was rankly spattered,
his byrnie gashed, some of the gilded iron scales missing. He was sweaty,
and his throat cried for drink.

"Where is Withucar?" he thundered.

The Saxon limped into view. He showed signs of hard fighting also,
but he'd seemingly fled the ramparts when he saw they were unavoid-
ably lost. His men had taken a massed position against the long wall
of the eating-hall. They were now outnumbered something like two to
one

"Here."

"*Where are your hostages!*"

"Within the hall, under trusty ward. Thus are you still where you
were before."

"Look around you and tell me that! Ha! I have you, traitor. I have
you by the throat and you will gasp out your last breath ere I loose my
grip." Cerdic's voice was a vengeful purr. "Yes, I have you, but you have
my wife and children. I made you an offer some days gone because of
that. You remember?"

"I remember." Withucar looked incredulous. "You are not making
it anew?"

"I am that. If you suppose I mean to stand here and argue back and forth with you over Giralda's body, you are misled. I haven't so much time to spend on you. Best agree, Withucar. Or are you as false to the men you lead as to me, whom you pledged to serve?"

The men at bay by the long hall murmured, for it was their lives too. Withucar saw that Cerdic had trapped him neatly. His men had fought for him as their chieftain. Now it was for him to repay them in kind. If he did not, they might well throw down their weapons and chance Cerdic's mercy. They all knew he'd show none if the hostages were harmed. And indeed, single combat now seemed to be Withucar's only chance.

"The same terms?"

Cerdic was too eager to refuse his enemy that. Like a great tawny lynx smelling prey, he sensed what he wanted within his grasp.

"Aye!" he shouted. "The very same, with one other. Send Giralda and the children to me now, before we fight!"

Withucar gave him shout for shout. "I'm to trust you?"

"Why not? I never made an oath to you and broke it!"

That stung more fiercely than Antonius's bees because it was too true. Withucar paled, then reddened.

"Bring them out!" he snarled to his henchmen. "We will see what a half-Jute's word is good for!"

Cerdic saw them led forth. He'd have croaked nonsense and run to them were he not his gesiths' war-leader with work still to finish and had he not been aware of Withucar's sneering gaze. The woman's hair wavered in his sight like a torch, as it had the first time he had set eyes on her in her father's hall—she the daughter of a Jutish chieftain of royal descent. How fearlessly Cynric trod beside her! A show, of course, abetted by unwillingness to shame his parents—but how many boys his age could have done as much? One of Withucar's traitors growled and stamped his foot to make the atheling jump. Rage burned in Cerdic. He marked that man's visage well lest they should ever cross paths in the future.

Then they were safe on the platform. Cerdic seized Giralda in his arms. Let Withucar stare his fill and be cursed! She held him equal-strongly and returned his kiss with a hunger like starvation, caring no whit for the hardness of his byrnie or the blood-reek upon him. The children jostled for his attention as children will. Fain's voice carried when she said, "What did you fetch me home?"

Cerdic sat her on his knee and began a game, making her guess.

"By Wotan!" roared Withucar. "This burg has not again become your home yet, Cerdic! Suppose you step down here and fight me before you take it on yourself to dandle your brats!"

Cerdic grinned broadly and stood. Fain now sat in the crook of his arm, her hands on his mailed shoulder. Hair as red as her mother's blew wild.

"I am going to rest a while," Cerdic said, "and wet my throat." He passed his sword to Lanfrith. "Meantime I'll let my blade be cleaned and sharpened, just for you. Never fret, Withucar. Enough and to spare of the afternoon is left. It won't be dusk before we settle this."

Ulfcetel passed him a brimming ale-horn. He smacked his lips and drank it steadily until its contents were a memory, save for foam in his mustache. The second he waved away, although he could gladly have emptied it too. Nor did he eat. It was unwisdom to fight on a full belly.

The grindstone ended its song. Lanfrith brought back the heavy sword with its edges shining. Cerdic tried it by hewing into the top of one of the palisade logs and then smiled with baleful satisfaction at the result.

"Good lad," he said. "This will do." To Giralda he said, "I'll not fall, my beautiful. Not to such as Withucar. But if it could happen, I'd command you to see that my word was kept."

"And let him live?" Her smile wavered a little, but nonetheless, it was as fierce as Cerdic's own. "Then am I glad it cannot happen. Slay him, Cerdic!"

"Indeed I will." The big man swaggered down from the platform and thence from the ramparts. Withucar awaited him. All sensations seemed clearer, from the gold-yellow hue of the hall's thatch to the smells of dunghill and midden and thickening blood. High, clean, untouched, a wind drove clouds across the sky.

"He carries no shield!" Giralda cried.

"He fights without one," Ulfcetel spoke bluntly, and yet his voice held compassion. "Those are the terms."

"No! This is madness!" Giralda rounded on them, raging. "You, his companions, sworn to him—you let him do this? You had not the manhood to protect him even from himself? Now may your luck and all the gods forsake you!"

"Enough," the steersman said harshly. "I'd not have had him do this, but it wasn't my wife and children Withucar held."

Giralda gripped her face between her hands so wildly that her nails drew blood.

Withucar had taken a new shield, and it untouched. The linden orb had been painted red and bore the figure of a raven, shown as sitting on the iron boss. The bird's pose was restless, ready to fly.

Cerdic's battle-experienced eyes took note of other things: the number and spacing of rivets that held the boss in place, the shield-rim's heavy leather binding, the thickness and probable weight of the linden wood. It all mattered, though none of it so much as Withucar's prowess.

"Was your meeting with Giralda happy?" the Saxon asked. "Did she maybe tell you that her howls of joy in my bed were heard clear to the south cliffs? Or that after the second time, I had to fend her off? Oh, you'd find her a changed woman—if you were going to live."

Cerdic said contemptuously, "You talk a good lay. You talk a good fight too. I've heard you. Now let us see."

Withucar trod forward. His sword slanted back over his shoulder; the red shield covered him from chin to groin. Their swords belled together. The shield turned a little, and Withucar drove it slanting, smashing down at the side of Cerdic's knee. Cerdic straightened that leg smartly to step the other way. He moved into a shrewd cut from his enemy and had to check it, sword on sword once more. The iron shield-boss slammed cruelly into his side. Even through scale and leather

and heavy tunic, it jolted breath sickly from the lung. Cerdic backed
three swift paces, circling. This was the tactic, then. Occupy sword
with sword, meanwhile battering with the shield until flesh could no
longer endure it. Not bad. But Cerdic's left hand was free. It opposed
Withucar's sword-hand, of course—and yet by his own chosen tactic,
Withucar's sword-hand would be engaged a deal of the time.

Clash of metal! Stamp and shuffle of hide-shod feet!

The swords joined again, a diagonal cross ablaze with light. Cerdic
forced the cross from erect to horizontal, his blade screeching down the
length of Withucar's to split the wooden guard. Enduring the slam of
the shield-boss, he held his enemy's sword engaged—and seizing Withucar's sword-wrist with his left hand, Cerdic freed his own weapon.

The shield flashed edge-on between them, rushing to break the bones
of Cerdic's forearm. He threw that hand high, raising Withucar's with
it. The shield missed. Cerdic chopped down at the hurtling edge. He
cut through the leather binding and notched the wood, that was all.
The shield had been made in two layers, with the grain running in
opposite ways. One blow could not split it.

Withucar used his knee. Cerdic lifted a thigh in time to take the
impact, but it cost him balance. Withucar rammed him with the shield-
boss, hurling him back. The two men broke apart.

The death fight went on.

I'll stomach no more of this, Giralda thought.

She glanced about. Almost at once she saw a spear resting forgotten
against the rampart. She could throw one, strongly and straight. Yet
Withucar made a nigh-invulnerable target. His neck was too small a
mark. Besides, it was constantly moving. His byrnie shielded his torso.
That left the legs.

She couldn't miss those.

Yes! It wouldn't be instantly fatal, but all she had to do was to make
him stumble. Cerdic would do the rest. His blood heated by the fight,
he'd never stop to think if it was honorable or not. When he knew
what had happened he'd be more than angry. He'd be enraged... well,
let him be! She wasn't afraid of his rages, and he'd be alive.

She slipped into the background. All there had eyes for nothing but the fight... as Giralda supposed. Her fingers closed on the spear shaft.

Much larger fingers closed on her wrist. The strength of them was terrifying. Giralda looked up into a coldly handsome face and a pair of ice-pale eyes, shadowed under the scalp and muzzle of a wolf skin.

No!

Of all men, this one!

"Let me go, you oaf!"

Tosti Fenrir's-get removed the spear from her hand. "Be quiet," he said calmly. "The fight goes to its fated end, and none may meddle."

Giralda struggled. Tosti took her by both of her upper arms and held her in a grip that warned he could splinter her bones if he chose. Giralda did not heed the warning. In this extremity she cared for neither honor nor fate—and she knew in hatred that they did not concern Tosti either. He was simply enjoying the fight.

She raged, kicked, tried to bite, promised riches, threatened, begged, and finally cursed Tosti Fenrir's-get as few had ever ventured to do. She wondered afterward why he hadn't just cuffed her senseless. She supposed it had suited his cruel humor to make her watch the combat.

Cerdic had suffered four small wounds. Although none were disabling, they were painful and they bled. He knew now that he was not going to get past the red shield without a shield of his own. Withucar was too skilled.

Then he must reduce the shield or destroy it.

Recklessly Cerdic hewed, spending his strength because there was no more reason to hoard it. The swords chimed and clashed. Cerdic used his unweaponed left arm as bait, tempting Withucar to strike at it. Barely in time he snatched it aside and cut strongly into the shield-rim. A segment of the top layer of wood split straight across, decapitating the painted raven. Then Cerdic had to jump smartly backward to avoid his enemy's sword. He felt the wind of that stroke. Had he been fresh, he could have disabled Withucar's sword-arm then; but both men were slowing. They were not made of unfeeling iron. Cerdic missed the chance.

Wielding his glaive two-handed, he rained blows on Withucar's sword until his own hands stung. The Saxon's single grip must surely be numbed. Chancing all, Cerdic swung two mighty strokes on Withucar's shield, calculating them as nicely as he could with hot brain and sweat-blurred eyes. Then Withucar's sword caught Cerdic over the ribs, on his left side. He croaked; he reeled. And struck two-handed again. Withucar's sword was knocked from his grasp. A wild yell went up.

Dogged, unthinking, Cerdic hewed at the shield. The weakened segment fell away, held only by the hide lacing. Then that unraveled and burst. Withucar circled sideways. Quickly he dropped to one knee, reaching for the sword that lay behind him, covering his forward knee with what remained of the shield.

Cerdic brought one terrible blow down from on high. It hacked through the finger's length of partly splintered wood that still protected Withucar's shield-arm, and it smashed his elbow to bone fragments in a tube of broken meat. Withucar screamed. Somehow he regained his feet, and the sword was in his right hand again.

The shield fell from his useless arm. It thudded on the earth.

Withucar never thought of crying for quarter. Snarling, he flung himself upon Cerdic, careless now of death so long as he took the other with him. Their swords jonted together for the last time. Cerdic seized Withucar about the waist and toppled the Saxon over his hip. Withucar let fall his sword, flinging out his sound arm to save the shattered one from impact. With a grunt of agony, he sprawled helpless.

Cerdic had ample time and space to swing his weapon. He did so decisively; one blow slew.

To stop was to almost collapse, so fierce had been the contest. Shuddering, sucking air through his raw throat, Cerdic leaned on his sword while his gesiths bellowed their jubilation and rattled spearheads on shields. Ulfcetel rushed down from the ramparts at the head of twenty warriors. Cerdic straightened and waved them back with his encarnadined sword. Glaring, he spoke to the dead man's followers.

"You," he said, gasping. "I gave you gifts... fed you... and you gave me your oaths. Well, I gave mine that you should be free to go where you wish. So you may. Take your ships. Go." His powerful voice steadied; he brought his panting under control. "I give you leave, but know this. The day I see any of you again will be an ill one for you. Even if it never comes, I do not think your luck will be good hereafter. What chieftain would trust you?"

"Lord, take us back!" one man cried. "Give us the hardest tasks, the brunt of all danger, until you deem us worth trusting again!"

Cerdic said wearily, "Get out."

Lacking a leader, bereft of hostages, and twofold outnumbered, they had to obey. They formed a body and marched through Wiht-gara-byrig's gate. Cerdic entered his hall, bloody and sweaty but triumphant. His arm was around Giralda's lithe waist.

Then and ever after, she let him suppose the savage bruises on her arms where Tosti had squeezed them black and blue were relics of Withucar's treatment. She had no wish to provoke trouble between her husband and Tosti after all else that had happened that day. Besides, as she soon saw, her bruises were nothing to Cerdic's.

PRETTY BABY

by Ray Peekner

Editor's Introduction

When a stupid man does something he knows is wrong, he always claims that it is his duty.

—George Bernard Shaw

This has been the era of social engineering; a time of high purposes, when the very nature of man will be transformed; a time to create a beautiful world, in which there will be no poor, no ignorant, none in want; there will be no suffering. A world of beauty is struggling to be born. Naturally there will be birth pains, dislocations, even horror; but we have only to sweep away the old to bring forth the new.

Thus inspired, both foolish and learned have acted like beasts in the name of humanity. Soviet troops in the Ukraine took the food from the homes of starving peasants. The Nazi regime ordered euthanasia for the aged, incurably ill, and the insane. Yellow rain falls in Laos and Afghanistan. Prisoners in Iran are used as human mine detectors.

The democracies have not been blameless. Dresden was fire-bombed. Mushroom clouds bloomed above Hiroshima and Nagasaki. "Operation Keelhaul" returned hundreds of thousands of Russian expatriates to the Soviet Union where they were either murdered or worked to death in labor camps. There were other incidents, in Korea and later in Viet Nam, to suggest that civilization is a thinner veneer than we like to suppose. For all that, Lieutenant Calley was charged and tried; individual soldiers may have committed atrocities, but indiscriminate murder of the helpless has never been a policy of the US or Britain.

And yet—could it happen here? Whatever one's views on the rights and wrongs of abortion, twenty years ago the notion that abortion on demand might some day be legal throughout the land would have been laughed down as absurd. Now we hear of doctors who with parents' consent have treated defective newborns with "benign neglect"—i.e., have allowed them to starve to death. Phrases like "quality of life," and "it's better this way," are heard in courts of law. Perhaps infanticide on demand will never be legal here—but it is not impossible. The moral absolutes crumble before a barrage of words, and no one knows where the erosion of values will end.

Pilate asked, "Is it not better that one should die for the sake of all?" And if one—then why not two? Or four, or a thousand. Rationalizations come easy once begun. It remains only to convince those who must do the bloody work.

Good soldiers do not often make good butchers. Sometimes those in command may believe there is no choice; but they do not lightly order good troops into a human charnel house to be stripped of their human feelings, for to do so is to risk losing their effectiveness. The most hardened professional soldiers must feel loyalty to some purpose higher than themselves, be it no more than the honor of the regiment; else they will not risk their lives as good soldiers often must.

Nations that order their soldiers to dishonor themselves are then defended by dishonorable troops.

I would like to convince myself that this story could never happen. I want to comfort myself with the thought that American soldiers, professional or conscript, would never carry out these orders.

———

PCC Vet Slays Wife, Son, Self

Ferndale, Iowa—AP

Kenneth MacCarter, 18, who served with the Population Control Corps in India, today shot his wife, Nancy, and his 10-month-old son, Kevin, six days after his return home. After slaying his family, he put the service automatic into his mouth and took his own life.

From the hillside, the village of Sanphura was now visible in the distance. The dilapidated bamboo huts with the plastic sheeting stretched upon the rooftops glistened wetly beneath the driving rain.

"Damn it all," muttered Private George Hansen to the soldier alongside him. "With this mucking rain, we won't be able to fire the huts. We'll have to go in after them."

Private Ken MacCarter at that moment wished he were back home, or at least secure in warm, dry barracks. His lean fingers hugged the M-19 in readiness. He was acutely conscious of his anxiety and he hoped Private Hansen would keep talking. Hansen, at twenty, was only two years his senior, but he was a veteran; the distance separating them seemed more like twenty years.

"Yeah," said Private Hansen, spitting cleanly. "It's easier when you can burn them out. But going in after them, it's not so bad. Takes longer, that's all. Kick the door and spray in every direction, low and steady. Drop a fire grenade and get the hell out. That's all there's to it."

The squad halted. The village of Sanphura was about a hundred yards away. It appeared to be empty.

The sergeant withdrew, addressed his squad. "Move out, in pairs. I want a clean mop-up. Understand? I don't want to find anything moving when it's over, not even a goddamn flea wiggling on the fur of a rat. Understand? Move out!"

"Stick with me, kid," Private Hansen said, and he started toward the village.

Private Ken MacCarter realized suddenly that in a few moments it would all start happening. Still, a vague sense of unreality crowded him.

This was not a war, and these emaciated villagers were not the enemy. The American unit was there to perform "humane actions" at the
request of the Indian Government, as were the Russian, the English,
the Chinese units—all of them.

Their mission was to wipe out the excess population that was dragging India into ever greater poverty. Scientific experts had assured the
greater powers that they were helping to rebalance the ecology of the
planet. It was dirty work, but necessary, like thinning out the herds
on the great game preserves. Sooner or later, without this cropping,
thousands more would die of starvation. "This operation is a humane
action," he kept telling himself.

MacCarter became aware that he and Hansen were being followed.
He turned quickly. The friendly face of a news photographer beamed
a quick smile. The man was husky, a bit overweight, red-faced, about
forty. He carried a network film camera.

Hanson stopped, grimaced, his already narrow eyes closing to thin
slits. "Ah, it's you, Farley," he said to the man. "Damn it, do you have
to tag along with us? MacCarter here is a new man. This is his first
mission."

"I know it," acknowledged Farley. "I thought there might be a story
in that. Don't get uptight about it, I'll stay out of the way."

As they were almost to the village, Hansen warned, "Sometimes one
of them might have a knife or an old revolver and try to put up a fight.
Don't take any chances. Shoot them all, moving or not."

Suddenly shots exploded. The mop-up had begun.

"Watch it," shouted Hansen. "Now some of them are running out."

From behind a bamboo hut an emaciated old man, his ribs visible,
stumbled into the muddy street. His hands were outstretched, reaching.
MacCarter realized that the man was blind. Trachoma in these rural
villages affected eighty to ninety percent of the inhabitants. Then he
watched the thin figure jump suddenly and collapse in the mud.

"Fire!" screamed Hansen.

More figures in the street. Another old man. A child, its belly hung
and distended from starvation. A woman carrying a baby. She fell with

it still in her arms. The figures toppling. MacCarter felt the vibration as the M-19 kicked in his hands, saw the shots ripping through the frenzied mass, plunking noiselessly into flesh. He saw, but he did not believe. It seemed too simple and clear-cut a proposition for the mind to logically accept.

Twenty people down, thirty. Thinning out now.

He saw a small boy down on his knees, crawling for cover. He noticed that the boy's foot was missing and he wondered whether it had been shot away.

He hesitated.

At that moment Farley moved into view, his camera aimed at the crawling boy.

"No," murmured MacCarter. "Don't…"

Hansen aimed a shot at the boy's head, and the boy fell suddenly face-down in the mud, the dark-red blood oozing from his temple and mingling with the brown water.

"Stop!" he heard himself saying. Something inside him was rebelling at the idea that Farley was recording an action that should not be recorded. And he found himself aiming at Farley's camera, firing.

The camera flew into the mud. Farley's hand clutched his wrist, a look of astonishment contorting his face.

"The crazy bastard shot at me," Farley whined. Then, more precisely, "He shot the camera out of my hands."

"I saw it," said Hansen. "You'd better get to a medic, Farley."

"I asked him to stop," insisted Ken. "He was… filming that boy dying." He knew these were not accurate statements. The boy had died instantly. And Farley had not heard his warning. What really disturbed him most, however, was his own impulsive act.

Anguished screams shot out from the flames as the small village burned. Soon after the rains, the Khari River, one of the many tributaries of the Ganges, would overflow its banks and flood the entire area.

"Okay, now watch me," instructed Hansen calmly.

Hansen kicked a hut door, and with his M-19 cradled low in his arms, sprayed a volley of shots inside. Behind him, MacCarter looked into the shack, saw an old man slump forward, two red stains budding in his chest. An old woman lay stretched across the floor. Her throat had been cut.

"He got to her first," explained Hansen.

As they left, Hansen chucked a fire grenade inside. They hurried away, feeling the heat of the bursting flames.

A woman ran from an adjoining shack toward the hillside, toward the rice paddies.

"Take her!" ordered Hansen.

MacCarter was conscious only of his arms lifting his weapon, firing, watching her being hit. Her body was so emaciated, the bullets went through without resistance. As she toppled back into the mud, Mac-Carter was unable to determine how he felt about it.

"Okay! Okay!" shouted Hansen encouragingly.

The mop-up completed, only the tagging remained to be done. As Hansen explained, it was very important to tag all your victims so that when the body-counters came in they could attribute the right count toward your K.Q. Each man was assigned a Kill Quota of 1000. After that his active-duty assignment was terminated.

Private George Hansen already had 1047 on his K.Q. count, and he needed fifty-three more. His K.Q. had been raised by 100 as a disciplinary measure. When tagging the bodies, Hansen suggested they put both of their numbers on each body. That way the body-counters would total them and split the count between them.

MacCarter found that marking the bodies was a relatively easy job if he avoided looking at the faces. But some of them couldn't be ignored. One face, the face of a baby, was undamaged. The trouble was, the head had been severed from the body. The sight of it stirred his guts. He stopped, steadied himself by leaning on his rifle and, hunched over, let the sour vomit come out.

Hansen looked up from his marking, released a knowing smile.

It had been a good day, he felt. The count might be fifty or sixty, which would be twenty-five or thirty for him. The kid had been all right too, once he'd gotten into it.

The temporary, prefabricated barracks were reasonably comfortable, with radiant heating, lights, clean chemical toilets and folding beds. This all moved in the cargo choppers when the weather was good or, as now, in the trucks. Generators supplied adequate electrical power, and the processed food was plentiful.

Private George Hansen was lying propped up on his bed watching a videocomic on a portable set. At the far end of the room a poker game was in progress. MacCarter sat idly on the bed next to Hansen's, looking forlorn.

"Why don't you call your wife?" suggested Hansen. "You're married, aren't you?"

"Yes," said Ken, "but..." His thin, boyish face, topped with curly, reddish-brown hair, lighted with eagerness. "You mean I can call my wife from here?"

"Personnel on active duty may exercise the prerogative of making not more than two videocalls per week," read Hansen from an operations manual. "It's all in the book. Only who gets a chance to read that crap?" Every few days they handed you a supplement. He tossed the book to the floor, got up.

"I'll walk over to the Com shack with you," Hansen volunteered.

"You're not married, are you, George?" Ken asked, as they walked. It was the first time he had called Hansen by his first name, which he pronounced a bit hesitantly.

The videophones at the Communications post were equipped to receive picture transmissions, via satellite, from the States, but at this end they were able to send only voice transmissions.

"They're not supposed to know we're in India," said Hansen. "They'll bleep you if you mention it."

When Nancy's soft, tired face appeared, Ken felt a deep stab of nostalgic homesickness. He wished he were able to reach out and touch her, feel the grainy texture of her dark, black hair. She wore a loose yellow housedress, open at the throat. Not picking up a picture, she was tapping the receiver with agitation. Anonymous videophone calls could really bug a person.

"It's me, honey," Ken repeated.

"Ken?"

"There's no way to send the picture from here, Nancy, but I can see you. You look beautiful."

Hansen watched with interest. "She's not bad, your wife."

"Thanks. Wait'll you see my boy."

Suddenly the face of an angry, mewling infant being held by two thin, feminine hands filled the screen. His open mouth released his cries of distress at being awakened.

"Can you see him?" Nancy yelled.

"Yes, I can see him. He's really getting big. What do you think of that, Hansen?"

Hansen nodded. "Nice baby. What can you say about a baby?"

"Who are you talking to, Ken?"

"A buddy. George Hansen. He's from Wisconsin. Say hello, George."

Hansen said hello, then left to allow them to relay their kisses in private.

In the Com shack lounge, Hansen found Farley helping himself to a cup of coffee from the large aluminum percolater. They nodded to each other. Ken MacCarter came in a moment later.

Farley looked directly at him, switched his coffee to his left hand, reached for a handshake to show he held no ill feeling over the morning incident. "MacCarter."

"Yeah," muttered Ken, clasping the hand. He noticed a bandage on Farley's wrist. "Look, I'm sorry about…"

Farley waved aside the apology. "Forget it. Things like that happen. I understand what you're going through, son. Even some people back home think that taking pictures of this operation, showing the blood and death, isn't right."

Hansen interjected, "Well, it isn't. Why is it necessary to show these things on television?"

Farley took a sip of coffee, rinsed his teeth with it. "These films are a social document, not only for now, but for generations to be born. Sure it's a dirty business, but don't you see, unless people are told the cold, hard facts, see the chaos, it could happen to us. Seeing the stark effects of overpopulation, it's a valuable lesson." Farley tossed the paper cup into the trash container. "You boys want to see what you did today?" He looked at Ken. "The film wasn't destroyed. In fact, it's quite good." He hitched up his pants. "Come along, I'll show it to you."

Inside the screening room, Farley ran a videotape of the morning's action, the villagers hitting the street, reeling and spinning under the impact of the bullets. To Ken it seemed even more unreal now.

There, intact, was the shot of the one-legged boy, crawling, that Hansen had shot in the head. Farley informed them that the clip was being used on all three network newscasts.

As Private Ken MacCarter watched, he felt no animosity toward Farley, nor Hansen, but thought, oddly, of—it was only an image—the bawling face of his son Kevin superimposed on the film. He turned away. "There must be a better way than this," he pleaded.

"True," agreed Farley. "On a clear day, the choppers can drop gas. That's relatively painless. But with heavy winds, or this rain, it has to be this way. Those people were warned to evacuate. They had to be eradicated. That land is needed. It's a race against time. Those people, they resigned themselves to dying." He looked at MacCarter. "You haven't been here long enough. You don't know the whole story, the way it is."

"Maybe not."

Farley replayed the clip of the crawling boy. "See that? The missing foot, I mean."

MacCarter nodded. He felt sick inside, as though his soul had left him.

"The city syndicates, they buy these kids. They maim them in various interesting ways to look pathetic when they are begging. It's a bizarre operation, picking them up and distributing them in the cities each morning, collecting them at night. Don't you think that kid is better off where he is?"

"I don't know," said MacCarter. He imagined Kevin's tiny face again, saw him crying for all humanity.

Morning came gray and wet. Today the objective was Dahkangar, a village three miles northeast, across the Khari River. Like the others, a pesthold of bleak starvation and disease, a population blight that had to be eradicated.

The procedure was the same. When the shooting began, some of the villagers ran into the streets. You picked them off first. Then you hit the shacks.

MacCarter was working with Hansen again, and they had already run up a good kill in the street. Hansen was likely to meet his K.Q. and be relieved this week. He envied Hansen that.

MacCarter kicked a door, was about to fire the M-19 when he saw the baby.

Two thin, feminine hands lifted a crying infant beneath its arms. A memory, an image, impelled itself on his mind.

The baby seemed to be floating toward him.

He couldn't shoot.

The baby's wet, open mouth sucked air.

The baby screamed. MacCarter's hands reached to take the child when, suddenly, the baby was flung to the ground like an empty box.

He was conscious of watching the baby strike the floor, instantly still, but did not see even the glint of the knife as it entered beneath his breastbone. Sharp pain exploded inside him and his mind collapsed under the pressure.

Life at the Rehabilitation Center was pleasant enough. The staff was friendly, almost solicitous. Best of all, Private Ken MacCarter knew that in a few days he would be going home. It was a good feeling. Occasionally the thought of the heart transplant bothered him, but they all said he was doing fine. He hadn't been confined to bed for over two months. He did feel good.

One thing, his memory, seemed a bit confused. He no longer re-membered how he had been hurt, but the doctors told him it didn't matter. They explained they had helped him to forget; something about memory probing. He did remember Hansen coming to visit him the first days after the operation.

Hansen, knowing that it wouldn't matter anyway, told MacCarter everything that had happened. He told Ken how he had caught and wounded the bitch who had knifed him, how he'd gotten help, and how it was her very heart that was now beating in Ken's chest. That seemed just in a way. But it didn't matter, the doctors would help MacCarter to forget.

Private George Hansen returned to Wisconsin and work at a fish hatchery, and he tried to forget about India and MacCarter and looked for a girl to marry.

Private Ken MacCarter came home to Iowa, to Nancy and Kevin, to his job at the printing plant. All his friends in Ferndale told him he was looking just fine. A few inquired about where he had been and what he had done, but when he declined to answer, no one pursued the matter.

For five sweet days Ken resumed his old life. Everything was falling into place. In the fall he would begin studying at the state technical college. The company was sponsoring him.

It sometimes made Ken nervous when Kevin cried, but Nancy did not notice anything. His return had had an exhilarating effect on her.

On the sixth day after his return, Ken MacCarter came back from the plant—he would begin work the following Monday—and he looked for Nancy to tell her the good news. He found her in the kitchen giving Kevin his afternoon bath in the portable bassinet.

The inexplicably sensual image ripped hard and uncontrollably through his mind: tearing, violent glimpses of dead faces, hot fires, screams, rain, an open mouth...

It happened exactly when Nancy lifted a protesting Kevin in her fine, thin, feminine hands to show Ken his pretty baby.

The Man in the Gray Weapons Suit

by Paul J. Nahin

Editor's Introduction

The weapons of war are forever changing. We are today engaged in a technological war which could of itself be decisive; which is why military research is so vital to our survival. The Falklands War demonstrated two things: that wars cannot be won without good soldiers; but good soldiers are not enough. One needs high technology, particularly computers and electronics.

When a truck broke down during World War II the British and French had little choice but to send for mechanics. Automobiles were much more common in the United States, and in any truckload of American soldiers there was generally at least one with sufficient experience to fix the vehicle unaided. Those familiar with technology are generally best able to use and maintain it. It will be so with computers and electronics; which poses an interesting dilemma for the Soviet Union and other tyrannies.

When Germany invaded Poland, the first thing the soldiers did was to disable the telephone system. Control of communications is vital to modern totalitarian states. Soviet citizens must register their typewriters with the police, and possession of an unregistered mimeograph machine is an offense worth five years in a labor camp; but how can communications be controlled if small computers are widely dis-

tributed? The Soviet economic system desperately needs computers—
but the political system probably can't withstand their side effects.

Whatever the effect of the computer on the totalitarian, the technological war continues. Artificial Intelligence, "fifth generation" computers, and "expert systems" may well be the decisive weapons of the
future.

Dr. Paul Nahin, Professor of Electrical Engineering at the University
of New Hampshire, has worked in weapons system design and evaluation, and is well qualified to show us this picture of the future at war.

———————

The warrior gently ran his hands over the smooth flanks of his love.
She responded not in any physical sense, but still he knew that deep
within, under the flawless skin, she felt his presence. With a single
flowing, graceful motion, he mounted her. She opened wide and he
slipped inside. The fit was narrow: his bulk squeezed tightly against
her sides. But to the warrior, it was cozy, snug, warm. The plexiglass
cockpit housing slid back down over his helmeted head with barely a
hissing of its electric motor.

He inserted the digital communication umbilical cable from his
biosensor body box into the female connector on the floor and became
as one with Red Striker Five.

Snapping the throat mike down against his neck, he called the Com-
bat Information Center on the nuclear carrier. "CIC, this is Red Striker
Five. All weapons stores on board, fuel topped off, and set for launch.
Give me your ready-status readouts."

"Roger, Red Striker Five, we have you on first launch. For your ready
status—wind over the bow at forty-two knots, sea state at level three,
cloud cover starts at five thousand, solid to eight thousand five hundred,
and clear from there up. You are initially on weapons tight, with a
required visual verify of a bogey before authorized to perform a weapon
release. No voice communication in the clear allowed—perform all
data transmission to the fleet on GPS LINK Ninety-nine. Set your

security-level switch to antijam position three. Ship radars show a clear screen out to one-five-five miles. Prepare to launch."

The warrior felt the passing of a momentary irritation. *Weapons tight, with a visual verify! Damn!* His air superiority platform could detect, lock on, and track twenty-three simultaneous targets out to three hundred line-of-sight miles. His frequency hopping, pulse-doppler, lockdown radar could pick enemy infiltrators out of the massive clutter background echo of the ocean, even if they attempted to penetrate fleet defense by coming in 100 feet off the deck at Mach two. His "fire-and-forget" Eagle-Six missiles, with home-on-jam radiation-seeker heads, could attack and kill with probability point nine, nine, nine at 170 miles, at hypersonic speed.

And he had to identify a hostile visually before weapon release! Even with his electro-optical visual aid, that meant a maximum attack range of ten miles. Maybe fifteen if he used the narrow-field zoom lens with autovideo tracking. Damn! It was *his* ass on the line, not those of the political toadies who soiled their pants at the thought of a mistaken ID. Having to close that near to a potentially deadly hostile dropped his survival probability by at least ten percent.

But maybe the hunting will be good today. The use of the Global Position System satellite, and its antijam, encrypted digital data link meant that something was up. His pulse rate elevated and the surface of his skin wetted slightly with perspiration. Small biosensors in his body box picked these reactions up and routinely filed them away in the on-board flight computer. The gray weapons platform called Red Striker Five would need to know everything if it was to help the warrior survive.

The flight-deck tractor was already hooked up to his aircraft, and the warrior waited as the twenty-one-ton Red Striker Five was attached to the steam catapult. Eight hundred feet ahead, just faintly visible in the dim, early glow of daybreak, was the edge of the flight deck. From there it was 93,000 feet straight up to his operational limit and possible death, and ninety feet straight down to certain death. No in-between. Just up or down. He briefly thought of what it would be like, sealed in his cockpit as he made that short, yet long fall into the water, and then he imagined the essentially infinite inertia of the 87,000-ton CVN as its stately mass crushed him under at thirty knots. No real need to worry about that—the fall alone would kill him all by itself, without any help.

His eyes and mind turned to the red-glowing cockpit displays. Soon, as he climbed out of the cloud cover and burst into sunlight, he would turn the night-vision lights off. As the final seconds before launch slipped away, he made the last run through his checklist. Red Striker Five was ready, a deadly air and near-space machine of precise, electronically guided death. Her companion tensed as CIC warned him of launch, and he braced for the high gee acceleration that would fling them up to takeoff speed. Theoretically, it would take only a bit more than half the flight-deck length. But the warrior had witnessed launches that hadn't worked. His mouth felt dry and his heart pounded as he brought the throttle levers up to sixty percent of full military power. More than that would dangerously stress the catapult mechanism. Red Striker Five roared her pleasure as she gulped the JP-4/nitro mix.

The blast of launch pressed him back into the body-contour seat, the details of his peripheral sight faded in a tunnel-vision readout as blood flowed away from his optic nerves, and the edge of the flight deck rushed toward him at incredible speed. And then, as Red Striker Five lifted free of the launcher coupling, the warrior's left hand shoved the throttles forward, his right pulled back on the stick, and he accelerated up and away. Pulling a thirty-degree attack angle, he rode the twin jet-engine exhausts at an initial climb rate of 20,000 feet per minute.

He could feel the whining turbine shafts under his buttocks, one cheek over each roaring monster. He used the feedback through his backside to even-up the shaft rpms to balance out the engines. Balanced engines gave better handling, less fuel consumption, and minimum vibrational abuse to his spine.

The rear-view closed-circuit screen showed the carrier rapidly falling behind and below him. As he hurtled toward the clouds, the massive ship was soon no larger than a postage stamp, and then, as he flicked on the afterburners it disappeared in seconds. He was riding a tornado now, each engine thundering 42,000 pounds of thrust. At two pounds of thrust per pound of platform weight, Red Striker Five was like no aircraft that had ever flown before. Her limits were set by the endurance of the warrior, not by technology.

He punched through the top of the cloud cover with a vertical velocity vector of 30,000 feet per minute, and the airspeed needle passed the Mach-one line. His only indication of breaking the sound barrier in a climb was the funny behavior of the altimeter—first it lurched upward 2,500 feet, and then wiggled its way back to normal. The engine vibrations on his butt, the pounding roar in his ears, and the instant response of his craft to the stick, throttle, and foot controls gave him the same pleasures a passionate woman would have. Except that no woman could ever be so perfect.

When Red Striker Five passed 30,000 feet, the warrior returned to normal engine power as the afterburners wasted too much fuel for just cruising. He nosed the craft over gently until he was in level flight at 33,000, with an indicated airspeed of 1,200 knots.

He flipped off the night-vision lights, set the surveillance radar to its long-range search mode, and turned his MARK XII/IFF beacon transponder on. The beacon could be interrogated by coded transmissions from properly equipped observers, and Red Striker Five would automatically broadcast her mission number, altitude, bearing, and airspeed. Her echo would also be enhanced on the observer's radar screen. Failure of an interrogated aircraft to respond to such requests could bring an infrared missile up the tailpipe!

"CIC, this is Red Striker Five. I'm at start of mission run. Going now to GPS LINK Ninety-nine."

"Roger, Red Striker Five, we have a solid track and now going with you to LINK Ninety-nine." There was a pause, and then, "Good hunting, Red Striker Five. Take care." The warrior heard the strange metallic bang on the voice circuit as the digital link took over—he was now in direct communication with CIC's computer. It would talk to

him by audio tone cues through his headset, which he could react to
faster than an oral command. He was now getting the situation normal
cue of a continuous up-down frequency sweep from one kilohertz to
five kilohertz each three seconds. The sound was comforting to the
warrior, like the humming of a mother to a baby. He snuggled happily
in his seat.

Red Striker Five flashed through the sky, serving as the eyes of the
mighty naval fleet miles below and behind. Part of the always-flying
combat air patrol, CAP war missions were top-priority tasks. A billion-
dollar carrier, and its hundred-million-dollar companions of missile
destroyers and cruisers couldn't afford to let the enemy get close enough
to launch a tactical nuclear-tipped cruise missile. CAP missions extended the fighting reach of the fleet from the fifteen-mile range of
naval gunfire to the hundreds of miles that were Red Striker Five's
combat radius.

Ten minutes after launch, the warrior heard the audio tone cue in his
ears change to a frequency-sweep period of one second. The first-stage
alert cue. Three bogeys were beginning to edge onto his cockpit radar
screen, and the pre-engagement weapons program in the fire-control
computer switched the radar from surveillance to track-while-scan. All
of Red Striker Five's radar updates were now being automatically fed
up to the GPS satellite, 22,000 miles over his head, and then back to
the CIC computer. There, integrated with sensor data from surface,
subsurface, airborne, and space platforms, CIC had an accurate, real-
time picture of everything that moved in a water-air-space volume of
over 2,000,000 cubic miles.

The bogeys were flashing red on the multicolored radar screen now,
the computer's visual cue to the warrior to pay attention. His left hand
punched the Mark XII interrogate button—seconds later, the flashing
red switched to the steady yellow of a friendly response. Good. But
the enemy had been known to spoof the IFF by making recordings of
friendly replies and then retransmitting them when their penetration
aircraft detected the interrogation request.

The warrior went to the HOARSE GOOSE mode and hit the interrogate button again. Now a new, special-coded signal was included that would *inhibit a friendly from replying. A reply would be a fake.* But these were friends, as their images on the screen now changed to green and the audio tone cue reverted to three seconds. The radar returned to routine surveillance, the tracking computer dumped the stored trajectories of the identified bogeys, and the fire-control computer relaxed its electronic finger on the trigger. Red Striker Five streaked on.

Four hundred miles out, with the radar's constantly searching fan beam picking up nothing, the audio tone cue went into a continuous ping-ping-ping. LINK Ninety-nine was calling. The warrior pushed a red button next to the cockpit video screen, normally displaying a rear view of the aircraft. The screen cleared of the flashing sky, and an encrypted digital message streamed down from the GPS. LINK Ninety-nine was a spread spectrum, time-division, multiple-access channel, with hundreds of users tied into it on a time-sharing basis. With a spectral width of four gigahertz, and a signal level forty db below the background noise, there was no way the enemy could jam it, even if he could find it in the infinite electromagnetic spectrum. Unless he was willing to devote the entire electrical output of a 2,000-megawatt nuclear power plant to the task—a highly unlikely event. The decoded message scrolled in milliseconds onto the screen:

MULTIPLE HOSTILES AT HEADING 079. SUBSURFACE ACOUSTIC SENSORS INDICATE VELOCITY VECTOR OF 1450 KNOTS, AT 500 FEET, ON FLEET INTERCEPT BEARING WEAPONS. FREE DOCTRINE NOW IN EFFECT. ENGAGE AND DESTROY.

This was more like it! This is what he was waiting for—he punched the red button again to acknowledge the message, and the audio tone cue changed to a rhythmic six-kilohertz pulse, with a period of one-half second. The GPS would watch for surface-launched missiles directed at Red Striker Five and warn the warrior by modulating the pulse rate, intensity, and tone frequency in each ear.

He put the radar in its high-power burn-through-jam, track-while-scan mode, five degrees around both sides of 079, from Sea level to 1,000 feet. Eleven flashing red spots appeared on the radar screen in a vee pointed back toward the fleet. They were 620 miles from the warrior's home ship and 215 from Red Striker Five, to his left. The warrior pushed the HOARSE GOOSE button. There was little doubt: the attack pattern was characteristic of the enemy, and no friendlies would roar into the fleet in such a clearly provocative, hostile way. But he was going to kill them, and he had time to be sure. Red crosses appeared, superimposed over the flashing hostiles! They had replied to HOARSE GOOSE, thinking they were being normally interrogated. *Too bad for them*, thought the warrior. *Let's go get'm, baby!* The warrior snapped on the power switch for his heads-up display. Normally a clear plastic shield extending from the top of his instrument panel to just below the canopy, it now became a remote projection output of the fire-control computer. Once combat started, there was no time to keep moving eyes and head between instrument display and cockpit windshield. The HUD showed the warrior the radar-screen image, Red Striker Five's gun-cannon status, and projections of the proper launch envelope for the Eagle-Six missiles against all tracked enemy targets.

The warrior looked at the computed intercept course and saw that he was already within attack range. He elected to go in closer. That was his only mistake.

Hitting the afterburner switch, he lit the tail of Red Striker Five and went into a sixty-degree banking turn-dive. As he passed through 20,000, he was hitting 1,900 knots and accelerating. The titanium/boron fiber skin of Red Striker Five was a dim, yet visible cherry glow. The projected intercept course, computed by the dedicated radar computer operating at a memory cycle time of forty-three nanoseconds, kept pace easily.

The warrior flipped the red plastic cover off the missile arming/firing switches with his left thumb and threw the leftmost of three exposed toggles. He couldn't hear the cryogenic pumps, but he knew the infrared sensors on the missile-seeker heads were now rapidly cooling down to the ten degrees Kelvin, where they operated optimally for the terminal-attack phase. He asked for a launch countdown from fire control to achieve missile intercept at approximately seventy miles' range, and large numerals projected on the HUD. As the numbers flickered by, he flipped the middle target-attack toggle to designate all displayed radar tracks as hostiles. When the flashing red zero appeared on the HUD, he threw the rightmost toggle on the missile switches, and the Eagle-Six weapons came off their wing pods, two at a time, from each side.

Fump! The first double pair streaked off, each missile locked onto its own target. Guided by control signals from Red Striker Five's radar computer, they would fly their own way in on the last 2,000 meters of intercept with the infrared seekers.

Fump! The second double pair raced out and away, their exhaust trails leaving a crazy, swiftly dispersed pattern. Each missile quickly accelerated to 4,000 knots, its body glowing red-hot with the air friction. The warrior loved night-attack missions; the blazing missile skins looking like jewels. But even in the daylight he could follow them for a few split seconds. Then they were gone.

Fump! The last three missiles launched, two from the right wing, the eleventh from the left.

The warrior watched, fascinated, as thin, spidery purple lines, marking the missile paths, weaved their way on his HUD toward the flashing-red, hostile symbols. At first the enemy vee stayed on course, but then their electronic warning systems picked up the inbound missiles. The vee started to break up, the pattern spreading apart. The warrior knew that some were diving, others climbing, but all were being flown by men as good as dead. An Eagle-Six missile could pull thirty-seven gees in a chase-down maneuver; greater even than Red Striker Five could take without disintegrating. And the enemy platforms were inferior to Red Striker Five. But the doomed men tried. And the warrior had no pity. They were the enemy!

One after the other, the purple filaments reached out and touched a desperately twisting, whipping, spinning red dot. And then they both slowly faded from the display. The searing explosion, the vaporizing metal, the carbonized flesh—all were reduced to a quiet decay of glowing colored light reflected in the cold eyes of the warrior. The tracking radar computer performed an automatic-kill assessment of each strike, looking for the highly characteristic fragmentation pattern of a successful intercept. As a backup, for attempted kills at ranges under 100 miles, a spectrum analyzer also examined the radiation from the explosion fireball, looking for a suddenly enhanced carbon line. The last blaze of glory of an enemy warrior before the mist that was once a man's body dispersed forever. A low-level kill assessment would bring a secondary missile attack, but none was needed. All eleven hostile markers had vanished. He flicked off the afterburners and let his machine coast down to 1,000 knots. No need to waste fuel.

And then the warrior felt Red Striker Five shudder, and his surprise was unbounded as he saw fireballs bigger than his fist stream by his cockpit above and to the right of his head. He'd been jumped from the rear and was taking high-cyclic 37mm cannon fire! With his attention diverted to the earlier attack, a twelfth enemy aircraft had somehow avoided detection. *The bastards must have learned how to defeat LINK Ninety-nine! Maybe those were decoys I just took out!*

As he realized his peril, the right wing took two hits: one on the tip and one on the trailing edge near the wing root. Red-hot, searing metal fragments tore through Red Striker Five's body, and one, the size of a man's thumb, ripped into the warrior's right leg, just below the knee. Muscle tissue, bone, and arterial fragments, mixed with shreds of flight-suit fabric, splattered the cockpit, and blood gushed from the wound. Instrument-glass splinters ripped into his body. Blinding pain tore at the warrior, and he would have screamed but for the paralyzing shock.

The warrior knew, just before he passed out, that his survival was out of his control. He retained enough strength to slap the emergency combat palm switch at the side of his seat, and then he rapidly slid into unconsciousness. It was up to Red Striker Five to get them both home.

The palm switch activated the autonomous-combat program in the flight computer. Immediately Red Striker Five examined all biosensor outputs on the warrior's body, determined the presence and location of blood loss, and pumped compressed air to the proper imbedded circular tube in the right suit leg to create a tourniquet. The blood flow slowed to a seeping.

Simultaneously Red Striker Five lit her afterburners, blew away all external weapons pods, and dove for the deck. The enemy war plane followed her down, too close for a missile attack but well within gun range. It was the enemy's mistake.

Red Striker Five leveled out at two hundred feet, moving at 1,500 knots, weaving, jinking, humping in a manner determined by a random-number generator in the computer software. Desperately trying to keep those 37mm fireballs away from her warrior!

The enemy pilot was good—but Red Striker Five was better. Hurt by the loss of streamlining from the ragged metal edges where she'd been hit, Red Striker Five was melting at 1,500 knots. The enemy was 1,000 meters behind and closing at 1,600 knots. Red Striker Five dropped to twenty feet above the ocean, letting her surface-following radar keep her at altitude. The enemy stayed on her tail. The enemy pilot was very good, rough-riding through the near-surface thermals on an attack run.

The two screaming metal bullets raced over the water, cannon bursts rocking Red Striker Five violently. The acoustic shock wave each was dragging along was incredible, and a boiling wake of dead fish bobbed to the surface long after the hunter and the hunted had passed. And then Red Striker Five fought back.

When the enemy was only 700 meters behind, Red Striker Five popped her air brakes and lost 300 knots almost immediately. Simultaneously she pulled into a climb and did a full inside loop, coming down behind and on the tail of the snookered enemy aircraft. The defeated foe had a few milliseconds to realize his fatal error, and then Red Striker Five ripped him apart with two dozen strikes from her dual 20mm cannons. The flaming enemy debris flared out along a ten-mile track, but by then Red Striker Five, bearing her dying warrior home, was gone.

Racing for altitude, she climbed to 5,000 feet and started squawking on all clear broadcast channels:

EMERGENCY-EMERGENCY-EMERGENCY. RED STRIKER FIVE CAP WOUNDED PILOT ABOARD. REQUEST PRIORITY LANDING. REQUIRE FLIGHT-DECK MEDICAL.

Over and over she transmitted her urgent message as she bore in toward the fleet with her burden. The warrior flickered in and out of consciousness, but knew neither where he was nor what his fate would be. He put his trust in Red Striker Five and passed out.

She didn't fail him. The flight deck was cleared, and with guidance signals from CIC's computer, Red Striker Five made a perfect landing. The Navy medical personnel gently lifted the warrior's torn body from the shattered cockpit and placed him carefully on the deck. After emergency aid, as they prepared to take him below for permanent surgery, he temporarily regained his senses once more.

"Take it easy, son," said the medic. "You're hurt pretty bad, but you'll be okay. I saw it all on the radar screen—that's some aircraft you got there. She fought her way out and back like nothin' I ever seen!"

The warrior smiled weakly through a pale white face lined with pain and shock. He looked up at Red Striker Five and saw not a technological marvel of electronics, armament, metallurgy, and computer programs. He saw both a warm and loving creature, and a being that had killed to save him. Killed with savagery and intelligence. His body filled with emotion, a feeling of passion that only later he would just barely begin to understand.

He looked at the battle-ravaged Red Striker Five, and just before he slipped into darkness again, he knew. He knew she'd be there when he came back. She'd wait for him, and he loved her.

And he knew she loved him too.

REAGAN VS. THE SCIENTISTS

by Robert Jastrow

Editor's Introduction

Robert Jastrow was the founder of NASA's Institute for Space Studies and was its director until his retirement in 1981. He has taught astronomy and geology at Columbia, is co-author of a standard astronomy text, and is now professor of earth sciences at Dartmouth. Dr. Jastrow was chairman of NASA's Lunar Exploration Committee and received the NASA Medal for Exceptional Scientific Achievement.

Strategic Defense is probably the most important issue to face the United States in this decade.

---

1. The Threat

When President Reagan announced his proposal last spring for defending the United States against Soviet missiles, the reaction from scientists, politicians, and journalists was almost uniformly hostile. Dr. Richard Garwin, who has had a great deal of experience in defense technology, said, "It won't work." Former Defense Secretary Robert S. McNamara called the plan "pie in the sky," former National Security Adviser McGeorge Bundy described it as "astonishing," and Senator Edward Kennedy said it was "misleading" and "reckless." Anthony Lewis wrote in his column in the New York *Times* that President Reagan was indulging in "a dangerous fantasy" and James Reston entitled his *Times* column on the President's speech, "The April Fool."

This was pretty strong language. Why was everyone so irritated by President Reagan's suggestion? There were two reasons. First of all, missiles travel at very high speeds and are difficult to shoot down in full flight. As a consequence, no defense against missiles is likely to be 100-percent effective; in any full-scale attack, one or two missiles are bound to get through. Since each one carries enough nuclear explosives to destroy an entire city and kill a million people, the President's critics accused him of misleading the public when he spoke of a defense that could "intercept and destroy strategic ballistic missiles before they reach our own soil."

The other reason for opposition to the plan stemmed from the fact that many defense advisers believe the best way to defend yourself against a missile attack is to have no defense against missiles. Although this idea seems to be contrary to common sense, there is a certain logic to it. If both superpowers leave themselves entirely undefended, the Soviets will know that if they launch a missile attack against us, our own missiles will lay waste their homeland in reprisal. And, of course, we will know that if we attack the Soviet Union, our nation will be destroyed by Soviet missiles. This knowledge will deter both countries from starting a war, and will make for a very stable situation.

If, however, either side acquires an effective defense against enemy missiles, it can attack the other side with impunity, secure in the knowledge that this defense will protect it from retaliation. Therefore, runs the reasoning, the best way to avoid a war is for both sides to leave themselves entirely undefended.

In other words, a watertight defense against missiles would upset the nuclear balance between the two superpowers. In the language of the nuclear strategists, seeking to defend your country against the enemy's missiles is "destabilizing."

On the basis of this reasoning, American arms-control experts pressed the Soviets, during the SALT talks, to sign an agreement outlawing any large-scale defense against ballistic missiles. The Soviets accepted this, and the result was the ABM treaty of 1972—ABM meaning anti-ballistic missile—in which the U.S. and the USSR agreed that neither country would undertake to protect itself from a missile attack by the other. In this way, it became the official policy of the United States to keep its people undefended against nuclear attack.

Most Americans do not know that this has been our government's policy for the last twelve years. If they did, I believe they would be astounded. As Henry Kissinger has said: "It cannot often have occurred in history that it was considered an advantageous military doctrine to make your own country deliberately vulnerable."

* * *

It takes a person with an idealized view of the world to think up something like the ABM treaty. The logic of the arms-control experts was impeccable, but if you are not an arms-control expert you see the weakness in the idea right away. Suppose one side cheats on the treaty, and secretly builds up its defenses against missiles anyway. Now it can launch its own missiles without fear of retaliation. The country that continues to honor the treaty is then vulnerable to a nuclear attack. This is exactly what happened to the United States.

Starting almost immediately after the ABM treaty was signed, reports began to come in that the Soviets were testing their surface-to-air missiles at altitudes close to 100,000 feet. Some 50 to 60 tests of this kind were carried out between 1973 and 1975. Surface-to-air missiles are supposed to be used for defense against aircraft, but aircraft do not travel at an altitude of 100,000 feet. However, missiles do. The Soviets were testing their air-defense missiles in what is called an "ABM mode." Such tests are specifically outlawed by the ABM treaty.

The first Soviet ABM tests used a surface-to-air missile called the SA 5, which is not very powerful. However, the Soviets continued to work away at improving their ABM system, and a few years ago they began to test a better surface-to-air missile, the SA-12, which can accelerate to the speed of an ICBM—about 12,000 miles an hour—from a standing start in a matter of seconds. The SA-12, used as an anti-ballistic missile, is a serious threat to the security of the United States because it has the potential for shooting down our submarine missiles, which are the mainstay of the American nuclear deterrent.

All this added up to a clear Soviet violation of the ABM treaty and the SALT I agreement. Several Senators complained about this, but nothing happened.

Last summer, evidence came to light of Soviet cheating so blatant that even cautious State Department officials were ruffled. One said bluntly about the Soviets, "They've busted the SALT agreement!" The new evidence was provided by Big Bird, one of our best reconnaissance satellites. Big Bird had discovered a radar of a special type called "phased-array," deep in the interior of the Soviet Union, near the village of Abalakova in south-central Siberia.

A phased-array radar, which consists of thousands of little radars connected so that they sweep the sky electronically, is a major improvement over the rotating radars which can be seen at airports. This kind of radar is particularly useful in shooting down enemy missiles because it can create a highly detailed and accurate picture of a missile attack. One phased-array radar, backed up by a large computer, can keep track of hundreds of separate attacking missiles, figure out their paths, and assign defending missiles to intercept and destroy them.

Phased-array radars are also useful in providing warning of a missile attack. We have several of these so-called "early-warning" radars on the East and West Coasts of the United States. To be useful in giving warning of a missile attack, a radar must be located where it can pick up reflections from the attacking missile at the earliest possible moment. In other words, it has to be placed on a country's borders. The ABM treaty, recognizing this fact, says that each country is permitted to have large phased-array radars provided they are located "along the periphery of its national territory," and are therefore usable for early warning.

However, the treaty forbids locating such radars in the interior of the U.S. or the USSR. That is why everyone was upset about the phased-array radar at Abalakova. It is located smack in the middle of the Soviet Union, 1,900 miles from the Pacific, and far from the periphery of the Soviet national territory. There is no conceivable reason for placing an early-warning radar in that spot. But there is every reason for putting a missile-defense radar there, especially since Abalakova is located near a field of Soviet heavy intercontinental ballistic missiles (ICBM's), which would be one of the top priority targets of any American attack on the Soviet Union.

In fact, the radar at Abalakova has every characteristic of a radar intended for defense against enemy missiles. It is just the kind of radar that is outlawed by the ABM treaty.

Some Soviet violations of SALT have exploited loopholes in the language of the treaty, violating the spirit rather than the letter of the agreement. The radar at Abalakova rips the very heart out of the treaty. Senator James A. McClure calls it "the most flagrant Soviet SALT violation yet."

The Abalakova radar is disturbing for another reason. Radars of this kind are mammoth devices, requiring years to construct. The appearance of this radar indicates that the Soviets decided years ago to go in for a big system of missile defense, in violation of the ABM treaty. Apparently they decided to cheat on the treaty rather than withdrawing from it formally, in the hope that we would continue to honor it and thereby be placed at a disadvantage.

The Abalakova incident has discouraging implications for the future of arms-control negotiations with the Soviet Union. It is difficult to see useful results coming out of these negotiations, when, as Fred Iklé of the Department of Defense has said, "The very party with which we are currently negotiating treaties has been caught violating a treaty." The Soviet violations of the ABM treaty confirm the impression of many Americans that the arms-control process has been cynically exploited by the Soviet Union as an instrument for achieving military superiority over the United States.

Other Soviet actions reinforced the impression that arms-control discussions with the USSR were not turning out very well. Immediately after the SALT I agreement was signed, (The SALT agreement and the ABM treaty are distinct documents, although Nixon and Brezhnev signed them on the same day.) as the Soviets proceeded to develop their defenses against American missiles, they simultaneously began to build up their own missile forces to an awesome level. By 1980, Soviet missile strength had reached the point where a surprise attack by the USSR could cripple a large part of our missile forces and weaken our power to retaliate. That knocked the stuffing out of deterrence. The American arms-control negotiators thought they had secured a commitment from the Soviet Union that it would not menace the survivability of our retaliatory forces in this way. But almost as soon as the ink had dried on the SALT I agreement, the Soviets had begun to slide into their old silos a new generation of ICBM's—the so-called "fourth generation"— that were heavier, more destructive, and more accurate than previous models. The warheads on these missiles were accurate enough to give them a capability for destroying our missile silos and other key military sites. The result was a nightmare for American security. Our adversary had created a great force for the destruction of the military power of the United States, and we had signed away the right to defend ourselves.

One of the fourth-generation Soviet missiles, the SS-18, is twice as big as an MX missile, about as accurate, and carries 8 to 10 nuclear war-heads with an aggregate explosive power of five megatons. (A megaton, the unit of explosive energy commonly used to describe the size of a nuclear warhead, is the energy released by the detonation of a million tons of TNT.) At last report, the USSR had 308 monster SS-18's in the field. The Soviet Union also has in the field 360 missiles of the new type known as the SS-19, each as large as an MX missile and equally accurate. The megatonnage, or power for destruction, residing in just these two types of Soviet missiles—the SS-18 and the SS-19—is far greater than the megatonnage of the entire U.S. missile and bomber force. All this has happened since the signing of SALT I and in the name of arms control.

The new Soviet missiles are a greater threat to American security than any other weapon in the Soviet arsenal. For twenty years the United States had relief on the three legs of the famous American "strategic nuclear triad" as our means of discouraging the USSR from an attack on the American homeland. The elements of the triad are Minuteman missiles on the land, B-52 bombers in the air, and Poseidon and Trident submarines in the sea. The Minuteman missiles are housed in silos— underground hollow cylinders of reinforced concrete. Most of the warheads on the Soviet SS-18 and SS-19 ICBM's are sufficiently accurate to land within 250 yards of these missile silos and the underground bunkers that house the men and equipment needed to launch the missiles. The Soviet warheads are also sufficiently powerful to cave in a missile silo at a distance of 250 yards and destroy it, even if the silo has been "hardened" by tons of concrete and steel. As a result, according to General John W. Vessey, Jr., chairman of the Joint Chiefs of Staff, the Soviet Union can now destroy 70 to 75 percent of our Minuteman missiles in a surprise attack.

Moreover, the accuracy of Soviet warheads, which is the key factor in destroying hardened targets, has improved by about a factor of two from one generation of Soviet missiles to the next. (A twofold gain in warhead accuracy has the same effect on a hardened silo as a tenfold increase in the destructive power of the warhead. Calculations show that if the accuracy of a Soviet warhead improves from 250 yards to 125 yards, the chance of destroying a Minuteman silo jumps from 57 persent to 95 percent.) The newest Soviet missiles of the fifth generation, currently being tested in the Pacific, may be able to eliminate 90 to 95 percent of American ICBM's outright. When to these prospects for the destruction of the missiles themselves are added the potentials for destroying, with highly accurate Soviet rockets, the launch-control centers that house the American officers who would press the buttons, and for destroying the communication links to the President that would relay the order to execute the counterattack, the chances for effective retaliation with our ICBM's dwindle to the vanishing point.

The upshot of the matter is that our Minuteman missiles—the land leg of the U.S. strategic triad—are vulnerable to a Soviet attack and becoming more so every year.

The air-based leg of the triad is even more vulnerable to a Soviet surprise attack. Seventy percent of all B-52's are normally not on the alert at any one time, and are likely to be destroyed by Soviet missiles at the outset. Of those escaping, few would get across the border of the Soviet Union. Soviet air defenses, comprising nearly 3,000 fighters, 7,000 radars, and about 12,000 surface-to-air missiles, are the most massive in the world. Our B-52's are antiquated planes, twenty-five years old on the average, and have lots of nooks and crannies in their contours that reflect radar waves strongly and cause the planes to show up clearly on Soviet radars. B-52's also fly at high altitudes, which means they can be picked up by a radar at a considerable distance. Finally, they fly at the slow, subsonic speed of a commercial airliner. As a result, they are easy targets for Soviet fighter-interceptors and surface-to-air missiles. Secretary of Defense Caspar Weinberger reported a year ago, "The aging B-52's G/H bombers will not be capable of effectively penetrating the Soviet air defenses in the mid-1980's."

The air-launched cruise missile is intended to restore the usefulness of the B-52's in the triad. The cruise missile is a pilotless jet aircraft that navigates itself without human assistance, checking its radar signals against a map of the terrain stored in an onboard computer. Cruise missiles do not have an intercontinental range, but they can be carried to the borders of the USSR by B-52's and launched from the air.

Once across the border, the cruise missile is supposed to be able to penetrate Soviet air defenses more effectively than the B-52 because it flies very low, hugging the terrain and staying out of sight of Soviet radars. However, it is vulnerable to an attack from above by the new Soviet Foxhound fighter, with its look-down, shoot-down radar. The current version of the cruise missile is also as slow as a B-52, and can be shot down by the Soviet SA-10, a relatively new surface-to-air missile. Some years ago the Department of Defense said the Soviets would need up to 1,000 SA-10's to have an effective defense against our cruise missiles, and predicted that the USSR would not have that number until the 1990's. However, as of 1982, the Soviet Union already had 1,200 SA-10's in the field. The implications for the effectiveness of the air-launched cruise missile are not encouraging.

Improved cruise missiles—supersonic, and with a "stealth" design making them nearly invisible to Soviet radar—are under development, but will not be available in large numbers before the end of the decade. Until then, the air-launched cruise missile is not likely to make a major contribution to the viability of the U.S. strategic triad.

The new B-1 bombers, just going into production, will go far toward restoring the effectiveness of the air leg of the triad. The B-1 had been cancelled by President Carter on the ground that the cruise missile made it unnecessary, but the Reagan administration brought it back to life. The B-1 is designed to be considerably less visible to Soviet radar than the B-52. It also flies lower than the B-52, and is considerably faster. But Congress has only approved funding for 100 B-1's, and because of the cancellation of the B-1 program in the previous administration, even this reduced force will not be fully available until 1987. In the interim, the bomber leg of the triad will be severely compromised by Soviet air defenses.

So, of the three legs of the U.S. triad, two—the land leg and the air leg—are weak, and will remain weak until later in the decade. That leaves the sea leg—the nuclear-missile submarine—as the only fully effective deterrent remaining. For the present, the triad had been reduced to a monad.

That does not seem like a bad idea. The newest submarines have extraordinarily quiet engines, and therefore are very hard to pick up on sonar. They also have a long range that gives them an enormous volume of ocean to hide in; a Trident missile can reach Moscow from anywhere within 40 million square miles of ocean. As a result, submarines on station are essentially undetectable, and can be counted on to survive a Soviet attack. Of course, all American submarines in port, about half the current fleet of 33 boats, will always be an easy mark for Soviet missiles; but the remaining 15 or 20 submarines can safely hide at sea, at least for the present. (Some experts are concerned about a possible Soviet breakthrough in anti-submarine warfare that would reveal the location of submerged submarines by means other than the underwater sounds they make—for example, a change in water temperature in the wake of the sub, or a trail of plankton churned up by its motion. If that breakthrough occurs, it is more likely to be on the American side than the Soviet; but, on the other hand, what we discover, the Soviets soon steal. However, the consensus among Navy experts is that none of this will happen in the next few years.)

The survivability of the Trident submarine makes it an excellent deterrent to a Soviet attack, especially since the warheads carried on a single Trident can destroy every major city in the USSR. Yet even the Trident has problems as a deterrent. One weakness is its limited ability, when submerged, to communicate with the world above. A submerged submarine is very hard to reach by radio because radio waves do not penetrate sea water. To receive a message, the submarine must rise up to or just under the surface of the ocean. But near the surface it leaves a wake, increasing the risk of detection. (The Navy tries to overcome this handicap in several ways. In one procedure an airplane flies low over the water, trailing a wire several miles long, while the submerged submarine reels out a buoy that rides just under the surface of the ocean and picks up the message. Another technique broadcasts messages to the submarine on extremely low radio frequencies, which can penetrate water to a considerable depth. In time of war, all these methods would be more vulnerable to Soviet disruption than communications on the land. The recent report by the Scowcroft commission on strategic forces concludes that "communication links with submarines, while likely to improve, will still offer problems not present for land-based systems.") If the submarine actually rises to the surface, it becomes visible to Soviet satellites and can be picked off at will. For this reason, American submarines loaded with nuclear missiles must spend much of their time at sea incommunicado, cruising at depth. Radio contacts with the world above are sporadic, and may be separated by long intervals. This means that if a Soviet attack occurs, some submarines may not receive the message authorizing launch of their deadly cargoes until a considerable time has passed.

Perhaps a suspicious captain, observing that his radio links are dead, will take a chance on surfacing to catch a news broadcast or sample the air for radioactivity, but with Soviet planes and radar satellites reconnoitering the oceans continuously, that will be risky. And suppose the submarine captain decides he has reason to fire off his missiles. That will bring a fearsome retaliation from the Soviet Union. Do we want to entrust the fate of the American people to a naval officer out of touch with civilian authorities? Is it our intent to delegate authority for starting World War III that far down the chain of command? The problem is a serious one.

Our submarines have another weakness as a deterrent to a Soviet attack. A missile launched from a submarine is relatively inaccurate, and is not likely to land close enough to a "hardened" or protected target to do it any serious damage. That means that submarine-launched missiles cannot be used against missile silos, command bunkers, or other military installations, which are always "hardened." They are mainly useful for destroying "soft" targets, like cities and people. (This situation will change when an advanced submarine missile called the Trident 2 comes into use. The new missile has an improved guidance system with the accuracy necessary to destroy hardened targets in the USSR. But that will not happen until late 1989 or 1990.) But suppose the Soviet Union were to launch an attack against our military sites while avoiding our cities. We would be deterred from launching our submarine missiles against Soviet cities in reprisal, because the USSR would then surely respond by attacking American cities with the full power of its huge arsenal. The result would be a devastating loss of perhaps 100 million American lives, far greater than if we had withheld retaliation. That millions of Soviet civilians also lay dead or dying would not be a gain

to the United States. These circumstances severely limit the value of
our submarine deterrent.

Many people mistrust this analysis because they feel that a Soviet
nuclear attack on military targets will produce nearly as many casualties as an attack on cities. But the facts say otherwise. Suppose the
Soviet Union were to direct its highly accurate SS-18 and SS-19 rockets
against the American forces capable of nuclear retaliation—missile silos,
B-52 airfields, submarine bases, nuclear-weapon storage depots, and
military-command posts—while attempting to spare American cities.
Since most of those military sites are in sparsely populated areas, civilian
casualties in the U.S. would result mainly from radioactive fallout on
cities lying downwind. Calculations on the effects of nuclear explosions
indicate that casualties in such a Soviet attack on military sites would
be very great, between 2 and 14 million according to estimates by the
Department of Defense. However, they would be far fewer than the 80
to 170 million deaths that would result from a deliberate Soviet attack
on our cities in response to an American attack on Soviet cities. In spite
of the enormity of the two disasters, a real distinction exists between
them. One case means the possibility of a recovery for the U.S., and
the other case means the annihilation of the American people.

How would an American President respond to such a limited attack by the Soviets, with American military power crippled but the
cities largely intact? With only our surviving submarines available for
retaliation, he would be limited to two options, and both would be
painful. In Henry Kissinger's words, "A President could initiate the
extermination of tens of millions of people—first Soviet citizens and
then our own—or he could give in." The choices, Kissinger concludes,
are "suicide or surrender."

It is sometimes said that a "surgical" nuclear attack on our military
sites is impossible, because some Soviet warheads are bound to miss
their targets by wide margins. In the words of one critic, Soviet missiles
"would be falling all over our country." This is not correct. If the accuracy of a warhead is, say, 250 yards, that means that half the warheads
will land outside the circle. But the warheads that land outside will still

be clustered in the neighborhood of the aiming point. In fact, in the case above, 99.9 percent will land within a mile from the target.

So, urban areas will not be destroyed accidentally in a Soviet attack against our military sites. But is it possible that the Soviet Union, in planning an attack on the United States, will decide, nonetheless, that its interest is served—for the purpose of intimidating the remnant of the American population, or whatever reason—by the greatest possible devastation? Will the Soviet Union elect, as part of a calculated plan of attack, to explode megaton warheads over American cities? It seems clear that this can never happen. The leaders of the USSR must know that the one action certain to provoke an attack on their cities would be a Soviet attack on American cities. They must know that some elements of our submarine force are bound to survive their surprise attack, and are sure to visit fearful retribution on Soviet civilians for an attack on American civilians.

And such an attack on American cities will be counterproductive for the USSR in other ways as well. At the least, it will reduce Soviet prospects for extracting food, technology, and industrial loot from a subdued America. At worst, it will damage the atmosphere's fragile ozone layer, cool the climate of the globe, and visit ruin upon the agricultural lands and people of the Soviet Union. The USSR has everything to lose by an attack on American cities, and little to gain.

The essence of the matter is that American submarines are an effective deterrent to a Soviet attack on our cities, but are not a deterrent to an attack on U.S. armed forces. It is a sobering fact that if the USSR should launch a massive strike against our military installations, we could do little about it, short of a suicidal strike against Soviet cities, in the current state of disrepair of our strategic triad.

Experts count and recount missile silos, bombers, submarines, warheads, and megatonnage. They argue over whether we will have a kind of parity with the Soviet Union, in spite of the vulnerability of our ICBM's and B-52's. But there can be no argument about one basic fact: Soviet missile power has been growing faster than ours, and has succeeded in placing a large part of the American strategic deterrent at risk. The trend is frightening. If continued, it will lead to the possibility, a few years hence, of a preemptive Soviet attack aimed at the total destruction of American military power.

2. The Response

How is the United States to respond to this threat? One way would be by a massive build-up of our own missile forces, sufficient to match the threat of the Soviet ICBM's on equal terms. The result would be a nuclear stand-off between two adversaries, each armed to the teeth, and each capable of delivering a knockout blow if it can get in the first punch. That would be a balance of sorts, but the balance would be unstable. There is a better way, and that is the way President Reagan chose in his speech on missile defense.

Suppose a brilliant inventor could devise a method to defend the United States against Soviet ICBM's. Then our own ICBM's— Minutemen and MX's—would no longer be vulnerable to a surprise attack. These ICBM's are accurate enough to destroy many hardened targets in the USSR, including the 700 hardened leadership centers sheltering the Soviet elite. If our missile silos were defended, Soviet leaders could not eliminate this threat to their existence by knocking out American ICBM's in a preemptive first strike. If nothing else deterred the Soviet leadership from an attack on the United States, that circumstance would certainly do so.

Where can we find this invention? The answer is that we already have it. Critics of President Reagan's plan spoke as if he were proposing a defense of entire cities and their populations, but he made no suggestion of that kind in his speech; and, in fact, such an "area" defense, while very comforting, would not be necessary at the start. For the protection of our Minuteman missiles, it is only necessary to establish a "point" defense—i.e., a defense of the few square acres surrounding each missile silo, and the small areas surrounding a limited number of communication centers, command posts, and other military installations. The means for such a point defense of critical military sites are in hand today. The basic technologies have been proven, they are inexpensive, and they can be put into use with relative rapidity.

The key to these technologies is the miniaturized computer. Extraordinary developments in the miniaturization of computer circuits enable millions of transistors and other electronic components to be packed into a space the size of a thumbnail. As a result, defense technicians now have the means for building elaborate computer brains into a very small missile—a mini-missile—so that it can steer itself toward its target. Sensing the target either by its delicate emanation of heat waves, or by its radar reflections, the mini-missile analyzes the product of its senses within its highly capable computer brain, and directs a succession of messages to small rockets arranged around its circumference. Delicate thrusts of these rockets steer the defending missile into the path of the oncoming ICBM warhead. The result is either destruction of the warhead by a direct impact, or an explosion of the mini-missile in the vicinity, releasing a cloud of flying metal fragments. The warhead, moving ten times faster than a bullet, tears into the cloud of fragments; the skin of the warhead is punctured in many places; its electronics are disabled; and the nuclear bomb inside it is disarmed.

In essence, the defense consists in tossing into the path of the speeding warhead some TNT and a keg of nails. What makes this simple defense work is its computer brain.

The amount of TNT need not be very large. One mini-missile of the kind described, currently being tested by the Army, contains less than 100 pounds of explosive. The reason is that the defending missile does not have to destroy the warhead to be effective; it only has to prevent the nuclear bomb inside the warhead from exploding. That happens to be fairly easy, because nuclear bombs do not go off very readily; elaborate arrangements and a great deal of fragile electronics are needed to make one explode. Accordingly, a small charge of TNT, or a cluster of high-speed metal pellets, will usually be sufficient to disarm the bomb's mechanism.

In fact, it is not even necessary to keep the bomb from going off. Suppose, for example, Soviet technicians devise a countermeasure to the

American defense by wiring the warhead so that the nuclear bomb inside it explodes automatically whenever a defending missile approaches. As long as that happens at a high altitude, far above the atmosphere, the effects of the explosion will not be very damaging at ground level, either in radioactive fallout or in blast damage. An altitude above 100,000 feet is sufficient to achieve this. Progress in developing the smart little missiles indicates that making the kill at altitudes above 100,000 feet is not an especially difficult task.

Thanks to the newest ultra-miniaturized computers, the defending missile can exercise a formidable amount of brain power. Suppose the Soviet technician tries to confuse our defense by arranging to throw off decoy warheads—lightweight imitations of the real thing. The decoys, necessarily thin and flimsy in their construction (if the decoy weighs as much as a real warhead, you might as well put a bomb inside), will tend to lose their heat more quickly than the real warheads as they fly through the cold of space. By the time the cluster of Soviet warheads reenters the atmosphere, the decoys will be appreciably colder than the real warhead. The brain of the mini-missile, analyzing these differences in temperature from one "warhead" to another, will have no trouble in telling the decoy from the real McCoy. And once the real warheads have been identified, the computers can even sense which warheads are headed for empty silos, and instruct their defending missiles to ignore these and concentrate on the warheads headed for silos still loaded with ICBM's.

* * *

This kind of technology is not visionary. Its important features are already in operational use in the Pershing-2 missiles being deployed in Europe. The warhead of the Pershing 2 contains a radar "camera" that looks at the terrain beneath it, compares what it sees with an image of the target stored in the warhead's computer brain, and, guided by this comparison, changes its course and steers straight toward the target in the final moments of its flight. On the average, Pershing-2 warheads hit the ground within 30 yards of their targets, compared to an average error of 250 yards for the best missiles with old-fashioned dumb warheads. When the same kind of computer technology is used in mini-missiles for defense against ICBM warheads, the error comes down to a few yards, or even feet, or even inches.

Incidentally, the clever warheads on the Pershing 2's explain the intensity of Soviet anger at the deployment of these missiles by NATO. Warheads of this kind, which can figuratively drop down the air vent of a Soviet command bunker, place at risk the military and political leadership of the Soviet Union—and they are the only weapons in the NATO arsenal with the accuracy and range required to do that. And being mobile, the Pershing 2 is also survivable; it cannot be entirely eliminated in a preemptive attack. These properties make the Pershing 2's a very effective deterrent to a Soviet attack on Western Europe.

Getting back to President Reagan's speech, one of the main criticisms of his plan was that a defense against ICBM's can never be 100-percent effective. This criticism also applies to the smart mini-missiles. If these missiles were intended for the direct defense of American cities, they might not be of much value, because even a few ICBM warheads leaking through such a defense would kill millions of Americans. However, the situation is very different when a defending missile is intended only for the protection of missile silos and other military sites. Suppose, for example, that the defense of the silos is only 50-percent effective—a conservative estimate for the technologies described above. This means that roughly half the attacking warheads will accomplish their purpose. Therefore, the USSR will be required to make its ICBM arsenal twice as big as it is today, to regain the level of threat it possessed before the defense was put in place. In other words, it will have to buy another ICBM for every one it already has. The Soviet Union has spent about $500 billion on the build-up of its ICBM arsenal over twenty years and might be hard-pressed to spend another $500 billion in a short time. Even if the USSR does increase its missile forces in an effort to overwhelm our defense, we can increase the number of defending missiles around each silo and once again reduce to an acceptable level the number of Soviet warheads that would reach their targets. This response is practical because each defending little missile costs considerably less than the warhead it is aimed at. Estimates by a team of scientists at Los Alamos indicate that if the Soviet Union tries to overcome an American missile defense by building more rockets and warheads, its costs will increase at least twice as fast as ours. In this situation, in which the ratio of costs heavily favors the defense over the offense, the Soviet Union may be led to rethink its whole strategy of striving for military dominance with weapons of mass destruction.

With the feasibility and cost-effectiveness, there is still the troubling possibility that a defense of our missile silos will be "destabilizing" and will undermine the policy of deterrence. According to this theory, which is held by a number of American scientists and arms-control specialists, the Soviets will perceive the defense of American silos as a signal that the United States is preparing to attack them, and is therefore protecting its military sites against the inevitable Soviet retaliation. Feeling nervous about that possibility, the Soviet Union will move quickly to attack us before our missile defenses can be completed. In other words, so the reasoning of the arms-control experts goes, a defense of American missiles brings the United States closer to war.

It seems to me, that nothing could be farther from the truth. As usual, facts determine the situation, and the main facts here are first, that the Soviets have many more ICBM warheads than we do, and second, that ICBM's are the most valuable kind of missile from a military point of view, because of their great accuracy and ability to destroy hardened targets. (It is often mentioned that we have the same number of warheads, about 4,600, on our submarines as the Soviets have on their ICBM's. However, the submarine-based warheads are inaccurate and have relatively low explosive power, about one-sixteenth that of Soviet ICBM warheads. Consequently, they are completely ineffective against Soviet missile silos, which are even more hardened than our silos.) We have 1,650 accurate Minuteman warheads, too few in number to do much damage to the several thousand important Soviet military targets, but the Soviets have at least 4,560 equally accurate and far more powerful ICBM warheads, that can do a great deal of damage to our military targets. If we lived in another world, in which the Soviet Union had not constructed all these late-model ICBM's and many thousands of accurate and powerful warheads, an American system for defending our missile silos might be perceived as destabilizing and a weakening of deterrence. But in the real world, in which the Soviet missiles and warheads exist, an American missile defense restores our retaliatory force, and thus strengthens deterrence.

It is not clear why the Soviets have built up this mammoth ICBM force, because the build-up has been very costly—to repeat, about $500 billion over the years—and goes far beyond any reasonable level of military power they would need as a deterrent to an American attack. Whatever the reason, the fact is that they have done it. As a result, the Soviet Union is in a position to launch an attack on the United States aimed at destroying our means of nuclear retaliation—missiles, silos, B-52 airfields, submarine bases, and military command posts. In other words, those 4,560 accurate ICBM warheads look like the beginning of a Soviet drive to acquire a nuclear war-winning capability. We may not understand how the Soviets think they can possibly emerge victorious in a larger sense from a nuclear war in which they suffered "only" a few million to 10 million casualties, but apparently they do think that.

In any case, the USSR has built a large number of missiles and undermined our capability for retaliation and therefore our deterrent. Protecting our forces against the Soviet missiles will not give us a nuclear war-winning capability—the nuclear warheads of the Soviet Union are too numerous and powerful for that—but it will give us a continuing capability for retaliation against Soviet attack, which is the very basis of deterrence.

There are other gains for deterrence in a point defense against Soviet ICBM's, in addition to the protection of our missile silos. The dish in California that receives the signal from our early-warning satellites can be protected. The communication lines that connect the President and top military commanders to the Minuteman launch-control centers can be protected. Our bomber airfields and submarine bases can be

protected. Just two bases—one in Kings Bay, Georgia, and the other
in Bangor, Washington—will support our entire fleet of Trident submarines. If these bases are undefended, half the Trident fleet—the part
in port when a Soviet surprise attack occurs—must be written off at
the outset. A point defense of the Trident bases against Soviet missiles
will double the effective strength of the American submarine deterrent.
(When there are only a few targets, and the destruction of each one
is very important to the Soviet Union, it can always try to overwhelm
our defenses by allotting a large number of warheads to each target.
However, by the same token, a few sites, each of enormous value to the
United States, can be ringed by exceptionally strong defenses comprised
of not one or two but perhaps dozens of mini-missiles or more; and
this can be done at acceptable cost to the U.S., because only a few such
highly valuable sites exist.) All these measures improve our chance of
being able to retaliate against a Soviet attack, and therefore make an
attack less likely.

A point defense decreases the vulnerability of our missiles, and is
good. An area defense, directly shielding our cities and their populations, would be better. Can inventive genius find still another device to
accomplish this task as well? Once again, the answer is that we already
have the invention. It is called the laser. Unlike the smart mini-missile,
the laser defense is not inexpensive; it is not yet a proven technology;
but it has the promise of protecting our cities against destruction.

A laser is like a searchlight; it produces a beam of light. This beam of
light, focused on the metal skin of an ICBM, can burn right through
it, just as the light of the sun, focused to a narrow spot by a magnifying
glass, can burn through a piece of wood or paper. The difference
between a laser beam and an ordinary beam of light is that the ordinary
beam spreads out as it leaves its source, so that by the time it has
traveled several thousand miles—for example, from the United States
to the Soviet Union—the beam is dispersed over an area several miles
in diameter. As a result, the intensity of light in any one part of the
beam is too weak to hurt anything.

A laser beam on the other hand, has the remarkable property that all parts of the beam travel in the same direction, so that the beam doesn't spread apart as it travels through space. (Even in a laser beam, the light waves spill out over the edge of the beam to a limited degree and blur it somewhat, but the spreading effect is quite small. In the laser beams being designed for use against Soviet rockets, the spreading effect will be no more than a few feet over a distance of a thousand miles.) If the energy in the laser beam is intense enough at its source to burn through the metal skin of a Soviet ICBM, it will still be that intense, and still able to burn through metal, after it has traveled thousands of miles.

Laser beams have the advantage that they travel at the speed of light, which is 670 million miles an hour, and can cross a continent in a hundredth of a second. Compared to the speed of laser beams, even an ICBM is slow, and the laser beam has no difficulty in catching up to one and intercepting it. One of the disadvantages of a laser beam is that, being a beam of light, it is blocked by clouds and haze. For that reason, laser guns work best if placed in a space station or satellite, far above the atmosphere. But putting a laser gun in a space station means that a large amount of equipment and fuel for the laser must be ferried into orbit at great cost. Another disadvantage is that the laser beam must track the moving ICBM with great precision, equivalent to hitting a dime at a distance of 100 miles, so that the beam will stay on the target long enough to melt it.

Because of these and other difficulties, a team of MIT scientists led by Kosta Tsipis concluded a few years ago that "lasers have little or no chance of succeeding as practical, cost-effective weapons." When President Reagan announced that he was proposing to set the country on this course anyway, Professor Tsipis denounced the President's plan as "a cruel hoax." Many other prominent scientists also jumped on the President for his suggestion.

But scientists do not have a very good track record when it comes to making predictions about the feasibility of bold new ideas. In fact, they seem to have a talent for rejecting proposals that later turn out to be of great practical value. Examples abound. In 1903, just before the first flight of the Wright brothers, an American astronomer named Simon Newcomb announced that the laws of physics proved man could never fly. A little later, after airplanes were flying, another American astronomer ridiculed the notion that some day there might be "giant flying machines speeding across the Atlantic... and carrying innumerable passengers." In 1926, A. W. Bickerton, a British scientist, said that it was scientifically impossible to send a rocket to the moon. Just before the Soviet Union put the first Sputnik into orbit, the Astronomer Royal of Great Britain announced that the idea of launching artificial satellites into space was "utter bilge." In the weapons field, Admiral Leahy—not a scientist, but a qualified technician—said to President Truman, just before the first successful test of an atom bomb, "That bomb will never go off, and I speak as an expert on explosives." And Vannevar Bush, who directed the government's science effort during World War II, offered the following wisdom after the war:

> The people who have been writing these things that annoy me—have been talking about a 3,000-mile rocket shot from one continent to another carrying an atom bomb... I think we can leave that out of our thinking... I wish the American people would leave that out of their thinking.

Among the experts actually working on laser defense or advising the government on it, the consensus is that no basic scientific obstacles stand in the way of success. George Keyworth, Science Adviser to the President, said recently, "The major fundamental problems in every area [of laser defense] have been removed." Two committees, set up to advise the President on the matter after his speech, have reported that the feasibility of several kinds of laser defense against missiles can be tested in the next three or four years, and if all goes well, a complete defense can be in operation ten years after that. According to Dr. Keyworth, there has been "tremendously broad technical progress" in this area.

When the final system is constructed, it will probably be a so-called layered defense, with the first or outermost layer consisting of laser beams aimed from space at enemy ICBM's in the first minutes of flight, shortly after blast-off. A second layer of defense, either a laser or a smart mini-missile, will hit the ICBM's that have gotten through the first layer, as they fly across the void en route to their targets. A third layer of mini-missiles, with the "keg of nails" or similar technology, comes into play in the final minutes or seconds of flight as the Soviet warheads reenter the atmosphere, to destroy the intruders that have penetrated the second layer. If the "leakage-rate" in each of the three layers is 10 percent, only one warhead in a thousand will reach its target.

If the Soviets acquire an effective defense against American missiles, so much the better. They will not even have to steal it. The President has suggested that his successor can give the new technology to the Soviet Union, just to prove that there is no point in both sides keeping bulging warehouses of these deadly weapons any longer. Then, the President added, his successor can say to the Soviets, "I am willing to do away with all my missiles. You do away with all yours."

These are encouraging possibilities for the long run. The problem facing us in the short run, between now and the end of the 1980's, is the vulnerability of American ICBM's and other military installations to a Soviet surprise attack. The smart mini-missile, with its TNT and keg-of-nails technology, is less exotic than a laser defense, but it is already state-of-the-art, and can be available on relatively short notice for the protection of our missile silos, submarine and bomber bases, and command posts. In doing that, the mini-missile will strengthen and preserve the American deterrent to a Soviet attack. By strengthening our deterrent, this simple defense will also protect our cities.

For nearly forty years, since the first atomic explosion at Alamogordo, the nuclear bomb has dominated strategic weaponry. But technicians make new facts, and new facts make a new strategic calculus. We are on the threshold of revolutionary gains in the accuracy of intercontinental ballistic missiles, created by the incorporation of computer brains into missile warheads. In the future, the smart ICBM warhead, equipped with electronic brains and infrared or radar "eyes," will hitch a ride to the general vicinity of the target on its ICBM bus; then, disembarking, it will steer itself into a particular spot on the target within a yard or two to accomplish its task with nice precision. Consider the possibilities opened for the military planner by this development. A Soviet charge of TNT, carried across the ocean by an ICBM, guides itself down the smokestack of the Consolidated Edison plant in New York; an American warhead of TNT, carried 5,000 miles in the nose of an ICBM, drops down onto a critical transformer in the Moscow power grid; a bridge is destroyed by a small explosive charge ferried across oceans and continents on an ICBM, and carefully placed at the foot of a pier. A small, artfully shaped charge of TNT is delivered to the door of a Minuteman or SS-19 silo; exploding, it pierces a hole in the silo door, spraying the interior with shrapnel and destroying the missile. It is not necessary to crush the entire silo with the violence of a nuclear warhead; missiles are fragile, and gentler means suffice to disable them.

Command posts, ammunition dumps, highways, and airport runways—all are vulnerable to conventional explosives skillfully targeted. Nearly every task allotted to nuclear weapons today can be accomplished in the future by missiles armed with non-nuclear, smart warheads.

And when nuclear weapons are not needed, they will not be used. That may seem unlikely, but consider the following facts. A nuclear weapon has many defects from a military point of view. Because of its destructive power and radioactivity, it tends to kill innocent civilians, even if used sparingly in a surgically clean strike at military targets. If used in great numbers, nuclear weapons stir up clouds of radioactive material that roll back with the prevailing pattern of the winds, carrying their poisons with them into the land of the attacker. Finally, these weapons generate emotional reactions of such intensity that the military planner can only hold them in reserve to use as a last resort; he cannot release his nuclear arsenal in gradual increments, adjusted to the military needs of each situation.

In other words, nuclear weapons are messy, and, other things being equal, the military planner will avoid them. They will never disappear

entirely, some blockbusters will always be stockpiled by the superpowers as a deterrent to a genocidal attack on their cities and civilians. But
as the accuracy on smart warheads increases, and more military tasks
can be accomplished by non-nuclear explosives the tasks assigned to
nuclear warheads will diminish, and the size of the world's nuclear
arsenals will decrease.

The shrinkage has already been observed in the armaments of the
U.S. and the USSR. Nuclear weapons in the American arsenal are now
one seventh their size twenty-five years ago, and the total megatonnage
of our arsenal is one-quarter what it was then. (Nuclear weapons were
mated to ICBM's originally because the early models of the ICBM's
wandered all over, and generally landed a mile or so from their targets.
Only a nuclear warhead—with its enormous radius of destruction—
could make such blunderbusses militarily effective.) Figures available to
me on Soviet nuclear weapons go back only ten years, but in that short
interval, while the number of Soviet warheads increased enormously,
the average size of an individual warhead decreased by a factor of three.

These changes in the sizes of the world's nuclear arsenals have resulted
from rather modest improvements in the accuracy of missiles, but the
technology of the smart warhead is still in its infancy. When it reaches
its maturity, and the precision of delivery of explosives across continents
can be measured in feet rather than in hundreds of yards, the military
uses of the nuclear bomb will dwindle into nothingness. And so it may
come to pass, as President Reagan suggested, that the scientists who
gave us nuclear weapons will also give us "the means of rendering these
weapons impotent and obsolete."

Joined the Space Force to Wear My Blues

by John Maddox Roberts

Editor's Introduction

Combat is not the only danger to a military unit. Boredom can destroy military effectiveness as thoroughly as any enemy. From time immemorial soldiers have sought relief from the monotony of their daily routine through wine, women, and song. This has not always endeared them to the local townsfolk. more than one us post commander has arranged to have his troops paid in two dollar bills in order to demonstrate just how important the soldiers are to the local economy. Sometimes that has worked; sometimes the local shopkeepers do not care. it depends on the military unit nearby...

There have been campaigns in which the local townsfolk were more dangerous than battle. Troop commanders then seek ways to prevent fraternization, mostly without success. One of the strangest of such methods was employed in the Moroccan campaign after World War I: the French government sent in a mobile force of prostitutes. this was the notorious *Bordel Mobile de Campaigne*, the "Mobile Military Brothel," known as the B.M.C., ten or twelve whores sent to entertain as many as 5,000 soldiers. In order to avoid bloody fights days were reserved for different branches of service: legion, spahis, tirailleurs, with armed guards to enforce order.

When women are not available there is always booze. For many years the traditional drink of the foreign legion was called "earthquake"; it consisted of raw white Moroccan wine laced with pernod.

There are always those who would deny soldiers their rightful rewards. They usually have no more success than did the temperance workers who sought to end drinking in the foreign legion by placing in each barracks room a poster showing a grinning death's head and the legend "Alcohol is deadly." The signs came down when it was found that in every barracks someone had printed under the inscription "but the legionnaire does not fear death!"

It has ever been thus; and John Maddox Roberts tells us that things will not have changed in the far future.

――――――――――

Leave on Moloch!

Was ever there a place like unto Moloch? Were not its iniquities manifold and its delights beyond number? Yea, though we lie in our tanks, will we not drink deep of these? Will we not cast our souls into the visible?

Quick, off duty and put on our class as, jump before the mirror and check gig line and spit shine. All perfect.

"Remember to shine your brass!" says Minton to Huang. All laugh. Huang has more brass than most. Pile into the briefing room for cautionary lecture from the chaplain.

Here he comes, and the arc lights glint from his insignia, cross inside six-pointed star inside crescent. It gleams like a halo from his shiny dome. He is Chaplain Hymnal 55, a legend in his own time.

"You go forth in sin!" roars Hymnal 55.

"That we do," comes their reply. "That we do."

"The enemy seeks merely to destroy your miserable, replaceable carcasses, but Moloch will devour your immortal souls!"

"So it must be, padre," they say.

"Moloch is a sink of vileness, and you shall wallow in drunkenness, gluttony, sloth and lewdness!"

"Yes!" they say. "Yes! Yes!"

"Go, you sinners, and come not to me for absolution!"

All pile out and tumble for the shuttle dock, pockets stuffed with payday cheer.   Line up for last-minute inspection by the OD.

"Did you polish all your brass, Twomey?" asks the OD. All laugh. Twomey's left buttock is brass.

Into the shuttle for the ride down. The descent begins. Leave on moloch! "You descend into the pit," comes Hymnal 55's voice from behind their ears. They pay no heed. They were soldiers, heroes all, and they were bound for R&R, for the basic, raw stuff of which fun and guilt are made.

They left the shuttle at the port, and as they left, they saw other soldiers waiting to board for the trip back up. The others looked tired. Many were damaged. Some were in pieces. All were singing happily, for this was Moloch, and they had just enjoyed leave on Moloch.

Outside the port they were met by purveyors of all manner of delights. There were pimps and pushers and perversion mongers. There were bar shills and gamblers. Mostly there were taxi drivers. They grabbed one such.

"Take us where there is large-scale dissipation to be had," said Twomey. "We are heroes on leave."

"There is no small-scale sinning on Moloch," said the driver. "What kind do you crave?"

"Take us to the big-stakes games," said Dungeness. "To the sharpers and the high rollers, to where the dice click and the cards shuffle and the roulette balls whirl about."

"Take us to where there is blood and riot," said Twomey. "We've been fighting the enemy for many a day, and would fain fight our friends."

"The hundred-year-old crap game is still going strong in Whistler's Alley," said the driver. "There's a riot between Army and Navy in Skid Row Plaza that's been in progress for three days."

"That's what we want!" shouted Huang. "And we want women! Women with the bodies of houris and the minds of Port Said sewer rats."

"Such are to be had," said the driver. "Come with me, my heroes, and sample the homeric delights of Moloch." All piled into the cab and were off, singing.

They stopped at the notorious divine veil of Ishtar Bar & Grill, and there they swilled demijohns of delectable Olde Rocket Nectar. They crammed down cheeseburgers smeared with paté de foie gras and Ishtar's famed caviar milkshakes.

Thus fortified, they descended to the next level, lower middle gambling hell. There a fight promoter spotted the many rows of decorations adorning Twomey's chest.

"You must be the one I've searched for these many years, Sergeant," he said. "Come with me and make your fortune! Here we have sword-fights and knifefights, fistfights and gunfights. There are blood and cheering crowds and great piles of money to be won!"

"Not I," said Twomey. "But Spinetti, here, is the greatest pistolero of all. He's your man."

So they all tramped along, Spinetti warming up his draw and the others laughing.

"You'll be put out of action, Spinetti," said Burgess, "And miss the rest of the leave."

"It matters not," said Spinetti. "I must try my skill."

The arena was bright with floodlights and smelly with the crowds. There was money flying about as the bets were placed. Spinetti took the ring and challenged all comers. The hands dashed and the pistols zapped and stinky black smoke and prickly ozone filled the air. They laid bets on Spinetti and won hugely as he disposed of one opponent after another. Then they stopped betting because Spinetti was never good for more than ten fights per night. Eventually a Marine got him with a horizontal beam-slash and they carried him off to a body shop, blood dripping from his right arm and sparks and melted copper from his left. They promised to return for him when their leave was up.

They descended through the riot in Skid Row Plaza, duking it out with Army and Navy impartially. here the great Twomey came to the fore, his bronze fists smiting merrily as the flying wedge crossed the plaza, leaving a trail of broken, bleeding, smoking, sparking, tooth-spitting, circuit-fusing men in its wake. They found the drop and descended farther.

It was dim. It smelled sweet. It was quiet and infinitely enticing. It was New Storeyville.

The women came and took them by the hand. They were not ordinary women. Their skin was of a smoothness not to be seen outside dreams. Their curves defied geometry. There were violations of gravity in the way their various projections swayed. And their voices, their voices…

"Come with us, heroes," said one. "You are weary. You are worn. You are sated with lesser pleasures." They could not but agree. "*The lips of a loose woman drip honey, and her speech is smoother than oil,*" said the voice of Hymnal 55 behind their ears.

"Sweeter than any honey, Rev!" they sent back. "Smoother than any oil. Soothing balm to our afflicted sensibilities." They were led to a spacious villa. Quiet music played there, and they were served cool drinks in tall glasses as they reclined on couches and listened to the sound of wind chimes.

"Which among you is the greatest hero?" asked a green-eyed beauty with blue skin.

"Do you not see Twomey's KIA badge?" said Minton. "Do but note that it bears twenty-seven stars."

"Killed in combat twenty-seven times!" exclaimed the houri. "You surpass the records of the greatest heroes i have ever known!" "*beware the words of the flatterer,*" says the voice of Hymnal 55 behind their ears.

"We love flattery," they say back. "We want more!"

The women proceed with their ministrations. The men are delighted. "You seem to have been long deprived of female company," says an houri.

"Not so long," says Twomey. "But we are men of flesh and blood."

"Well," qualifies Minton, "Partly flesh and blood."

"That is to say," says Huang, "A good deal of plasti-flesh."

"And metal," says Twomey, "But nonetheless men withal. In fact, Huang there will require some specialized attentions."

The women opened Huang's trousers, observed and conferred among themselves. Some went out and returned with the agreed-upon equipment. They attached wires and plugs and tubes to Huang's midsection. "There," beamed one. "You'll never know the difference."

"We never worry about the difference," said Twomey. "for are we not heroes, and are not these our mortal carcasses dedicated to the heroes' calling, while the vital parts of us reside elsewhere?"

"Elsewhere," sighed the houri. "Yet you enjoy as if you were here."

"We are here," said Minton. "Meat and blood, plastic, wires, circuits and such, we are here. And come you here also, little wiggly one." And the houri complied, for was this not leave on Moloch?

Later, much later, they picked up Spinetti at the body shop on the way back to the shuttle. They were weary but exultant.

"You missed one of the great experiences, Spinetti," they said. "Now we must return to the war to rest up for the next leave, though it will never be such a leave as we had on Moloch."

"I am content," said Spinetti. "The nurses here are houris too. And some of the mechanics aren't bad either."

So, carrying spinetti, they returned to the shuttle. And as they returned, they sang the old, old song.

Oh, my heart belongs to Mama,
But my brain just orbits Rama,
And the chaplain tends the welfare of my soul.
Got my ass shot off on Thule,
And replaced on Finn McCooley,
And there's always something there when they call roll!

PSYOPS

by Stefan T. Possony

Editor's Introduction

Stefan Possony received his Ph.D. in International Relations in Vienna shortly before the German Anschluss. His anti-Nazi activities put him high on the list of those wanted by the Gestapo, but he managed to escape, first to Czechoslovakia, then France, finally to the United States, where he became a valued Pentagon intelligence expert. One of his accomplishments was to predict, almost to the day, when the Soviets would detonate their first atomic bomb.

With Robert Strauss-Hupe and William Kintner, Possony co-authored the important work *Protracted Conflict*, one of the first books to recognize the nature of the "cold war." After a long career in the Pentagon and at Georgetown University, Possony became a Senior Fellow at the Hoover Institution on War, Revolution, and Peace located on the campus of Stanford University. In 1970 we collaborated to write *The Strategy of Technology*; a new edition of that book is in preparation.

Steve Possony has long been an expert on Soviet strategy and tactics. This essay on psychological warfare was part of his presentation to the DEFENSE 1983 seminar.

Psyops is too large a subject for one article. So I will concentrate on two or three aspects that I think are crucial for the immediate and the more remote future.

I am using the expression "psyops" in distinction from "psychological operations," which, naturally, are included in the term. It embraces the whole range of operations relating to all strategically relevant aspects of individual and collective minds and behavior. It relates to mental and behavioral consequences of military operations and significant events. It includes mental operations undertaken in support of military and other strategic activities. It is at the core of conflict management. In addition, it comprises different types of psychological, intellectual-conceptual, and political undertakings. Lastly, it is executed by means of techniques and equipments, and it strives through deliberate actions, most of which are standardized, to attain goals on all levels of importance.

First Conclusion: Psyops is not a limited or subsidiary activity. It is an "operational universal" in that it interrelates with all other strategic undertakings. It is a weapon in its own right and may not be vulnerable to being disarmed. It is not limited geographically. It ranges over all the fields of the intellect. It may influence feelings and will; it may activate and paralyze; and it may be the decisive factor in conflict. Its importance is badly underrated.

To be effective, psyops should be organized as a system, more precisely as a holistic system. Fragmentary, sporadic, point-oriented, and improvised psyops are bound to be unsuccessful. Psyops by bureaucratic management tend to be boring, disappointed, and usually belated.

Military principles should henceforth include this one: "All offensive and defensive operations must be supported by, and be integrated with, psyops."

I also propose a principle of grand strategy (military plus…): "Psyops can be defeated by psyops. The side with inferior psyops probably is at the same time the side with inferior command and leadership. Other things being equal, this side is likely to suffer defeat."

Military-political history bears this principle out, from the time of Sun Tzu and Alexander the Great to the present time. Yet no such principles are reflected in NATO defense planning.

Second Conclusion: Franklin, Lincoln, Wilson, and, up to a point, Roosevelt understood wartime psyops. International-conflict management was more or less bungled, by American presidents except, to an extent, Eisenhower. Reagan is a first-class communicator personally. But he is frequently in trouble because he lacks advisors and staffs with psyops capabilities.

Lenin may be regarded as the originator of modern psyops. According to him, it consists of propaganda, agitation, and organization, all being interrelated. Propaganda deals mainly with "theory" or ideology, agitation with "practice" or attacks on human targets who are to be crippled to decide an issue, and organization with subversion or attacks on the enemy from within.

Leaving Stalin out of consideration (we don't have space here), Soviet psyops demonstrated astounding continuity. One man who influenced the project during the late 1920s, when he was still a youngster, is still in charge today—just one rung below Numero Uno. This is Boris Ponomarev, who displays signs that he advocates a strategy in which psyops is the dominant factor. Andropov and Ponomarev launched a major psyops offensive based on the revival of Marx and on Lenin's formula for disarmament: Disarm the bourgeoisie and arm the proletariat. I will publish an analysis of Moscow's strategy shift and of the new psyops high command in *Defense & Foreign Affairs*.

As a psyops factor, Marxism signifies ideology and little else. The renewed emphasis on Karl Marx means that ideology will be a focus of Soviet psyops. To the CPSU rulers, Marxism is ideologically crucial because it teaches that the victory of communism is ultimately inevitable. Marxism makes the CPSU look immortal.

The second focus of Soviet psyops is the Leninist policy of disarmament, compounded by deception and bluff. In the Aesopian lingo,

"Leninist policy of disarmament" differs from "disarmament policy." This Leninist policy is banked upon to accelerate the coming of the triumph. The disbelievers in Marx as a prophet should be cautious: Since the outcome of the historical process is not predestined, no outcome of the conflict is predictable. Either side may win or lose.

Americans tend to discount ideology; they do not realize that they are highly ideological themselves. Nor do they understand the true meaning of ideology, which is "science of ideas." Such a science is legitimate and needed, and it does not contain elements that are necessarily erroneous.

In any serious conflict, a rationale of success or victory is required, together with a horizon of knowledge and of ideas that are action concepts.

The Soviets are embarking on an ideological offensive because they aim to control the world's horizon of knowledge and action concepts, and victory-defeat rationales.

The Free World does not understand the crucial point at issue: Unless a conflict is first won spiritually, it is unlikely that it can be won materially. Ideology is the bridge to spiritual victory.

Here is my Third Conclusion: The U.S. and NATO do not understand the meaning of a psyops offensive. They have not, publically at any rate, recognized the fact that such an offensive is underway. They have not analyzed it. They do not realize the resultant threat to military security. They seem unable to visualize how a psyops defensive or counteroffensive could be mounted. They don't even think about the problem. There are radio programs and the like, but the real psyops arena has been virtually abandoned to the enemy. It makes eminent sense for Andropov to upgrade ideology. It would make still more sense for the U.S. and NATO to inquire why their power to persuade has been allowed to atrophy, and to terminate their voluntary muteness.

The history of psyops technology is about two hundred years old, and this technology will continue to progress. Hence it is most important to look into the future.

It is no longer really difficult to send messages to the targets, that is, the persons who are to be influenced. The target cannot be reached if he is not interested in the originator or in his message, or if his interest is perfunctory. He is unattainable also if he is bored and if he finds it more pleasurable to listen to competitors, who are multiplying.

The target cannot be *persuaded* to listen. It is the other way around: He may listen if he already is fully or partially persuaded, and if the program is attractive in addition to informative, and if it helps him in his activities.

Fourth Conclusion: Psyops technology is more or less in hand. Its better utilization is at present precluded in most instances by political ineptitude and by international opposition. The importance of better programming is recognized as a theory, but new ideas and fundamental improvement are rare. Hence success often is a matter of hit or miss.

At this point let us forget about history and current events, and let us resolutely turn to the future. I want to alert you to the possibility that psyops technology may advance from communicating to direct signaling.

X rays and gamma rays are located at the upper portion of the frequency spectrum. What is at the lower end? THE BRAIN, the most important of all of nature's phenomena. Suppose it becomes feasible to affect brain cells by low-frequency waves or beams, thereby to alter psychological states and possibly to transmit suggestions and commands directly into the brain.

Who is so rash as to doubt that technological breakthroughs of this general type would not be put promptly to psyops use? More important, who would seriously assume that such a technology would not be developed to accomplish political and military surprise?

A few years ago there was much excitement about the Soviet microwave "bombardment" of the American Embassy at Moscow. Why did the KGB, under Andropov's leadership, embark on this seemingly scurrilous—and very prolonged—effort? There was no answer to this question, except that the KGB must have wished to harass American diplomats and cause them to worry about their health. This theory was never convincing.

The question was raised as to whether the Soviets had discovered a technique of using microwaves for psychological purposes and whether they were experimenting with this technique on American specialists on the USSR, who might unwittingly be pressed into Soviet service as guinea pigs. Impossible, replied the State Department; the waves can't break through the blood-brain barrier, and thermal effects are so negligible that the body would not be affected. Nevertheless, embassy personnel was indemnified for health damage.

By 1979 at the latest, it was known that electromagnetic fields raising body temperatures by less than .1 degree Celsius may result in somatic changes. It was most surprising that such a trivial temperature rise was having any effects and even more astonishing that those effects were significant.

Chemical, physiological, and behavioral changes can occur within "windows" of frequency and energy continua. One of those windows is connected with navigation in marine vertebrates and with biological rhythms of humans. Another is at the level of the human electroencephalogram, i.e., in the range of extremely low radio and sound waves, around 20 Hertz.

Those findings remained unexplained. They seemed to require energy amplification of the initial stimulus by some twelve orders of magnitude. No such amplification was deemed to be feasible, and none was discovered.

Let us cut the story to the minimum. The original model, according to which the blood-brain barrier cannot be broken, was derived from the axiom that electromagnetic waves interact with tissue in a linear manner. However, it turned out that the molecular vibrations caused by a stimulating extracellular electromagnetic field are nonlinear. Utterly unexpectedly, they take the form of soliton waves that can transfer energy along long molecular chains.

By 1982 the term "soliton" finally made it to the technical dictionaries. Here is a definition from the 1982 McGraw Hill scientific-technical dictionary: "A soliton wave... propagates without dispersing its energy over larger and larger regions of space." As I understand it, it would be more correct to say: "A soliton wave propagates suddenly acquired energy, or energy imparted by shock, without dispersing it."

Soliton waves have recently been found to be relevant in high-energy physics and in the fusion program.

In biology the solitons occur as electro-solitons and as acoustic solitons, and they form only at certain high- and low-energy levels, or "windows." The solitons, which can be depicted as spikes, are dynamically stable; they participate in vital processes; they have long lifetimes; and their vibration has a long persistence. Those characteristics permit the formation of a soliton and the associated boost of energy.

Significance? Extracellular disturbances such as acoustic or electro-magnetic bursts can be propagated across the cell membrane. In this, nonlinearities in molecular dynamics rather than chemical kinetics are the key. Put differently, the twelve-magnitude energy deficit is overcome not by brute force, but by the formation of solitons.

Visualize the brain and its environment as structures of waves, and assume that shock waves create solitons. Then imagine that modern electronics with their flexibility, accuracy, and speed are put to work.

In addition, the range of resonances probably will be increased. Hence many frequencies, as well as several options for the transmission of energy across the membranes of brain cells, may become available. This may imply that the brain cells will be reachable diversely and flexibly, and perhaps routinely.

The discovery of cross-membrane coupling may be compared to the discovery of oxygen in 1772, which allowed the proof that phlogiston, the supposed element of fire, does not exist. Once the phlogiston was buried, chemistry and the chemical industry began their triumphal march across the world.

The exploration of the cross-membrane phenomenon is only at the beginning, and it is not yet possible to anticipate practical applications. As of now a new phenomenon has been discovered, probably. Nothing is as yet known, or is known publicly, on how the soliton can be aimed to produce desired effects. Only a hypothesis can be stated: If the phenomenon can be utilized, this will in due time have crucial bearing both on the body and on the brain, and on defense.

The theory of cross-coupling was formulated by A.S. Davydov, who, it seems, published the first purely theoretical version in 1976 and followed this with a study on "Solitons as Energy Carriers in Biological Systems." By 1979 Davydov appeared to be linked to the Ukrainian Academy of Science.

It should be noted that Russian mathematicians were concerned with solitons before Americans ever became interested. It is therefore conceivable that Davydov achieved his results long before publication, and also that the experiments that involved the U.S. Embassy produced findings that led to subsequent progress.

In the U.S., the pioneering work seems to have been done by Albert E Lawrence and W. Ross Adey, writing in *Neurological Research*, 1982, Vol.4, 1/2

After writing this text, I learned that the Max Planck Institute for Biochemistry (Martinsried bei Muenchen) also discovered that cell membranes can be crossed. Eberhard Neumann and Guenther Gerisch found that a shock wave passing through an electric field may create ultra-quick processes within the membrane and that through such "jumps in the field" (Feldspruenge—this probably means solitons), genes can be transmitted and cells fused.

There is a differential in the tension of the inner and outer membrane that averages 1/70,000 volt. This corresponds to 70,000 volt per (theoretical) membrane thickness of one centimeter. (The real thickness of a membrane is .1–8 centimeter.)

The discovery was made unexpectedly in the course of research on electric fields in membranes and their impact on vital processes. This research requires measurements of events lasting not more than one nano-second (one billionth of a second), and it suggested that solitons generally increase the permeability of membranes. Thus, new perspectives on genetic "engineering" were suddenly opened. Moreover, it was possible to fuse no less than fifty cells into one supercell with fifty nuclei and one single membrane. We might as well forego assessing this monstrous novelty.

The Max Planck Institute broke into the membrane, so to speak, either without knowing about Davydov, Lawrence, and Adey, or after learning about them while pursuing a different goal. In either event, a fundamental scientific rule is being confirmed once again: If the time comes for a fundamental innovation, a breakthrough discovery or invention will be made several times, at different places, and by persons working independently from one another.

It is futile to speculate on who stands where in a race that has barely begun. But it can be postulated that the USSR probably has an ambitious research program, whereas in the U.S., while work is being done, no program—let alone a crash program—is in existence.

It is predictable that in the wake of Andropov's upgrading of psyops, the relevant programs in the USSR will be given an early and powerful boost.

My Fifth (and last) Conclusion is that future psyops will have to be planned for perspectives that cannot be formulated before the United States embarks on a major and totally novel R&D program. Meanwhile, it must be assumed that psyops will grow worldwide in strategic importance, and in new forms.

THE BRAIN WAVE MACHINE, by Stefan T. Possony

May 23, 1983

On May 20, 1983, American newspapers printed an AP story from the Veterans Hospital at Loma Linda, California, stating that the Soviets had developed a device, called Lida, to bombard human brains with radio waves. The radio beams are expected to serve as a substitute for tranquilizers and to treat sleeplessness, hypertension, and neurotic disturbances.

It is not yet determined whether Lida affects the immune and endocrine systems.

Lida is reported to change behavior in animals.

Lida is on loan to Dr. Ross Adey, chief of research at Loma Linda. Adey started testing the machine three months ago and hopes to complete his investigations within a year. According to Dr. Adey, who repeatedly visited the USSR, the Soviets have used the machine on people since at least 1960.

The machine is technically described as "a distant pulse treatment apparatus." It generates 40 megahertz radio waves that stimulate the brain's electromagnetic activity at substantially lower frequencies.

Dr. Adey was quoted as saying, "Some people theorize that the Soviets may be using an advanced version of the machine clandestinely to seek a change in behavior in the United States through signals beamed from the USSR." No reference was made to the protracted microwave bombardment several years ago of the U.S. Embassy in Moscow.

On April 29, 1983, Associate Editor Stefan T. Possony, addressing the Defense 83 meeting sponsored by the present publication, reported on Dr. Adey's work and on the work by Dr. A.S. Davydov of the Ukrainian Academy of Sciences. Davydov discovered how the blood-brain barrier can be penetrated by low-frequency beams and directly affect cells in the brain. Possony's remarks were delivered to a panel studying psychological warfare.

In the U.S., research on directed brain waves has scarcely begun, and the USSR has a lead of approximately twenty-five years. Once it is matured, the new technology will be extraordinarily significant in medicine. It also may have major impacts on communications, intelligence, and psychological operations, and permit deliberate physiological impairment.

The KGB is known to be interested in the program.

It is not known whether the U.S. and other governments are trying to determine whether their countries have become targets of clandestine brain waves beamed from the USSR. Nor are there any indications that work on countermeasures is being contemplated anywhere—except perhaps in the USSR.

For that matter, it is high time that the U.S. government tells the complete story of how and why the American Embassy in Moscow was "beamed."

THREE SOLDIERS

by D. C. Poyer

Editor's Introduction

The secret of empire is to make war feed war.

Militant religions have often employed the technique. The early followers of Mahomet offered captives the choice of "Islam or the sword." Those who chose Islam were recruited to go forth and conquer. Whole nations were swallowed up and retrained into fighting units. The result was an empire that stretched from the Himalayas to the Pyrenees and threatened Europe for nearly a thousand years until Lepanto.

The British were exceedingly effective at this, with the result that most of India was conquered by a handful of British soldiers leading a large army of Indian troops. As late as World War II the British were able to field brigades of Indian soldiers, and to this day the Ghurka mercenaries are an important component of British strength.

Employment of mercenaries doesn't always work so well. As Machiavelli observed, incompetent mercenaries will ruin you by losing battles; competent ones will be tempted to rob their paymasters and may eventually take over governing their employers. Still, those who for whatever reason do not care to fight for themselves will continue to look for someone to do it for them. They will look for exceptional loyalty, obedience, and competence; and will devise ever more elaborate tests to aid them in selecting the soldiers they employ.

The blackness opened, and von Rheydt swam up through inky velvet to a consciousness that he had never expected to see again.

He did not move, not even opening his eyes.

Von Rheydt remembered falling face down in the snow, fingers clutching the sudden wetness in the pit of his stomach, hearing the soft crunch of millions of six-pointed ice crystals as his face sank toward the Russian earth.

Hauptmann von Rheydt noticed, without surprise, that he did not feel particularly cold, nor could he feel anything where the bullet had struck him. He was waiting, eyes closed and mind blank, for a Russian bayonet.

The white-coated troops who followed the tanks always checked the fallen Germans for signs of life. That, he thought remotely, must be why he was now face up. One of the Red troops must have turned him over while he was unconscious to check on the seriousness of his wound.

It must be bad if they hadn't bothered to use a bayonet, he thought. Maybe that was why he couldn't feel anything in his stomach.

Minutes passed. Von Rheydt waited. It was very quiet.

Too quiet, he thought suddenly. He could hear nothing but his heart. No machine-gun fire, neither the tap-tap-tap of the Degtyarevs nor the high cloth-ripping sound of the German guns. No grunting of tank engines, no shouts of "Oooray!" as the Red Army charged. Not even—and this was the strangest of all—not even the sighing of the wind over the plains of Stalingrad in this year of struggle 1942.

He opened his eyes, tensing himself for the bayonet. Above him was a gray ceiling.

A hospital, he thought. German or Russian? That was easy to answer. The Soviets did not waste hospital space on wounded enemy officers. So he was in friendly hands. A smile creased his thin, blond-stubbled face, and he sat up without thinking. And stared down at the crisp, unstained gray of his battle-dress tunic. No holes. No blood. After several seconds he touched his stomach with one hand. He was unwounded.

Captain Werner von Rheydt, German Army, thirty years old, educated at Göttingen... *memory's all right*, he thought confusedly, still
looking down at his stomach. Had he dreamed it, then? His brow
furrowed. The University... the war... the draft... the Polish campaign, then France, then Yugoslavia, and so to the Russian Front. To
Stalingrad with the 44th Infantry, Sixth Army, after four years of war.
To the madness of Stalingrad in winter, an entire army surrounded,
abandoned, but still fighting...

No, it was not a dream, von Rheydt concluded silently. Line "Violet"
had fallen; and in the fighting retreat to "Sunflower," the Soviet tanks
had broken through. He had led a counterattack and had fallen, badly
wounded, on a snowy battlefield two thousand miles from home. And
he was now—here.

He swung his boots over the edge of the bunk and noticed it for
the first time. It was a plain Reichsheer-issue steel bunk, standard thin
pallet mattress with a dingy pillow and a gray wool blanket.

He stood up and the momentary sense of reassurance the familiar-
looking bunk had given him disappeared. He stared around at a room
that was far too strange for a dream.

It's gray, he thought, but the gray was strange. Not a painted color,
but a hard shininess like the dull sheen of polished metal. But the
shape—it was the shape of the room that was different. He stood at
the bottom of an octagon and at the center of one; the room had eight
walls, and its cross-section was an octagon as well. He counted, came
up with a total of twenty-six facets.

A pile of what looked like military equipment was stuck oddly to one
of the eight vertical walls. Von Rheydt walked forward to investigate,
stepped up on a slanted facet of the room to reach up—and found the
pile on a slanted face just in front of him. He looked back at the bunk.
It too was on a slanted face and looked as if it should come sliding down
on him at any moment.

And there was no question but that the facet he had stepped up on
was now at the bottom of the room.

Queer, thought von Rheydt. He walked on, stood next to the pile. Now that facet was the floor, and the bunk hung ludicrously on a vertical wall.

Feeling a touch of nausea, he bent to the heap of equipment. It was not his own, he saw, but it was all standard army. Helmet, battle, one, white-painted for winter wear. Canteen. Pack ration. An officer's dress dagger, which he examined closely, scowling as he saw the double lightning strokes of the SS; the army and Himmler's thugs had never gotten along, and of late there had been rumors… shadowy but horrible rumors. A dress sword, plain but of good Solingen steel. At the very bottom of the heap he found what he had been hoping for: a Luger. A quick investigation revealed six cartridges in its magazine.

Von Rheydt smiled as he buckled on the pistol belt. Having a weapon made him feel much more confident *wherever* he was. He buckled on the dagger too, and began walking again, continuing around the room. His boots clicked arrogantly on the hard surface.

Halfway around—the "floor," inexplicably, still underneath his feet—he noticed a grille set into its surface. He bent to look into it.

A black, grimacing face, horribly furrowed with scars and paint, stared back at him, teeth bared. Von Rheydt recoiled, drawing the dagger. At his motion, the face disappeared, drawn back from the grille.

Beyond wonder, he walked on. In the next facet of the room was a door, or hatch, set flush with the gray surface and of the same material. There was no knob or handle, and he was unable to get the point of the dagger far enough into the seam to pry it open. He went on and had almost reached the bunk again before he saw something else on the smooth sameness of gray.

It was another grille. This one he approached with dagger drawn, but there was no one at it. He bent and peered through it, seeing on the other side another room like his own.

"Anyone there?" he called loudly.

The quick pad of footsteps came up to the grille and a moment later a hard-looking, tanned face stared out. A second or so passed, and then the man barked out a question.

It took several seconds for von Rheydt to realize that the strong-jawed, dark-haired man on the other side of the grille had said, "Who are you?"—in *Latin*.

Von Rheydt searched his mind for the moldy words he had struggled over at Göttingen. "*Ego sum*... von Rheydt," he said haltingly. "Ah... *sum miles Germanicus*... *amicus*. *Amicus, friend*. *Et tu?*"

The other man spoke rapidly; not classical Latin, but a rough, corrupt-sounding tongue with a Spanish rhythm. Von Rheydt caught a word here and there, enough to piece the sense together: "Roman soldier... Nineteenth Legion. Into the forest, the battle against Arminius... spear wound... slept." The Roman passed a hand over his close-cropped, dark hair, looking puzzled as if trying to remember something. "Slept..."

Von Rheydt started to speak in German, stopped, said in Latin: "You are a *Roman soldier?*"

"*Centurio*," corrected the man, showing a massive gold ring on his powerful-looking hand. "Junius Cornelius Casca, centurion second rank, Nineteenth Legion, General Varus commanding."

"Centurion Casca... what year is this?"

The other man—Casca—frowned through the grille. "Year? What year? Why, 762, *ab urbe condita*, and thirty-eighth year of the principate of Augustus." His heavy brows drew together. "Where are we, German? What prison is this?"

Von Rheydt did not answer immediately for he was chasing a phrase down dusty corridors of his mind. Ab urbe condita... literally, from founding the city... yes, he remembered. The legendary founding of Rome, 753 B.C., the date used to reckon time by the Empire. This man Casca, then, could be... almost two thousand years old?

And then something else clicked in his mind. P. Quinctilius Varus, leading the Nineteenth Legion into Gaul. Sent to crush the Chirusci revolt under Arminius. *Surrounded and massacred without a survivor, late in the reign of Augustus Caesar...*

"Non certe scire—I don't know," he said slowly, trying to match stale school Latin to the cadence the other man used. The Roman laughed, a short, bitter sound.

Von Rheydt looked up from the grille. He looked at the bunk that stuck to the wall like a fly, at the strangeness of the gray metal walls, at the light that filled the room without visible source. He remembered the gravity that followed wherever he walked.

He had been wounded in 1942, on the frozen plains of Stalingrad. Just as this Casca, this Roman, had been wounded in the forests of Teutoburgium in nine A.D. They had been snatched away. *But to where?* he asked himself. *And what year is it in this strange cell—9, or 1942 A.D.?*

The Roman had left the grille, and von Rheydt slowly stood up. He looked vacantly around the room, then walked back to the bunk and sat down.

Fifteen minutes later he got up and went to the first grille, the one at which he had seen the black man. He was there again, big hands wrapped around the gray metal bars that separated the rooms. Von Rheydt wondered whether the other man was kneeling too, and if so— where did the room's gravity come from? From the gray metal of its walls?

"Verstehen Sie Deutsch?"

The man looked back at him without expression, and von Rheydt sat back on his haunches and studied him. The face was broad, thick-lipped and strong; though the paint stripes were obviously meant for adornment or intimidation, the scars looked like battle scars rather than tattoo or ritual mutilation. The man's hair was done up in a doughnut-shaped ring atop the wide skull, and his eyes, dark and intelligent, were studying the German with every bit as much interest as they were being given. Von Rheydt tried Latin after a time, and then French, of which he had picked up a few words during the 1940 campaign.

No luck. The man was listening intently though, and when von Rheydt paused, he placed his outstretched fingers on his broad, bare chest and said several words in a gutteral, clicking language:

"Ngi wum Zulu."

Von Rheydt tried to understand but ended by shaking his head in frustration. Did ngi mean "My name is"? If only they had a few words of some language in common!

"You... are English?"

Von Rheydt started. His roommate at school had been English; he had picked up a fair amount of the language. "No. German. Who are you?"

The warrior placed his hand on his chest again and said slowly, "Mbatha. Of... the Zulu. This is... gaol?"

The language lesson lasted for about an hour.

By the time he was fully awake, von Rheydt had rolled out of the bunk and had the Luger in his hand—safety off; Stalingrad reflexes. He scrutinized his surroundings from a crouch before he stood up, holstering the pistol. The room was as empty, the light as steady, as when he had gone to sleep. Only one thing was different: The door had opened. He approached it cautiously, one hand still on the butt of the weapon.

As far as he could make out, the door had disappeared. There were no hinges, and the inside of the jamb was smooth and featureless; it could not have slid inside the wall. He remembered how impressed he'd been with the automatic doors he'd seen before the war in Berlin department stores, and grinned humorlessly.

Feeling a little like a cautious ape, von Rheydt stepped though the door. He looked to either side, down a long, narrow, gray-lit corridor with four welcome right angles to the walls. To his left the corridor fell away into darkness; to his right it was lit with the same sourceless brightness, stretching away into the distance.

There was a high, almost musical note behind him... the sound, he realized, that had awakened him. He turned and found the door in place, locked. He could see no way to open it.

Shrugging, he loosened the dagger in its sheath, placed his hand near the pistol and walked down the corridor to the right. He passed the outline of another door, and then another. A thought struck him, and he tried to step up on a wall; no good. The every-wall-a-floor device wasn't used in corridors, then.

Octagonal rooms... doors... square corridors... the layout of the place came into focus as he walked. Von Rheydt visualized a grid of octagons, side to side, their corners forming four-sided longitudinal corridors. The corridors would lead the length of... what? The arrangement was an inhumanly efficient utilization of space, so space must be at a premium here. He walked along, staying alert, but thinking as well.

As a boy he had read Hermann Oberth's and Willy Ley's books about interplanetary flight. Read them avidly, until his father had thrown them all away and forbidden him to read such trash. Was he aboard such an interplanetary rocket? Or... and von Rheydt felt uneasy at the thought... was he, and the Zulu and the Roman, trapped in something as far beyond his imagination as Stukas and Konigpanzer tanks were beyond Casca's?

He came to an open hatch, stepped in and snapped to rigid attention, a look of surprise flashing across his face.

The room was gray and octagonal; but in the center of it sat a desk, and at the desk stood a man. A hard-looking man of middle age, dressed in the high-collared tunic and red- striped trousers of a general of the O.K.W.—the General Staff. A man with sharp eyes and a rocklike chin, who nodded to von Rheydt's astounded salute and motioned to a chair.

"Sit down, Captain," he said in clear, Prussian-accented German. "Smoke?"

Von Rheydt sat, shook his head. "Thank you, no, Herr General."

"Well," said the general, studying him for a moment while taking a long cigar from a box on the desk, lighting it carefully and exhaling a puff of aromatic smoke. "You are a bit confused, no doubt."

"That is an understatement, Herr General."

"I suppose so. We expected that you would be—you and your two companions. We owe you an explanation. You are here, Captain von Rheydt, because you are a brave man."

"For Leader and Reich," said von Rheydt automatically.

The man in the general's uniform glanced at him sharply. "Yes. Of course. But tell me, Captain. Would you fight as bravely as you fought at Stalingrad—surrounded, outnumbered, abandoned by your leader—if, say the future of your species was at stake?"

"I beg the general's pardon?" said von Rheydt.

"How did you come here, Captain?"

"Here... I don't know, Herr General. The last thing I recall is leading an infantry counterattack against Soviet tanks..."

"Against *tanks?*"

"Those were my orders, Herr General," said von Rheydt. "And then a strange thing happened. I thought that I was wounded."

"That is not quite correct. You were killed."

"Killed... but I am alive!"

"Are you, Captain?"

Frozen, von Rheydt stared at the general's face. He felt his heart beating, felt the breath that rustled in his throat and the hunger that was beginning to stir in his bowels. "Yes, Herr General, I am alive."

"You died at Stalingrad in 1942, Captain. I am sorry."

Von Rheydt gripped the arms of his chair. "Explain yourself, Herr General. This is going beyond a joke!"

The older man chuckled. "This is not a joke, Captain. And I am not a general. Those of your time would not even consider me a man. Especially—you will pardon the emphasis—am I not a German."

"Not a German..." began von Rheydt, presentiment growing in his mind. "You are not of my time?"

"Nor of your species," said the general. "But—just as one stoops down when addressing a child—I am addressing you in a form that you can understand, one that, to your mind, embodies authority and command. As a general officer of the O.K.W."

"What do you want?" asked von Rheydt harshly.

"Simply this," said the officer, rising from the desk. His chrome leather boots clicked on the floor as he paced back and forth, hands interlocked behind his back, a cloud of cigar smoke trailing be-

hind him.   He began to speak, looking sharply at the seated captain each time he turned.   "You are familiar with war, Hauptmann
von Rheydt. As are your two comrades.   Well, envision, if you
can, a war that encompasses a galaxy and that has lasted for well
over a million of your years. A war in which entire races are developed, deployed and used as weapons, as you develop new tanks or
rifles."

In spite of what it meant, von Rheydt knew the man was telling the
truth. He shook his head. "And the fact that, as you say, I am dead?"

"You were dead," the general corrected gravely. "Until we intervened.
But we are offering you, and your companions, the chance to return."

"How?"

"By fighting."

"Fighting for you? In this war of yours?"

"Not quite. Let me explain a little further." The general stopped
pacing, crossed his arms and looked down at the captain. A wreath
of cigar smoke gradually encircled the hard features. "Your race has
always been puzzled by its own killer instincts, plagued by its own love
for war. To you it was tragic, inexplicable. It seemed contrary to all the
laws of evolution, for it killed off not the old and weak, but the young
and strong. Correct?"

"Yes."

"Your race, Captain, has been, shall we say, in development. Forced
development. To forge a warlike race, one must have wars."

"That is obvious, Herr General. The Fuhrer has said that himself."

"Yes," said the general, looking at the ceiling. "The Fuhrer... we will
have to recall him soon and cover his disappearance in some convincing
manner. But back to the subject at hand. Your species has developed
very promisingly. It can be very useful, to us, if..."

"If?"

"If you prove yourselves to be an effective weapon in a test. Tell me,
Captain, if your army had developed two types of hand grenade and
wished to determine which of the two would prove a more effective
weapon, how would it go about it?"

"Well, the answer would be to conduct a comparative evaluation," began von Rheydt, and then he saw it. "There is another race of warriors," he said flatly. "Another one of your 'weapons projects.'"

"Very good!" said the general, smiling. "Correct. Please go on."

"Somehow, I don't know how, you've been able to... go back in time and pick up the other two men, Casca and Mbatha. Roman and Zulu and German—your choice for the most warlike races of earth's history, I suppose. And now you will match us against the others, I suppose."

"Exactly," said the general, raising his eyebrows in pleased surprise and perching one leg on the edge of his desk. "An intelligent species as well as a warlike one. Very good, Captain."

"But why pick us?" asked von Rheydt. "Front-line soldiers, all three of us. If you had all history to choose from, why not Napoleon, or Caesar, or Frederick the Great? They were true men of war."

"Not quite," said the general. He tapped the cigar into a glass ashtray and examined the glowing tip. "The men you name were leaders, not soldiers. Since, in this war, we will provide all necessary leadership, they would be of little value to us. No, what we value in our weapons is different. Take the three of you. Stalingrad, Teutoburgium, and Ulundi— all battles in which a body of professional soldiers, abandoned, almost leaderless, and greatly outnumbered, stood and fought to the death because they valued obedience above life."

Von Rheydt sat motionless. The general went on: "We need soldiers like that. So far in your history your three cultures have shown us what we can expect from the human race at its most disciplined, most obedient and most unthinking best."

"As you say," said von Rheydt slowly. "We are soldiers, then. But what good will our victory do for our race? Make mankind a pawn in a struggle we know nothing about?"

"It is that or extinction," said the general quietly. "To put it in army terms, Captain, the Human project is at the crossroads. It must now either be put into full production or it must be liquidated and the resources shifted to another project. I'm sure you realize, Captain, that in total war there is no other way."

Von Rheydt stood up stiffly, put one hand on his dagger and clicked his heels. His other hand shot out in a quivering salute.

"You will find us good soldiers," he said.

"I hope so," said the general. "Tell the others, Captain. Ten hours from now, the three of you will fight. I suggest that you all get some sleep." The high-pitched note of an opening hatch came from behind the rigid German, "Dismissed!"

Von Rheydt pivoted smartly and marched out. Outside, in the corridor, he turned. The door was not yet closed, and he caught a glimpse, not of a stiff O.K.W. general at a German army desk, but of something that sent him, mind reeling, stumbling down the corridor.

* * *

Von Rheydt's school Latin seemd to be coming back; Casca, listening at the grille, nodded slowly and frowned as he finished his explanation of the upcoming test. "I have been thinking, German. The *framea* (spear?) could not have healed like this." He drew up a dirty tunic and showed von Rheydt a smooth, unmarked chest covered with curly black hair. "When will we go into battle?"

"About nine hours from now."

"I am ready," said the centurion. "I found some arms in my room. I will sleep, I think, before the contest of the gods."

"The gods? ...Yes," said von Rheydt, realizing the inadequacy of his Latin to explain alien races and galactic wars to a man who thought the earth flat. "Yes, sleep well, Junius."

Mbatha was not at his grille. Von Rheydt drew his dagger, stuck it through the bars and rattled it to attract the Zulu's attention. An instant later he froze as the point of a broad-bladed, razor-sharp assegai touched his throat.

Von Rheydt smiled as he let go of the dagger, which the African took and examined critically, at last pulling back the assegai and returning the knife to the German.

"We must fight soon, Mbatha," said von Rheydt in English. "You, me, and Casca, the other man with us. We must win. If we lose, we die."

"Fight English? Fight you and Casca?"

"No, you do not fight us," said von Rheydt desperately, thinking that the three of them might have to act as a team in a very few hours; having one man suspicious of the other two might kill them all. The Zulu had fallen fighting white men; to him all whites were the hated English. "I am not English. Casca is not English. We three men fight three... devils."

"Devils?" said the African.

"Spirits. Ghosts."

"Ghosts," repeated the Zulu, deadpan. "Warriors cannot fight ghosts, u-Rheydt."

"We don't have a choice, Mbatha. We fight in the morning. In one sleep."

"I sleep now, u-Rheydt," said Mbatha and left the grating. A scraping sound came from his room for a few minutes, and then silence.

Von Rheydt went back to his bunk and sat down, eased his boots off. He had a light meal of tinned sausage and biscuit from the ration pack and found what tasted like vodka in the canteen. When he had finished his meal, he lay back on the bunk, placed the Luger under his pillow and fell into a heavy sleep.

"Captain von Rheydt," said the voice in his dream, and he jerked awake. "It is time," said the voice, and as its meaning sank in, he came slowly back to reality.

He went to the grilles and made sure that Mbatha and Casca were both awake. They were, looking around their rooms; they must have heard the voice as well. As von Rheydt pulled on his boots, he wondered, *In what language had it spoken to them?*

He stood up, stamped his feet into the boots and walked to the pile of gear. He buckled on the scabbard of the dress saber over his pistol belt and stuck the dagger under it. He tightened the belt of his uniform trousers and tucked the cuffs into his boots. Finally he walked back to his bunk, took the pistol from under his pillow, checked the chamber, tucked the gun into its holster and buttoned the leather flap over it.

He was tightening the leather chinstrap of his helmet when the door bonged. With a last look around, he picked up the canteen, slung it from his shoulder and stepped out into the corridor.

Mbatha was already there waiting, and von Rheydt's eyebrows rose. The Zulu was big—muscular as well as tall. His broad, bare chest was crisscrossed with dark, puckered scars. A short skirt of animal pelt fell from waist to mid-thigh, and at elbow and knee blossomed fringes of white feathers. The African was carrying a short thrusting spear at his waist, a slightly longer one in his right hand and an oval cowhide shield on his back. A necklace of yellow animal teeth clicked against his chest.

Before von Rheydt could speak, there was a rattle of metal, and the German turned to see Junius Cornelius Casca raise a hand in greeting to the Zulu.

The centurion's dirty tunic was gone, hidden by a burnished corselet of horizontal hoops of steel. Leather padding showed under half-hoops of deeply gouged metal protecting the shoulders; the swelling muscles of his arms were bare. A coarse brown-woolen skirt or kilt fell to his knees, and he wore heavy sandals. One big, tanned hand rested on the sheath of a short sword and the other was curled negligently around a square shield, embossed with a wing-and-thunderbolt design. A short, plain dagger rode at his waist, and in spite of the Roman's short stature, the plumes of his centurion's helmet nodded above the taller men. Casca reached out an arm and gripped their hands solemnly, one at a time.

Von Rheydt looked at the two of them, the tall Zulu and the stocky Roman. "If it is the fate of a soldier to die," he said aloud in his own tongue, "to do it with such men as you is an honor."

They did not understand his harsh German, but they understood that it was a compliment and they nodded grimly. At that moment, one end of the corridor went dark, and they began to march three abreast in the direction of the light. The clang of bronze and steel echoed away in front of them.

The hatch closed behind them, and von Rheydt whispered, "My God." A low grunt of surprise came from Casca. The three men stared around.

They were in a gigantic amphitheater, and it was empty. Von Rheydt looked back, seeing a high wall without a trace of the door through which they had entered. Firm sand grated under their feet, and a red sun above them cast a bloody glow over empty tiers of gray metal seats, stretched to meet a deep violet sky.

Metal scraped as Casca drew the short sword and balanced it at waist level. "In your country, German, do you have the circus?" he asked in his strangely corrupt Latin. "That is what this is like. I have seen the gladiators fight in the imperial city. And now we fight—before the throne of Jove."

Von Rheydt looked at Mbatha, who returned his look without visible expression. "The u-Fasimba do not fight ghosts," said the African slowly. Then the short spear pointed with the speed of a striking snake. "But those... those are not ghosts."

Across the flatness of sand, through the atmosphere shimmering with heat, three dark figures stood against the wall of the amphitheater.

Von Rheydt unslung the canteen from his shoulder, took a mouthful of vodka and handed the canteen to the Zulu. When Casca handed it back to him, it was empty, and he dropped it to the sand and drew his saber.

Mbatha started forward at a jog-trot, and Casca and von Rheydt followed, their steps thudding on the hard-packed sand. The figures opposite them swung into motion too, and the two groups, men and others, closed rapidly.

Fifty meters apart, they both stopped, and von Rheydt's eyes narrowed.

The enemy was not human. From a distance they had resembled men, upright, bipedal, two-armed. But from this distance the differences were horribly evident.

The aliens were taller and thinner than men, but there was no appearance of fragility. They had long hair of a brassy color. *Skin tone?* von Rheydt wondered. Thick, small footpads, like a camel's. The necks were long, leading to a ridiculously small knob of a head. There was no clearly defined face, though he could make out large, dark eyes fixed on the men.

A sound next to him made him turn his head. Casca, eyes fixed on the enemy, had fronted his sword and was murmuring a prayer; when he caught von Rheydt's eyes on him, he grinned but didn't stop. Mbatha had been silent, scrutinizing the enemy; but then he turned his back contemptuously to them and addressed the German.

"We fight, u-Rheydt?" he said. "You—Casca?"

Von Rheydt nodded. "We fight."

Casca finished his prayer and brought the square shield up to cover his breast. Mbatha turned back; and von Rheydt, drawn saber in his right hand, Luger in his left, walked between the armored Roman and the hide-shielded Zulu toward the waiting aliens.

As they closed, he could see variations in their equipment and dress. They must be of different times too, he thought. One of them seemed to be sheathed in a blue-metal armor and carried a long staff of the same material. Von Rheydt nudged Junius, pointed with his saber; the Roman nodded, teeth bared, and fixed his eyes on that one. Another was almost naked, and its weapons were two curved, glittering scimitars; Mbatha was already turning toward it when things began to happen.

In a second, the aliens seemed to shrink, from seven feet or so to almost human size. Von Rheydt blinked, then saw what had happened; the "heads" had been withdrawn into the deep chests, and the dark eyes peered over the edge of a protective carapace like a soldier peering from a trench. The brain must be inside the chest, he thought. Well, a bullet would reach it even there.

And even while von Rheydt blinked, the blue-armored alien had lifted a long arm and something swift left the long staff and fell toward him, too fast to dodge.

There was a terrifying loud clang, and a meter-long, blue-metal rod quivered in the sand at his feet. Casca's shield twitched back and the centurion sent a mocking laugh at the being that was drawing another missile from a quiver on its back.

"*Gratias*," said von Rheydt, and then the three men separated and he found himself face to face with the third alien.

Von Rheydt's opponent stood solidly on two feet, neck stalk slightly extended, large, dark eyes fixed on the German. The smooth, brassy-looking skin was bare at the arms and legs but the trunk was covered with a flat black garment that looked incongruously like carbon paper...

But these were details that the captain noted only with his subconscious, for his attention was centered on the short rod that one brassy hand was bringing up stealthily to cover him.

Von Rheydt fired twice, rapidly from the hip. The nine-millimeter jolted his hand and the flat crack of it echoed back from the circled walls of the amphitheater. His opponent reeled back, then steadied, shook itself, and stepped forward, one hand going to its chest and the other raising the rod.

Electricity snapped, and von Rheydt's whole body arced in a spasm. He fell heavily to the sand, face up but unable to move. The alien came toward him, towering up into the purple sky, and lowered the rod to point at von Rheydt's chest.

He recovered movement and brought the saber around in a whistling arc. The alien jumped back but not in time to avoid the stroke, and the German's arm tingled as if he had struck a lamp post. He scrambled back up, retrieving the automatic from the sand. The alien closed with him again, and the point of the saber grated against the black-jerkined chest. The alien backed off a little.

Von Rheydt looked at the saber point. Broken; the tip had gone with that wild slash to the legs. He looked again at his opponent, who was still backing away. Most likely it needed a little range to use the rod, which it was training on him again.

Von Rheydt switched the Luger to his right hand, aimed carefully and sent four bullets caroming off the thing's torso. None penetrated, but the sheer kinetic energy of the eight-gram bullets knocked it back with each hit, and at the last shot it fell, dropping the rod.

Von Rheydt was on the weapon in two bounds, crushing it into the sand under his boot. From the corner of his eye he caught a glimpse of Mbatha and the nearly naked alien, both weaponless, straining in hand-to-hand combat. Von Rheydt reached his alien, placed the muzzle between the wide eyes and pressed the trigger. Only at the empty click did he see that the toggle link was up; there was no more ammunition.

At the same instant a grip of iron closed around his leg and he was jerked off his feet. Dropping the saber and the useless pistol, he fell on his enemy, hammering with his fists on its chest. He had hoped it was the garment that had deflected his bullets, but it was too flimsy; it was the carapace beneath it that was like steel, impervious to his fists and his weapons alike.

He was being crushed in a close hug when he found the ceremonial dagger in his hand and managed to slice it into the softer flesh of the "neck." The grip loosened, and the two fighters sprang apart and circled warily under the red sun.

Von Rheydt panted, wiped sweat from his eyes with the back of his dagger hand. Pain began to throb in his crushed ankle and in his chest. His opponent's sad eyes watched him unblinkingly as they circled, crouched, arms extended like wrestlers. The cuts on his half-extended neck gaped, but there was no trace of blood. The dark eyes flicked away from von Rheydt once, noting the ruin of its weapon, then slid back to follow the limping German.

Von Rheydt, circling to his right, stepped on something hard, stooped quickly and retrieved it: Mbatha's short spear. He held it low, pointed up at those sad, interested eyes.

This makes it a little more even than hand-to-hand, thought von Rheydt. He felt quite cool, as he usually did once a fight had started.

But the odds certainly seemed to favor the alien; that metal-hard skin, its great strength he had felt in his leg, the lack of an exposed brain. The very deliberation with which the creature moved gave an impression of terrible strength. The deliberation of a tank...

Deliberation. Could it be the deliberation not of irresistible power, but of great mass? Anything hard enough to resist a steel-jacketed bullet *must* weigh more than flesh.

At that moment von Rheydt crumpled, as if his injured ankle had given out. He fell to the sand and groaned.

The alien hesitated for a moment, then strode forward, its camellike foodpads making deep impressions on the sand.

It reached the fallen German, and the quick stride turned to a stumble as his spear entwined itself in the long legs. It began to topple over him, and von Rheydt rolled, bounding up. The neck extended as the creature fought for its balance; and then the whole frame jerked as von Rheydt swept the short spear around and rammed its butt into the back of the alien's neck.

It hit the ground so hard that little gouts of dry sand flew up. Von Rheydt reversed the spear and leaned the point into the base of the neck stalk, but the creature did not even shudder. Von Rheydt smiled tightly; there had been a major nerve from the eyes to the brain.

He glanced around for the others and saw Casca grinning at him. The Roman was bareheaded, and blood covered his scalp and the right side of his face; but he was kneeling on the chest of the blue-armored alien and his short sword was at its throat.

Where was Mbatha? He looked around and saw, about twenty meters off, the last minute of that combat. The giant Zulu, body shining with sweat, had both hands interlocked on his opponent's back in a powerful full nelson. The alien seemed to sag suddenly; the Zulu's back and shoulder bulged with a great effort, and with a horrible tearing sound, one of the brassy arms was bent far back.

Mbatha dropped the unconscious alien, fell to his knees and was sick in the sand, his body shaking with the aftermath of his exertion.

There was a sound of clapping from above them, and von Rheydt looked up at the general, who was sitting alone on the lowest tier of seats.

"Well done, Captain!" he called down, honest admiration in his harsh voice.

Von Rheydt looked around at his companions. Casca had raised his palm in the air in salute; he looked surprised. Mbatha had risen to his feet and extended his spear arm. *What*, von Rheydt wondered, *were they seeing in place of a general of the O.K.W.?*

"Thank you," he said to the general. "And now—your part of the bargain?"

"Of course. Return to life for all three of the victors," the general said. "Finish these three off, and then–"

"No," said von Rheydt.

The general stopped in mid-stretch, arms in the air. "What did you say, Captain?"

"I said no. This—creature—fought bravely. It is not a soldier's way to kill when his opponent, though brave, is helpless."

The general lowered his arms and laughed. "And what do your less-civilized friends say to that noble sentiment, Captain?" He said something rapid, something von Rheydt couldn't catch, and they both looked at Casca.

The Roman looked down at the blue-clad warrior, slowly raised his hand and—turned his thumb upward.

Mbatha spread his hands and walked away from his defeated opponent. Von Rheydt turned back to the general. "You see?"

"This is insane," said the general, angrily. "This primitive chivalry has no place in modern warfare. Even in your time, Captain—do your enemies give quarter to the wounded?"

"No," said von Rheydt; then his eyes fell to the sand of the arena. "Nor... do some of my own countrymen. But the best among us, the professional soldiers, do. Obedience is not our only code, General. We also have honor."

"That's enough," said the general, who had turned white. "Your last chance, Captain. Finish this matter properly. Now."

Von Rheydt stepped forward and threw the spear violently to the ground. It stuck there, quivering. "You do it," he said flatly. "It's your war." He turned, motioned to the Roman and the Zulu. They walked away across the sand.

Von Rheydt felt the blackness coming, drawing closer to him, like a velvet curtain sweeping in to end the last act of a play. It reached him, and he sank into it.

He opened his eyes to the white coldness of snow against his face and to a warmth that glowed like fire in the pit of his stomach. His eyes blinked, focused on a face. A human face. The face of a white-clad soldier who shouted something and raised a submachine gun...

* * *

It had rather enjoyed the role of a General Staff Officer, and It still retained the appearance of one as It sat down to write Its report. The battered army typewriter rattled as It typed; It paused occasionally to refer to a document from the desk or to take a draw on Its cigar. The gray octagonal room gradually filled with drifting layers of smoke as It wrote:

...the directive embodied in paragraph [4], reference [a], was fully carried out in accordance with standard testing procedures as set forth in Ordnance Manual, latest revision... Evaluating officer personally observed comparative combat testing and was highly impressed with performance of Human soldiers. They proved the better fighters in three of three encounters.

However, the Humans evinced certain undesirable characteristics as far as suitability for front-line use is concerned. The most serious was a refusal to obey orders contrary to their primitive codes of fighting.

It leaned back in the chair and thought about that one for a while, absentmindedly blowing smoke rings. In all good conscience, It could not recommend immediate employment of the Humans in the Disputed Sectors; they simply wouldn't do if they couldn't take simple orders. But then, It thought, there's just too much combat potential here to simply close down and start over again with some other design.

It thought for quite some time and then stubbed out the cigar, tilted the chair forward again and typed, *Recommendations*:

What is needed now for this Project is an intensified, speeded-up program of development. To effect this, it is proposed that two great power blocs be created at the conclusion of the present war and that a situation of continuous conflict be maintained for as long as is necessary to produce a deployable Human weapon...

It nodded in satisfaction. Just the thing. And It could stay on to supervise, in a soft rear-echelon job, far from the front...

It smiled and began to change.

Interim Justice

by William F. Wu

Editor's Introduction

It is a fundamental principle of the common law that justice delayed is justice denied; which says volumes about what passes for justice in the United States today. We have more lawyers than any society in all history; indeed, nearly as many as all societies in all times combined. For all that it takes years for civil cases to come to trail, and if there is a large discrepancy of resources—if the aggrieved party is small and weak, and the other large and rich—the case may never come to trial at all.

When disaster strikes far away, the French send doctors, the Swedes send food, and we send lawyers. After the disaster at Bhopal, India, a dozen lawyers sued Union Carbide in the name of the victims. Some went to India to seek clients. At least one took the name of his "client" from a newspaper account, and only later tried to get the client's approval. Suits claiming billions of dollars were filed. It was ambulance chasing on a grand scale.

The worse the injury, the more the lawyers will collect—and the longer it will take to settle the matter. We all know this; but any attempt to change the system is fought tooth and nail by the lawyers. Since all judges are lawyers, it is not surprising that matters affecting the financial interests of lawyers as a class are not easily settled—especially when we note that a majority of both state and national legislators are also lawyers.

Nuclear power; release of new drugs; whether or not to conduct genetic experiments; building dams, closing steel mills, purchasing weapons, conducting research: no matter how technical the matter, lawyers are thought competent to settle it. Two teams of lawyers argue to convince yet another lawyer (called a judge). Usually none of the parties have any technical training, and often none can explain the technology of the matter in dispute. Nevertheless, in many cases all concerned are paid by the taxpayers. Certainly the judge will be.

Dr. Arthur Kantrowitz, development scientist, Dartmouth professor, and Chairman of the L-5 Society, has long advocated "science courts" staffed by professional scientists to settle complex technical matters. The concept has won considerable approval, but it seems no closer to implementation now than it did when first thought of.

An ancient Roman principle holds that it is to the benefit of the commonwealth that there be an end to litigation; that disputes be settled once and for all, rather than dragged on forever. Norman law allowed trial by combat: the litigants, or their champions, fought in the lists after priests and heralds prayed that "God grant the right." Whether or not the Almighty intervened, battle unambiguously settled the dispute. The loser was not generally in any condition to file an appeal.

Dr. William Wu writes of a time a few years hence; a time when people have had enough of lawyers and have turned to war games as a way to decide civil cases. Not everyone is satisfied that justice is thereby done—but then not everyone believes our present system dispenses justice.

Ken Li pushed buttons on the arm of the gaming chair to adjust its position and then looked down over the big white holographic playing field in front of him. He had already tuned out the presence of thirty-five thousand excited, eager spectators packed into the stands around the arena. Now he swung up the flat keyboard on a steel arm and worked it into exactly the right height and distance from himself.

Ten meters away, across the playing field, his opponent finished maneuvering his own keyboard and raised one hand, signifying that he was ready. Ken centered his keyboard and made sure the small videoscreen across the top row of keys was not obscured by any glare from the lights. Then he raised his hand.

An attendant seated on the left edge of the playing field pushed a button on his own keyboard. Instantly the blank field came alive with holographic terrain and miniature armies drawn up in battle formation. The little video screen read, "Culloden Moor, 1746. House of Stuart. Prince Charles Edward Stuart." A list of Victory Conditions followed.

Ken nodded to himself. As a Gamer of the Master class under contract, he was about to play a war game as the representative of a litigant in a civil suit. He had fifteen seconds in which to recall the details of the battle before the computer activated the game. Culloden? Yes…

"Lydia?" A month before, Ken had stood up behind his desk as his secretary ushered in his next appointment. "Why didn't you just call me at home? I didn't know you were coming until I checked the calendar this morning." His heart started pounding.

The slender, honey-blonde woman stood by the closed door across the room. "I'm here to see you professionally," she said coldly. She wore a simple dark-blue dress that he remembered.

"As a client then, please have a seat." Ken gestured toward the two padded armchairs in front of his desk.

"A *prospective* client." Clutching her purse in both hands, she walked primly forward and sat down. "I guess you know I wouldn't be here if I weren't absolutely desperate."

Ken sat down behind his desk, intensely curious. "Yes. I never expected that you, of all people, would volunteer your litigation for a Guild contract." He picked up a pen and nervously twirled it.

"Have you read about the case? It's been in the papers." She held herself stiffly erect.

"I saw some headlines. When I realized they were about you, I… quit reading." He smiled, a little self-consciously.

"I know you're good, and I know your fee. I'll pay you in full, of course." She opened her purse.

"You know it's customary to give discounts to friends."

"I'd rather pay you in full." She pulled out a checkbook.

"Even so, you're premature with that. Don't worry. I don't intend to turn you down. When you're in trouble, I'll still do anything for you. Now. What's the case about?"

The Battle of Culloden—that was where the House of Hanover, represented by the English and certain Scottish clans allied with them, defeated the Stuart heir and his rebel Scots and brought about the end of the traditional Highland way of life. Ken studied the disposition of his troops just as the game activated. He played the role of Prince Charles and had most of the limitations imposed on him that the Bonnie Prince had endured. His only edge over the Prince was his own tactical ability, of which the Prince had had very little.

The Victory Conditions were simple enough. The rebel Scots had to destroy a certain number of English, or drive them from the field. The English had to destroy a certain number of Scottish rebels, or kill the Scottish heir. If Ken withdrew with the Prince and his army intact, the game would be drawn and another one played. However, with the royal superiority in cavalry, the last possibility was too unlikely to consider.

Quickly Ken worked over the keyboard to correct certain flaws in his order of battle that had been allowed by the Prince's incompetent Irish advisor, John William O'Sullivan. For instance, the left of his lines angled away from the enemy so that they were farther from them than the right. It was nothing more than sloppy supervision, and he issued orders to have the clans there brought forward. They were anchored by the Macdonalds, a sullen lot who were angered over losing their position on the right, which had been theirs by tradition for many centuries. Ken could not move them there now. Nor could he do anything about the lack of food and sleep endured by his army prior to the time of the opening of the game, or about the rain and sleet falling out of a nonexistent sky. Their physical and emotional condition would be considered by the computer as it resolved conflict.

Ken's opponent was in the role of the English Duke of Cumberland, who gave the order for his artillery to fire. Ken gave a similar order and hurried to rearrange his right. He felt flushed now, and the sweat flowed freely down his face and back from the effort of concentration and from the tension. A flash of memory came to him—a quote from aged Lord Lovat, who had brought his Clan Fraser out for the Prince: "None but a mad fool would have fought that day."

A small stone house called Culwhiniac stood far to the right of the Prince's line. A long stone wall ran from the Prince's line all the way to the royal line. More stone walls ran from this wall to the right at a perpendicular angle, making them excellent barriers against the royal army, but O'Sullivan had failed to man them. Ken knew better, and he drew clans from his second line to hold the walls. He also sent his meager cavalry there—the Fita-James Horse that was down to squadron strength—and the half troop of Life Guards he still had. This was out of character for the Prince since the Life Guards were acting as his personal bodyguard, but Ken had the prerogative.

He had no other cavalry, however, and he was outnumbered overall by about 8,800 to less than 5,000. A third of the rebels had drifted away recently, driven by starvation and lured by the nearness of their homes. Historically, the House of Stuart had been routed in twenty-five minutes.

The royal lines began to advance.

Lydia settled back in the chair slightly. "It's about Johnny AA9. Remember him?"

"Mm—isn't he classified? You never said much about him."

"He's our most successful artificial life-form. I can't tell you much more than that."

"You're covered under gamer-client privilege, you know."

"He's still classified. The main thing is, Carnehan-Chang Labs contracted us to conduct certain experiments, and Johnny AA9 resulted from one of them. We don't want to proceed any farther because Carnehan-Chang won't commit itself to full responsibility for him and we don't want to give him up until we know he'll be taken proper care of." Lydia shook her head tightly. "The cell differentiation is... I can't tell you how advanced, but I can tell you we had to put the... put AA9 into cryogenic sleep when we first went to court. It's been six years and we're getting nowhere. So finally both sides agreed to a game."

Ken fought to keep his voice professional and to control the strong attraction he still felt toward her. "So you're resolving a simple ownership issue? Does the winner of the game take ownership or relinquish it?"

"It's not that simple." Lydia's voice was almost a whisper. "Johnny's *human*, Ken. He–"

"*What?* I thought that was just a nickname or something."

"If he reaches full term, as we expect, he'll have all the human needs. But who's responsible for him? The bureaucracy of a corporation? And who's going to protect him from being constantly experimented on by that collective bureaucracy? For that matter, will he be a person under the law? Or an animal that can be patented and owned by a corporation? We made him out of lab chemicals, not human gametes. I want some legal definitions before we go on, and the standard judicial process hasn't given me any."

"Well, as you so often told me, a game won't provide any legal precedent. So what are you asking if you win?"

"That the fetus—that Johnny stay in suspended animation until my lab gets all the legal decisions we're asking for."

"What does the other side want?"

"They want immediate and full ownership and the total control that goes with it." Lydia forced an ironic, unpleasant smile. "Why are you asking all these questions? Aren't you the one who said that playing war games was independent of the issues?"

"Well, that's true. As a gamer, I don't pass judgment on the controversy, but I do like to know the magnitude of the case." He shrugged slightly. "I know you still hate the Gaming Masters' Guild, not to mention me. If you didn't think this game was of extreme importance, I guess you wouldn't be here."

Lydia shook her head angrily. "Never! The system is terrible—it doesn't give us any kind of justice based on the issues."

"But you're going to pay me for it anyway." Ken couldn't help a little smile.

"Well… all the new technology just keeps outstripping the laws on the books. We have to have something to go by until society catches up with us."

Ken nodded. "Exactly. I'll take your case."

Smoke, rain, sleet and fog obscured the formations on the battlefield, but Ken could see that the royal artillery, with its light, snapping sounds, was tearing viciously into the motionless rebel line. On the rebel right, English dragoons and the Clan Campbell were advancing to the first stone wall of Culwhiniac. The Campbells, afoot as classic Highlanders, began to dismantle the wall for the mounted dragoons. At the next wall they would be met with a hail of fire from the rebel right.

Ken recalled, breathlessly, the kind of troops his Highlanders were; they had been the last feudal army to assemble in Britain. They wore kilts and plaids, and they carried muskets and claymores and dirks and targs. Their only effective tactic was the legendary charge of wild, screaming, furious clansmen down upon their enemy and the panic it sometimes caused.

It had not worked at the real battle.

The rebel artillery ceased firing. The Prince's guns had been in poor condition and his gunners inexperienced; they had silenced themselves early in the actual conflict, and the computer had silenced them again on that basis here. Ken gave the attack order to his restless warriors, keying in the cry, "Claymore!"

The first line of Scots rebels raced forward across the moor with cries that sounded in the arena's speaker system. A great roar of excitement rose from the spectators seated in the giant oval, even breaking through

Ken's concentration as his fingers danced over the keys. Then, blinking sweat from his eyes, he suddenly saw a chance for advantage.

The computer had been programmed to include all the historic personalities who were known on the particular day in question, their behavior and that of the ranks in general. Also, of course, Ken's opponent would be using his own knowledge of the battle to strengthen his advantages, though in this case the royal victory had been quick and easy. He was probably not making any significant changes. On the rebel right, where the Fitz-James Horse and the Life Guards were waiting behind a stone wall, Ken saw a chance to rewrite the conflict.

Historically, the skewed angle of the rebel line had caused the charging Highlanders to run somewhat to the left instead of straight at their enemies. The Macdonalds, on the left, had been slaughtered or driven back by artillery and musket fire even before they reached the enemy because of the great distance they had to cross. Just to the right of center, however, the charging Erasers, Appin Stewarts and Camerons had overcompensated by running too far to their right. This had cut off the charge of their allied Atholl men, who were charging down the moor with one of the stone walls next to them on the right wing of the line. They were driven into the wall by their Cameron fellows. There the enemy Campbells had turned the rebel flank, lined the stone wall and fired their muskets point-blank into the blunted Atholl attack.

Ken had already straightened his line, and the Highland charge before his eyes was running dead ahead, though the orderly musket fire and artillery fire from the royal lines sliced into it savagely. On the right, however, the Campbells were just beginning to line up along the stone wall. Afraid he was too late, Ken had the Prince send a messenger running to the rebel horse. Just in time, they, too, leaped their own wall and charged the Campbells and the English Dragoons.

To defend themselves, the Campbells turned to face forward, allowing the Atholl regiment, with the rest of the Highland line, to finish their great charge.

Now came a terrible moment for Ken, who was tense and nearly drained already and still drawing on reserves of energy. Just like a real commander, he had made certain choices and given certain orders. Also like a real commander, he could only wait and watch as his orders were carried out, looking through the rain and smoke and fog for any other order that he thought might help.

On the left, the Macdonalds had closed with the royal line, which they had never done historically. The battle was in the balance now. If the charge failed to break the royal line, the rebels had no second tactic.

In the center, Clan Chattan had closed with the English in the face of a furious fire of grape and the steady, disciplined, relentless volleys of English muskets. Even so, the Scots broke the first line and fell upon the second—upon their bayonets, which outfought the claymores when properly used. The English center held.

On the left, the Macdonalds simultaneously drove a shock wave into the English right, also under murderously heavy fire and disciplined lines of bayonets.

Ken raised his head to look through smoke toward the rear of his enemy. Historically, the Duke of Cumberland had sent the Kingston's Horse Regiment and two regiments of infantry from his rear around his right flank to smash the Macdonalds. Yes, Ken could see them moving. He could do nothing about it.

The day before the game, Ken had taken Lydia out for brunch. Giving one's client an encouraging talk before a game was part of the psychology of being a Master Gamer, and though he was uncomfortable with her, he wanted to be strictly professional. The conversation was awkwardly polite.

"I don't like to sound ungrateful," she said over coffee once the plates had been removed. "I know you'll do your best for me. I just wish we had laws that made the games unnecessary."

"I agree it would be better for everybody," said Ken with a shrug. "It's also impossible to rush the process. Science and technology are rolling right along, and the legislators have to be caught up before they can pass decent laws."

Lydia sighed and nodded. "So... how have you been?"

Ken remained motionless, looking down at the table in front of him for as long as he could. This was the last time he would be able to talk to her for a long time, maybe forever. He decided to sacrifice pleasantry for honesty.

"I miss your daughter. Very badly."

"She's fine. She doesn't need you."

"I helped raise her for three years. And it's not as though she remembers her father or that he's around somewhere. I'd just like to see her sometimes. Take her places."

"She doesn't need you. It's not like you think."

"You don't know what I think," Ken said angrily. "You never let me tell you. Every time I tried to talk about her, you just told me I was wrong. After years of telling me you couldn't read my mind, you suddenly decided you could when it served your own selfish purposes. Thanks a lot."

"You're not her father, you know."

"Have you told her you won't let me see her?"

"She hasn't asked."

"So you're just letting her wait to see if I come to visit her and letting her assume that when I don't, it's because I don't care about her. You don't even have the guts to tell her it's your decision, do you?"

"Forget it, Ken. Thanks for brunch." Lydia slid out of her chair and walked away quickly, slinging the strap of her bag over her shoulder.

Ken's thoughts raced wildly. *AA9*, he thought. *Johnny AA9.* I'll never see that little girl again. Maybe I can help that frozen little fetus, at least. Maybe.

Ken's only chance was on the right. The men of Atholl, led by the Prince's fine but disfavored general, Lord George Murray, had also pierced the front line of Barrel's regiment. That regiment was courageous, however, and was virtually the only one that had withstood the Highland charge in the last battle between these armies that had led to the rebel victory at Falkirk. Yet the odds were now just uncertain enough to offer hope.

Breathing hard and fast, Ken ordered his second line to charge. This was a group of Lowland Scots, Irish and dismounted cavalry regiments, the last because enough horses could not be found. In the real battle they had been of no consequence, and the computer would not figure them to have great combat power. They charged, however, before the Macdonalds were smashed by the enemy cavalry, before the Campbells and Dragoons overwhelmed the weaker rebel horse, and before the rebel center began to flee and obstruct the force of the second charge.

The Camerons and the Atholl men had driven the remnants of the royal front line back. Yet the royal lines stood three regiments deep, and the regiments of Sempill and Wolfe in the second line now poured their musket fire onto the clansmen.

Those Highlanders, however, rallied when their second line came charging up behind them. Again the shock of the Highland charge drove back the English line, with horrible casualties. If the rebels were to win, this was the spot that would bring victory.

Ken, still working fast over the keyboard, watched with clenched teeth as Kingston's Horse drove into the Macdonalds and scattered them. They fled, to be ridden down by the English. With grim satisfaction, Ken noted that Kingston's Horse gave chase, as would the English infantry behind them. They would take themselves out of the battle.

On the rebel right, beyond the stone walls and away from the rest of the battle, the numbers of the Campbells and the numbers and discipline of the dragoons broke the rebel horse. Ken sent the Prince out to rally his Life Guards and then realized that no one could do so against those odds. With both flanks collapsing, Ken had nowhere to send the Prince except after the Atholl men, into the battle itself.

Finally the improbable happened. The men of Atholl, still led by Lord Murray, burst around the right of Wolfe's regiment, where it had been anchored against the stone wall. The Prince charged after them, calling stragglers forward still. With the right of the line broken, the clansmen ranged across the center ran forward again, enraged by the fever of battle and encouraged by the partial success.

Courage in a common soldier was always a variable and unpre-dictable quality. At Falkirk, Barrel's had been almost the only royal regiment to withstand the Highland charge; historically, at Culloden, they had all stood fast and carried the day. The computer calculated the fragility of human courage and either provided it or withdrew it, according to its own complex judgment of the battle at any given stage.

Though the royal army had taken both flanks of the rebels, and though the dragoons on Ken's right were in position to return and fall upon the rear of his men and destroy them, the computer suddenly broke the morale of the royal flank that had been turned. The men of Semphill's Border Scots and Wolfe's regiment turned and fled yet another time from the triumphant, screaming Highlanders chasing after them. The royal army was still in the better position overall, but panic was contagious, and the royal lines collapsed like dominoes in a repeat of Falkirk. Cumberland could not contact and control the widespread wings of his army, but the Prince was now riding with his own most successful troops and was able to keep them together.

As the royal formation collapsed, Cumberland withdrew. A moment later the holograms all froze in place. Ken read across the little video screen over his keyboard, "Victory Conditions: House of Stuart."

Ken let out a long breath and slumped back in his seat. Exhaustion overtook him now that the game was ended. The crowd about him was cheering wildly. He closed his eyes, chest heaving, and indulged himself in a grin. Lydia would have her way, at least until the courts got to work.

A Guild attendant took Ken to the reception room in an electric cart, as was customary. Ken thanked him and hopped out, feigning more energy than he felt. As the crowd parted before him, waving and calling congratulations, he reflected that the bounce in his step resulted more from rubbery knees than from his exhilaration.

If he had lost, of course, he wouldn't have any bounce at all.

Ken made his way to the refreshment table where a smiling young female attendant had a cup of red punch to hand him. He downed it quickly and then stood with his back to the table, accepting hand after hand of good cheer, all from privileged spectators whose position with the Guild had in some way gained them entrance to the private reception.

One hand, suddenly, thrust a sealed envelope into his hand. Ken looked up into Lydia's face.

"Thanks. I do appreciate it," she said quietly. "That's a check for the balance of your fee."

"I'm glad I could help. Really. Thank you." Ken was uncomfortably aware of the grinning strangers milling around them.

"I still despise this method of reaching decisions. It proves nothing about the issues at hand. It's totally arbitrary." Lydia spun quickly and disappeared into the crowd.

"It's supposed to be arbitrary," Ken said lamely after her. Then he looked around at the crowd of people surrounding him, waiting with big smiles for some snappy comeback from their idol.

"Well." He smiled and shrugged. "Justice is justice… Isn't it?"

NO TRUCE WITH KINGS

by Poul Anderson

Editor's Introduction

The virtue of prudence is not much discussed today; yet it lies at the heart of one of the fundamental issues of our time, the conflict between ethics of intention and ethics of responsibility. The "intentionists" argue thus: "what I intend is good, and I do what I intend; therefore my actions are good." Their opponents say "what you intend is of little matter; it is the *result* of your action that must be judged. Just because you thought you were doing good does not excuse you. You must take forethought and act prudently, with due regard to the consequences of your action."

Much evil has been done for the sake of evil goals. Genghis Khan built a pyramid of over a million skulls. His Mongol horsemen devastated whole nations. Poland and Hungary were nearly depopulated. The lands that sustained the Persian civilization were returned to desert and have not recovered to the present day; nor were the Mongols the only evil empire in history.

For all that, it can be argued that as much harm has been done from noble motives as from evil ones. Evil is eventually self-limited. The Mongol royalty drank themselves into inactivity. One will eventually tire of rapine and pillage. In contrast, there is no limit to the resources of those who wish to do good. The more selfless they are the more tireless they become. There is no oppression worse than the rule of a theory.

I first met Poul Anderson at the Seattle World Science Fiction Convention in 1961. We hit it off instantly, and from that time on have been close friends.

A year later Poul told me of a story he was writing. "I'm partly doing it for you. The do-gooders get their comeuppance," he said. I could hardly wait.

The result was the Hugo-winning "No Truce With Kings," which may very well be the finest story Poul has ever done.

"Song, Charlie! Give's a song!"

"Yay, Charlie!"

The whole mess was drunk, and the junior officers at the far end of the table were only somewhat noisier than their seniors near the colonel. Rugs and hangings could not much muffle the racket, shouts, stamping boots, thump of fists on oak and clash of cups raised aloft that rang from wall to stony wall. High up among shadows that hid the rafters they hung from, the regimental banners stirred in a draft, as if to join the chaos. Below, the light of bracketed lanterns and bellowing fireplace winked on trophies and weapons.

Autumn comes early on Echo Summit, and it was storming outside, wind-hoot past the watchtowers and rain-rush in the courtyards, an undertone that walked through the buildings and down all corridors as if the story were true that the unit's dead came out of the cemetery each September Nineteenth night and tried to join the celebration but had forgotten how. No one let it bother him, here or in the enlisted barracks, except maybe the hex major. The Third Division, the Catamounts, was known as the most riotous gang in the Army of the Pacific States of America; and of its regiments, the Rolling Stones, who held Fort Nakamura, were the wildest.

"Go on, boy! Lead off. You've got the closest thing to a voice in the whole goddamn Sierra," Colonel Mackenzie called. He loosened the collar of his black dress tunic and lounged back, legs asprawl, pipe in one hand and beaker of whiskey in the other: a thickset man with blue wrinkle-meshed eyes in a battered face, his cropped hair turned gray but his mustache still arrogantly red.

"*Charlie is my darlin', my darlin', my darlin',*" sang Captain Hulse. He stopped as the noise abated a little. Young Lieutenant Amadeo got up, grinned, and launched into one they well knew.

I am a Catamountain, I guard a border pass.
And every time I venture out, the cold will freeze my—

"Colonel, sir. Begging your pardon." Mackenzie twisted around and looked into the face of Sergeant Irwin. The man's expression shocked him. "Yes?"

I am a bloody hero, a decorated vet:
The Order of the Purple Shaft, with pineapple clusters yet!

"Message just come in, sir. Major Speyer asks to see you right away."

Speyer, who didn't like being drunk, had volunteered for duty tonight; otherwise men drew lots for it on a holiday. Remembering the last word from San Francisco, Mackenzie grew chill.

The mess bawled forth the chorus, not noticing when the colonel knocked out his pipe and rose.

The guns go boom! Hey, tiddley boom!
The rockets vroom, the arrows zoom.
From slug to slug is damn small room.
Get me out of here and back to the good old womb!
(Hey, doodle dee day!)

All right-thinking Catamounts maintained that they could operate better with the booze sloshing up to their eardrums than any other outfit cold sober. Mackenzie ignored the tingle in his veins; forgot it. He walked a straight line to the door, automatically taking his sidearm off the rack as he passed by. The song pursued him into the hall.

For maggots in the rations, we hardly ever lack.
You bite into a sandwich, and the sandwich bites right back.
The coffee is the finest grade of Sacramento mud.
The ketchup's good in combat, though, for simulating blood.

(Cho-orus)!

The drums go bump! Ah-tumpty-tump!
The bugles make like Gabri'l's trump—

Lanterns were far apart in the passage. Portraits of former commanders watched the colonel and the sergeant from eyes that were hidden
in grotesque darkness. Footfalls clattered too loudly here.

I've got an arrow in my rump.
Right about and rearward, heroes, on the jump!
(Hey, doodle dee day!)

Mackenzie went between a pair of fieldpieces flanking a stairway—
they had been captured at Rock Springs during the Wyoming War, a
generation ago—and upward. There was more distance between places
in this keep than his legs liked at their present age. But it was old, had
been added to decade by decade; and it needed to be massive, chiseled
and mortared from Sierra granite, for it guarded a key to the nation.
More than one army had broken against its revetments before the
Nevada marches were pacified, and more young men than Mackenzie
wished to think about had gone from this base to die among angry
strangers. *But she's never been attacked from the west. God, or whatever
you are, you can spare her that, can't you?*

The command office was lonesome at this hour. The room where
Sergeant Irwin had his desk lay so silent: no clerks pushing pens, no
messengers going in or out, no wives making a splash of color with their
dresses as they waited to see the colonel about some problem down
in the Village. When he opened the door to the inner room though,
Mackenzie heard the wind shriek around the angle of the wall. Rain
slashed at the black windowpane and ran down in streams which the
lanterns turned molten.

"Here the colonel is, sir," Irwin said in an uneven voice. He gulped and closed the door behind Mackenzie.

Speyer stood by the commander's desk. It was a beat-up old object with little upon it: an inkwell, a letter basket, an interphone, a photograph of Nora, faded in these dozen years since her death. The major was a tall and gaunt man, hook-nosed, going bald on top. His uniform always looked unpressed somehow. But he had the sharpest brain in the Cats, Mackenzie thought; and Christ, how could any man read as many books as Phil did! Officially he was the adjutant, in practice the chief adviser.

"Well?" Mackenzie said. The alcohol did not seem to numb him, rather make him too acutely aware of things: how the lanterns smelled hot (when would they get a big enough generator to run electric lights?), and the floor was hard under his feet, and a crack went through the plaster of the north wall, and the stove wasn't driving out much of the chill. He forced bravado, stuck thumbs in belt and rocked back on his heels. "Well, Phil, what's wrong now?"

"Wire from Frisco," Speyer said. He had been folding and unfolding a piece of paper, which he handed over.

"Huh? Why not a radio call?"

"Telegram's less likely to be intercepted. This one's in code, at that. Irwin decoded it for me."

"What the hell kind of nonsense is this?"

"Have a look, Jimbo, and you'll find out. It's for you anyway. Direct from GHQ."

Mackenzie focused on Irwin's scrawl. The usual formalities of an order; then:

You are hereby notified that the Pacific States Senate has passed a bill of impeachment against Owen Brodsky, formerly Judge of the Pacific States of America, and deprived him of office. As of 2000 hours this date, former Vice Humphrey Fallon is Judge of the PSA in accordance with the Law of Succession. The existence of dissident elements constituting a public danger has made it necessary for Judge

Fallon to put the entire nation under martial law, effective at 2100 hours this date. You are therefore issued the following instructions:

1. The above intelligence is to be held strictly confidential until an official proclamation is made. No person who has received knowledge in the course of transmitting this message shall divulge same to any other person whatsoever. Violators of this section and anyone thereby receiving information shall be placed immediately in solitary confinement to await court-martial.

2. You will sequestrate all arms and ammunition except for ten percent of available stock, and keep same under heavy guard.

3. You will keep all men in the Fort Nakamura area until you are relieved. Your relief is Colonel Simon Hollis, who will start from San Francisco tomorrow morning with one battalion. They are expected to arrive at Fort Nakamura in five days, at which time you will surrender your command to him. Colonel Hollis will designate those officers and enlisted men who are to be replaced by members of his battalion, which will be integrated into the regiment. You will lead the men replaced back to San Francisco and report to Brigadier General Mendoza at New Fort Baker. To avoid provocations, these men will be disarmed except for officers' sidearms.

4. For your private information, Captain Thomas Danielis has been appointed senior aide to Colonel Hollis.

5. You are again reminded that the Pacific States of America are under martial law because of a national emergency. Complete loyalty to the legal government is required. Any mutinous talk must be severely punished. Anyone giving aid or comfort to the Brodsky faction is guilty of treason and will be dealt with accordingly.

Gerald O'Donnell, Gen, APSA, CINC

Thunder went off in the mountains like artillery. It was a while before Mackenzie stirred, and then merely to lay the paper on his desk. He could only summon feeling slowly, up into a hollowness that filled his skin.

"They dared," Speyer said without tone. "They really did."

"Huh?" Mackenzie swiveled eyes around to the major's face. Speyer didn't meet that stare. He was concentrating his own gaze on his hands, which were now rolling a cigarette. But the words jerked from him, harsh and quick:

"I can guess what happened. The warhawks have been hollering for impeachment ever since Brodsky compromised the border dispute with West Canada. And Fallon, yeah, he's got ambitions of his own. But his partisans are a minority and he knows it. Electing him Vice helped soothe the warhawks some, but he'd never make Judge the regular way because Brodsky isn't going to die of old age before Fallon does, and anyhow, more than fifty percent of the Senate are sober, satisfied bossmen who don't agree that the PSA has a divine mandate to reunify the continent. I don't see how an impeachment could get through an honestly convened Senate. More likely they'd vote out Fallon."

"But a Senate had been called," Mackenzie said. The words sounded to him like someone else talking. "The newscasts told us."

"Sure. Called for yesterday 'to debate ratification of the treaty with West Canada.' But the bossmen are scattered up and down the country, each at his own Station. They have to *get* to San Francisco. A couple of arranged delays—hell, if a bridge just happened to be blown on the Boise railroad, a round dozen of Brodsky's staunchest supporters wouldn't arrive on time—so the Senate has a quorum all right, but every one of Fallon's supporters are there, and so many of the rest are missing that the warhawks have a clear majority. Then they meet on a holiday, when no cityman is paying attention. Presto, impeachment and a new Judge!" Speyer finished his cigarette and stuck it between his lips while he fumbled for a match. A muscle twitched in his jaw.

"You sure?" Mackenzie mumbled. He thought dimly that this moment was like one time he'd visited Puget City and been invited for a sail on the Guardian's yacht, and a fog had closed in. Everything was cold and blind, with nothing you could catch in your hands.

"Of course I'm not sure!" Speyer snarled. "Nobody will be sure till it's too late!" The matchbox shook in his grasp.

"They, uh, they got a new CINC too, I noticed."

"Uh-huh. They'd want to replace everybody they can't trust as fast as possible, and De Barros was a Brodsky appointee." The match flared with a hellish *scrit.* Speyer inhaled till his cheeks collapsed. "You and me included, naturally. The regiment reduced to minimum armament so that nobody will get ideas about resistance when the new colonel arrives. You'll note he's coming with a battalion at his heels just the same, just in case. Otherwise he could take a plane and be here tomorrow."

"Why not a train?" Mackenzie caught a whiff of smoke and felt for his pipe. The bowl was hot in his tunic pocket.

"Probably all rolling stock has to head north. Get troops among the bossmen there to forestall a revolt. The valleys are safe enough, peaceful ranchers and Esper colonies. None of them'll pot-shot Fallonite soldiers marching to garrison Echo and Donner outposts." A dreadful scorn weighted Speyer's words.

"What are we going to do?"

"I assume Fallon's takeover followed legal forms; that there was a quorum," Speyer said. "Nobody will ever agree whether it was really Constitutional... I've been reading this damned message over and over since Irwin decoded it. There's a lot between the lines. I think Brodsky's at large, for instance. If he were under arrest, this would've said as much and there'd have been less worry about rebellion. Maybe some of his household troops smuggled him away in time. He'll be hunted like a jackrabbit, of course."

Mackenzie took out his pipe but forgot he had done so. "Tom's coming with our replacements," he said thinly.

"Yeah. Your son-in-law. That was a smart touch, wasn't it? A kind of hostage for your good behavior, but also a backhand promise that you and yours won't suffer if you report in as ordered. Tom's a good kid. He'll stand by his own."

"This is his regiment too," Mackenzie said. He squared his shoulders. "He wanted to fight West Canada, sure. Young and... and a lot of Pacificans did get killed in the Idaho Panhandle during the skirmishes. Women and kids among 'em."

"Well," Speyer said, "you're the colonel, Jimbo. What should we do?"

"Oh, Jesus, I don't know. I'm nothing but a soldier." The pipe stem broke in Mackenzie's fingers. "But we're not some bossman's personal militia here. We swore to support the Constitution."

"I can't see where Brodsky's yielding some of our claims in Idaho is grounds for impeachment. I think he was right."

"Well—"

"A *coup d'état* by any other name would stink as bad. You may not be much of a student of current events, Jimbo, but you know as well as I do what Fallon's judgeship will mean. War with West Canada is almost the least of it. Fallon also stands for a strong central government. He'll find ways to grind down the old bossman families. A lot of their heads and scions will die in the front lines; that stunt goes back to David and Uriah. Others will be accused of collusion with the Brodsky people—not altogether falsely—and impoverished by fines. Esper communities will get nice big land grants so their economic competition can bankrupt still other estates. Later wars will keep bossmen away for years at a time, unable to supervise their own affairs, which will therefore go to the devil. And thus we march toward the glorious goal of Reunification."

"If Esper Central favors him, what can we do? I've heard enough about psi blasts. I can't ask my men to face them."

"You could ask your men to face the Hellbomb itself, Jimbo, and they would. A Mackenzie has commanded the Rolling Stones for over fifty years."

"Yes. I thought Tom, someday—"

"We've watched this brewing for a long time. Remember the talk we had about it last week?"

"Uh-huh."

"I might also remind you that the Constitution was written explicitly 'to confirm the separate regions in their ancient liberties.' "

"Let me alone!" Mackenzie shouted. "I don't know what's right or wrong, I tell you! Let me alone!"

Speyer fell silent, watching him through a screen of foul smoke. Mackenzie walked back and forth a while, boots slamming the floor like drumbeats. Finally he threw the broken pipe across the room so hard it shattered.

"Okay." He must ram each word past the tension in his throat. "Irwin's a good man who can keep his lip buttoned. Send him out to cut the telegraph line a few miles downhill. Make it look as if the storm did it. The wire breaks often enough, heaven knows. Officially, then, we never got GHQ's message. That gives us a few days to contact Sierra Command HQ. I won't go against General Cruikshank... but I'm pretty sure which way he'll go if he sees a chance. Tomorrow we prepare for action. It'll be no trick to throw back Hollis' battalion, and they'll need a while to bring some real strength against us. Before then the first snow should be along, and we'll be shut off for the winter. Only we can use skis and snowshoes, ourselves, to keep in touch with the other units and organize something. By spring—we'll see what happens."

"Thanks, Jimbo." The wind almost drowned Speyer's words.

"I'd... I'd better go tell Laura."

"Yeah." Speyer squeezed Mackenzie's shoulder. There were tears in the major's eyes.

Mackenzie went out with parade-ground steps, ignoring Irwin: down the hall, down a stairway at its other end, past guarded doors where he returned salutes without really noticing, and so to his own quarters in the south wing. His daughter had gone to sleep already. He took a lantern off its hook in his bleak little parlor and entered her room.

She had come back here while her husband was in San Francisco.

For a moment Mackenzie couldn't quite remember why he had sent Tom there. He passed a hand over his stubbly scalp, as if to squeeze something out... oh, yes, ostensibly to arrange for a new issue of uniforms; actually to get the boy out of the way until the political crisis had blown over. Tom was too honest for his own good, an admirer of Fallon and the Esper movement. His outspokenness had led to friction with his brother officers. They were mostly of bossman stock or from well-to-do protectee families. The existing social order had been good to them. But Tom Danielis began as a fisher lad in a poverty-stricken village on the Mendocino coast. In spare moments he'd learned the three R's from a local Esper; once literate, he joined the army and earned a commission by sheer guts and brains. He had never forgotten that the Espers helped the poor and that Fallon promised to help the Espers... Then, too, battle, glory, Reunification, Federal Democracy; those were heady dreams when you were young.

Laura's room was little changed since she left it to get married last year. And she had been only seventeen then. Objects survived which had belonged to a small person with pigtails and starched frocks—a teddy bear loved to shapelessness, a doll house her father had built, her mother's picture drawn by a corporal who stopped a bullet at Salt Lake. Oh, God, how much she had come to look like her mother.

Dark hair streamed over a pillow turned gold by the light. Mackenzie shook her as gently as he was able. She awoke instantly, and he saw the terror within her.

"Dad! Anything about Tom?"

"He's okay." Mackenzie set the lantern on the floor and himself on the edge of the bed. Her fingers were cold where they caught at his hand.

"He isn't," she said. "I know you too well."

"He's not been hurt yet. I hope he won't be."

Mackenzie braced himself. Because she was a soldier's daughter, he told her the truth in a few words; but he was not strong enough to look at her while he did. When he had finished, he sat dully listening to the rain.

"You're going to revolt," she whispered.

"I'm going to consult with SCHQ and follow my commanding officer's orders," Mackenzie said.

"You know what they'll be... once he knows you'll back him."

Mackenzie shrugged. His head had begun to ache. Hangover started already? He'd need a good deal more booze before he could sleep tonight. No, no time for sleep—yes, there would be. Tomorrow would do to assemble the regiment in the courtyard and address them from the breech of Black Hepzibah, as a Mackenzie of the Rolling Stones always addressed his men, and.... He found himself ludicrously recalling a day when he and Nora and this girl here had gone rowing on Lake Tahoe. The water was the color of Nora's eyes, green and blue and with sunlight glimmering across the surface, but so clear you could see the rocks on the bottom; and Laura's own little bottom had stuck straight in the air as she trailed her hands astern.

She sat thinking for a space before saying flatly: "I suppose you can't be talked out of it." He shook his head. "Well, can I leave tomorrow early, then?"

"Yes. I'll get you a coach."

"T-t-to hell with that. I'm better in the saddle than you are."

"Okay. A couple of men to escort you though." Mackenzie drew a long breath. "Maybe you can persuade Tom—"

"No. I can't. Please don't ask me to, Dad."

He gave her the last gift he could: "I wouldn't want you to stay. That'd be shirking your own duty. Tell Tom I still think he's the right man for you. Goodnight, duck." It came out too fast, but he dared not delay. When she began to cry, he must unfold her arms from his neck and depart the room.

"But I had not expected so much killing!"

"Nor I... at this stage of things. There will be more yet, I am afraid, before the immediate purpose is achieved."

"You told me—"

"I told you our hopes, Mwyr. You know as well as I that the Great Science is only exact on the broadest scale of history. Individual events are subject to statistical fluctuation."

"That is an easy way, is it not, to describe sentient beings dying in the mud?"

"You are new here. Theory is one thing, adjustment to practical necessities is another. Do you think it does not hurt me to see that happen which I myself have helped plan?"

"Oh, I know, I know. Which makes it no easier to live with my guilt."

"To live with your responsibilities, you mean."

"Your phrase."

"No, this is not semantic trickery. The distinction is real. You have read reports and seen films, but I was here with the first expedition. And here I have been for more than two centuries. Their agony is no abstraction to me."

"But it was different when we first discovered them. The aftermath of their nuclear wars was still so horribly present. That was when they needed us—the poor starveling anarchs—and we, we did nothing but observe."

"Now you are hysterical. Could we come in blindly, ignorant of every last fact about them, and expect to be anything but one more disruptive element? An element whose effects we ourselves would not have been able to predict. That would have been criminal indeed, like a surgeon who started to operate as soon as he met the patient, without so much as taking a case history. We had to let them go their own way while we studied in secret. You have no idea how desperately hard we worked to gain information and understanding. That work goes on. It was only seventy years ago that we felt enough assurance to introduce the first new factor into this one selected society. As we continue to learn more, the plan will be adjusted. It may take us a thousand years to complete our mission."

"But meanwhile they have pulled themselves back out of the wreckage. They are finding their own answers to their problems. What right have we to—"

"I begin to wonder, Mwyr, what right you have to claim even the title of apprentice psycho-dynamician. Consider what their 'answers' actually amount to. Most of the planet is still in a state of barbarism. This continent has come farthest toward recovery because of having the widest distribution of technical skills and equipment before the destruction. But what social structure has evolved? A jumble of quarrelsome successor states. A feudalism where the balance of political, military, and economic power lies with a landed aristocracy, of all archaic things. A score of languages and subcultures developing along their own incompatible lines. A blind technology worship inherited from the ancestral society that, unchecked, will lead them in the end back to a machine civilization as demoniac as the one that tore itself apart three centuries ago. Are you distressed that a few hundred men have been killed because our agents promoted a revolution which did not come off quite so smoothly as we hoped? Well, you have the word of the Great Science itself that without our guidance, the totaled misery of this race through the next five thousand years would outweigh by three orders of magnitude whatever pain we are forced to inflict."

"—Yes. Of course. I realize I am being emotional. It is difficult not to be at first, I suppose."

"You should be thankful that your initial exposure to the hard necessities of the plan were so mild. There is worse to come."

"So I have been told."

"In abstract terms. But consider the reality. A government ambitious to restore the old nation will act aggressively, thus embroiling itself in prolonged wars with powerful neighbors. Both directly and indirectly, through the operation of economic factors they are too naive to control, the aristocrats and freeholders will be eroded away by those wars. Anomic democracy will replace their system, first dominated by a corrupt capitalism and later by sheer force of whoever holds the central government. But there will be no place for the vast displaced proletariat, the one-time landowners and the foreigners incorporated by conquest. They will offer fertile soil to any demagogue. The empire will undergo endless upheaval, civil strife, despotism, decay, and outside invasion. Oh, we will have much to answer for before we are done!"

"Do you think... when we see the final result... will the blood wash off us?"

"No. We pay the heaviest price of all."

Spring in the high Sierra is cold, wet, snowbanks melting away from forest floor and giant rocks, rivers in spate until their canyons clang, a breeze ruffling puddles in the road. The first green breath across the aspen seems infinitely tender against pine and spruce, which gloom into a brilliant sky. A raven swoops low, gruk, gruk, look out for that damn hawk! But then you cross timber line and the world becomes tumbled blue-gray immensity, with the sun ablaze on what snows remain and the wind sounding hollow in your ears.

Captain Thomas Danielis, Field Artillery, Loyalist Army of the Pacific States, turned his horse aside. He was a dark young man, slender and snub-nosed. Behind him a squad slipped and cursed, dripping mud from feet to helmets, trying to get a gun carrier unstuck. Its alcohol motor was too feeble to do more than spin the wheels. The infantry squelched on past, stoop-shouldered, worn down by altitude and a wet bivouac and pounds of mire on each boot. Their line snaked from around a prowlike crag, up the twisted road and over the ridge ahead. A gust brought the smell of sweat to Danielis.

But they were good joes, he thought. Dirty, dogged, they did their profane best. His own company, at least, was going to get hot food tonight, if he had to cook the quartermaster sergeant.

The horse's hoofs banged on a block of ancient concrete jutting from the muck. If this had been the old days... but wishes weren't bullets. Beyond this part of the range lay lands mostly desert, claimed by the Saints, who were no longer a menace but with whom there was scant commerce. So the mountain highways had never been considered worth repaving, and the railroad ended at Hangtown. Therefore the expeditionary force to the Tahoe area must slog through unpeopled forests and icy uplands, God help the poor bastards.

God help them in Nakamura too, Danielis thought. His mouth

drew taut, he slapped his hands together and spurred the horse with needless violence. Sparks shot from iron shoes as the beast clattered off the road toward the highest point of the ridge. The man's saber banged his leg.

Reining in, he unlimbered his field glasses. From here he could look across a jumbled sweep of mountainscape, where cloud shadows sailed over cliffs and boulders, down into the gloom of a canyon and across to the other side. A few tufts of grass thrust out beneath him, mummy brown, and a marmot wakened early from winter sleep whistled somewhere in the stone confusion. He still couldn't see the castle. Nor had he expected to, as yet. He knew this country... how well he did!

There might be a glimpse of hostile activity though. It had been eerie to march this far with no sign of the enemy, of anyone else whatsoever; to send out patrols in search of rebel units that could not be found; to ride with shoulder muscles tense against the sniper's arrow that never came. Old Jimbo Mackenzie was not one to sit passive behind walls, and the Rolling Stones had not been given their nickname in jest.

If Jimbo is alive. How do I know he is? That buzzard yonder may be the very one which hacked out his eyes. Danielis bit his lip and made himself look steadily through the glasses. *Don't think about Mackenzie, how he outroared and outdrank and outlaughed you and you never minded, how he sat knotting his brows over the chessboard where you could mop him up ten times out of ten and he never cared, how proud and happy he stood at the wedding... Nor think about Laura, who tried to keep you from knowing how often she wept at night, who now bore a grandchild beneath her heart and woke alone in the San Francisco house from the evil dreams of pregnancy. Every one of those dogfaces plodding toward the castle that has killed every army ever sent against it—every one of them has somebody at home, and hell rejoices at how many have somebody on the rebel side. Better look for hostile spoor and let it go at that.*

Wait! Danielis stiffened. A rider! He squinted at the distant man. One of our own. Fallon's army had added a blue band to the uniform. Returning scout. A tingle went along his spine. He decided to hear the report firsthand. But the fellow was still a mile off, perforce riding slowly over the hugger-mugger terrain. There was no hurry about intercepting him. Danielis continued to survey the land.

A reconnaissance plane appeared, an ungainly dragonfly with sunlight flashing off a propeller head. Its drone bumbled among rock walls, where echoes threw the noise back and forth. Doubtless an auxiliary to the scouts, employing two-way radio communication. Later the plane would work as a spotter for artillery. There was no use making a bomber of it; Fort Nakamura was proof against anything that today's puny aircraft could drop, and might well shoot the thing down.

A shoe scraped behind Danielis. Horse and man whirled as one. His pistol jumped into his hand. It lowered. "Oh. Excuse me, Philosopher." The man in the blue robe nodded. A smile softened his stern face. He must be around sixty years old, hair white and skin lined, but he walked these heights like a wild goat. The Yang and Yin symbol burned gold on his breast.

"You're needlessly on edge, son," he said. A trace of Texas accent stretched out his words. The Espers obeyed the laws wherever they lived, but acknowledged no country their own: nothing less than mankind, perhaps ultimately all life through the space-time universe. Nevertheless, the Pacific States had gained enormously in prestige and influence in San Francisco at the time when the city was being rebuilt in earnest. There had been no objection—on the contrary—to the Grand Seeker's desire that Philosopher Woodworth accompany the expedition as an observer. Not even from the chaplains; the churches had finally gotten it straight that the Esper teachings were neutral with respect to religion.

Danielis managed a grin. "Can you blame me?"

"No blame. But advice. Your attitude isn't useful. Does nothin' but wear you out. You've been fightin' a battle for weeks before it began."

Danielis remembered the apostle who had visited his home in San Francisco—by invitation, in the hope that Laura might learn some peace. His simile had been still homelier: "You only need to wash one dish at a time." The memory brought a smart to Danielis' eyes, so that he said roughly: "I might relax if you'd use your powers to tell me what's waiting for us."

"I'm no adept, son. Too much in the material world, I'm afraid. Somebody's got to do the practical work of the Order, and someday I'll get the chance to retire and explore the frontier inside me. But you need to start early, and stick to it a lifetime, to develop your full powers." Woodworth looked across the peaks, seemed almost to merge himself with their loneliness.

Danielis hesitated to break into that meditation. He wondered what practical purpose the Philosopher was serving on this trip. To bring back a report more accurate than untrained senses and undisciplined emotions could prepare? Yes, that must be it. The Espers might yet decide to take a hand in this war. However reluctantly, Central had allowed the awesome psi powers to be released now and again when the Order was seriously threatened; and Judge Fallon was a better friend to them than Brodsky or the earlier Senate of Bossmen and House of People's Deputies had been.

The horse stamped and blew out its breath in a snort. Woodworth glanced back at the rider. "If you ask me though," he said, "I don't reckon you'll find much doin' around here. I was in the Rangers myself, back home, before I saw the Way. This country feels empty."

"If we could know!" Danielis exploded. "They've had the whole winter to do what they liked in the mountains while the snow kept us out. What scouts we could get in reported a beehive—as late as two weeks ago. What have they planned?"

Woodworth made no reply.

It flooded from Danielis, he couldn't stop, he had to cover the recollection of Laura bidding him good-bye on his second expedition against her father, six months after the first one came home in bloody fragments:

"If we had the resources! A few wretched little railroads and motor cars; a handful of aircraft; most of our supply trains drawn by mules— what kind of mobility does that give us? And what really drives me crazy… we know how to make what they had in the old days. We've got the books, the information. More, maybe, than the ancestors. I've watched the electrosmith at Fort Nakamura turn out transistor units with enough bandwidth to carry television, no bigger than my fist. I've seen the scientific journals, the research labs, biology, chemistry, astronomy, mathematics. And all useless!"

"Not so," Woodworth answered mildly. "Like my own Order, the community of scholarship's becomin' supranational. Printin' presses, radiophones, telescribes—

"I say useless. Useless to stop men killing each other because there's no authority strong enough to make them behave. Useless to take a farmer's hands off a horse-drawn plow and put them on the wheel of a tractor. We've got the knowledge, but we can't apply it."

"You do apply it, son, where too much power and industrial plant isn't required. Remember, the world's a lot poorer in natural resources than it was before the Hell-bombs. I've seen the Black Lands myself, where the firestorm passed over the Texas oilfields." Woodworm's serenity cracked a little. He turned his eyes back to the peaks.

"There's oil elsewhere," Danielis insisted. "And coal, iron, uranium, everything we need. But the world hasn't got the organization to get at it. Not in any quantity. So we fill the Central Valley with crops that'll yield alcohol to keep a few motors turning; and we import a dribble of other stuff along an unbelievably inefficient chain of middlemen; and most of it's eaten by the armies." He jerked his head toward that part of the sky which the handmade airplane had crossed. "That's one reason we've got to have Reunification. So we can rebuild."

"And the other?" Woodworm asked softly.

"Democracy—universal suffrage." Danielis swallowed. "And so fathers and sons won't have to fight each other again."

"Those are better reasons," Woodworth said. "Good enough for the Espers to support. But as for that machinery you want—" He shook his head. "No, you're wrong there. That's no way for men to live."

"Maybe not," Danielis said. "Though my own father wouldn't have been crippled by overwork if he'd had some machines to help him... Oh, I don't know. First things first. Let's get this war over with and argue later." He remembered the scout, now gone from view. "Pardon me, Philosopher, I've got an errand."

The Esper raised his hand in token of peace. Danielis cantered off.

Splashing along the roadside, he saw the man he wanted, halted by Major Jacobsen. The latter, who must have sent him out, sat mounted near the infantry line. The scout was a Klamath Indian, stocky in buckskins, a bow on his shoulder. Arrows were favored over guns by many of the men from the northern districts: cheaper than bullets, no noise, less range but as much firepower as a bolt-action rifle. In the bad old days before the Pacific States had formed their union, archers along forest trails had saved many a town from conquest; they still helped keep that union loose.

"Ah, Captain Danielis," Jacobsen hailed. "You're just in time. Lieutenant Smith was about to report what his detachment found out."

"And the plane," said Smith imperturbably. "What the pilot told us he's seen from the air gave us the guts to go there and check for ourselves."

"Well?"

"Nobody around."

"What?"

"Fort's been evacuated. So's the settlement. Not a soul."

"But—but–" Jacobsen collected himself. "Go on."

"We studied the signs as best's we could. Looks like noncombatants left some time ago. By sledge and ski, I'd guess, maybe north to some strong point. I suppose the men shifted their own stuff at the same time, gradual-like, what they couldn't carry with 'em at the last. Because the regiment and its support units, even field artillery, pulled out just three-four days ago. Ground's all tore up. They headed downslope, sort of west by northwest, far's we could tell from what we saw."

Jacobson choked. "Where are they bound?"

A flaw of wind struck Danielis in the face and ruffled the horses' manes. At his back he heard the slow plop and squish of boots, groan of wheels, chuff of motors, rattle of wood and metal, yells and whip cracks of muleskinners. But it seemed very remote. A map grew before him, blotting out the world.

The Loyalist Army had had savage fighting the whole winter, from the Trinity Alps to Puget Sound—for Brodsky had managed to reach Mount Rainier, whose lord had furnished broadcasting facilities, and Rainier was too well fortified to take at once. The bossmen and the autonomous tribes rose in arms, persuaded that a usurper threatened their damned little local privileges. Their protectees fought beside them, if only because no rustic had been taught any higher loyalty than to his patron. West Canada, fearful of what Fallon might do when he got the chance, lent the rebels aid that was scarcely even clandestine.

Nonetheless, the national army was stronger, with more matériel, better organization, above everything an ideal of the future. CINC O'Donnell had outlined a strategy: concentrate the loyal forces at a few points, overwhelm resistance, restore order and establish bases in the region, then proceed to the next place—which worked. The government now controlled the entire coast, with naval units to keep an eye on the Canadians in Vancouver and guard the important Hawaii trade routes; the northern half of Washington almost to the Idaho line; the Columbia Valley; central California as far north as Redding. The remaining rebellious Stations and towns were isolated from each other in mountains, forests, deserts. Bossdom after bossdom fell as the loyalists pressed on, defeating the enemy in detail, cutting him off from supplies and hope. The only real worry had been Cruikshank's Sierra Command, an army in its own right rather than a levy of yokels and citymen, big and tough and expertly led. This expedition against Fort Nakamura was only a small part of what had looked like a difficult campaign.

But now the Rolling Stones had pulled out. Offered no fight whatsoever. Which meant that their brother Catamounts must also have evacuated. You don't give up one anchor of a line you intend to hold. So?

"Down into the valleys," Danielis said, and there sounded in his ears, crazily, the voice of Laura as she used to sing. *Down in the valley, valley so low.*

"Judas!" the major exclaimed. Even the Indian grunted as if he had taken a belly blow. "No, they couldn't. We'd have known."

Hang your head over, hear the wind blow. It hooted across cold rocks.

"There are plenty of forest trails," Danielis said. "Infantry and cavalry could use them if they're accustomed to such country. And the Cats are. Vehicles, wagons, big guns, that's slower and harder. But they only need to outflank us, then they can get back onto Forty and Fifty—and cut us to pieces if we attempt pursuit. I'm afraid they've got us boxed."

"The eastern slope?" said Jacobsen helplessly.

"What for? Want to occupy a lot of sagebrush? No, we're trapped here till they deploy in the flatlands." Danielis closed a hand on his saddlehorn so that the knuckles went bloodless. "I miss my guess if this isn't Colonel Mackenzie's idea. It's his style, for sure."

"But then they're between us and Frisco! With damn near our whole strength in the north!"

Between me and Laura, Danielis thought.

He said aloud: "I suggest, Major, we get hold of the C.O. at once. And then we better get on the radio." From some well he drew the power to raise his head. The wind lashed his eyes. "This needn't be a disaster. They'll be easier to beat out in the open, actually, once we come to grips."

Roses love sunshine, violets love dew,
Angels in heaven know I love you.

The rains that fill the winter of the California lowlands were about ended. Northward along a highway whose pavement clopped under hoofs, Mackenzie rode through a tremendous greenness. Eucalyptus and live oak, flanking the road, exploded with new leaves. Beyond them on either side stretched a checkerboard of fields and vineyards, intricately hued, until the distant hills on the right and the higher, nearer ones on the left made walls. The freeholder houses that had been scattered across a land a ways back were no longer to be seen. This end of the Napa Valley belonged to the Esper community at St. Helena. Clouds banked like white mountains over the western ridge. The breeze bore to Mackenzie a smell of growth and turned earth.

Behind him it rumbled with men. The Rolling Stones were on the move. The regiment proper kept to the highway, three thousand boots slamming down at once with an earthquake noise, and so did the guns and wagons. There was no immediate danger of attack. But the cavalrymen attached to the force must needs spread out. The sun flashed off their helmets and lance heads.

Mackenzie's attention was directed forward. Amber walls and red tile roofs could be seen among plum trees that were a surf of pink and white blossoms. The community was big, several thousand people. The muscles tightened in his abdomen. "Think we can trust them?" he asked, not for the first time. "We've only got a radio agreement to a parley."

Speyer, riding beside him, nodded. "I expect they'll be honest. Particularly with our boys right outside. Espers believe in non-violence anyway."

"Yeah, but if it did come to fighting—I know there aren't very many adepts so far. The Order hasn't been around long enough for that. But when you get this many Espers together, there's bound to be a few who've gotten somewhere with their damned psionics. I don't want my men blasted or lifted in the air and dropped, or any such nasty things."

Speyer threw him a sidelong glance. "Are you scared of them, Jimbo?" he murmured.

"Hell, no!" Mackenzie wondered if he was a liar or not. "But I don't like 'em."

"They do a lot of good. Among the poor, especially."

"Sure, sure. Though any decent bossman looks after his own protectees, and we've got things like churches and hospices as well. I don't see where just being charitable—and they can afford it, with the profits they make on their holdings—I don't see where that gives any right to raise the orphans and pauper kids they take in the way they do; so's to make the poor tykes unfit for life anywhere outside."

"The object of that, as you well know, is to orient them toward the so-called interior frontier. Which American civilization as a whole is not much interested in. Frankly, quite apart from the remarkable powers some Espers have developed, I often envy them."

"You, Phil?" Mackenzie goggled at his friend.

The lines drew deep in Speyer's face. "This winter I've helped shoot a lot of my fellow countrymen," he said sadly.

"My mother and wife and kids are crowded with the rest of the Village in the Mount Lassen fort, and when we said goodbye, we knew it was quite possibly permanent. And in the past I've helped shoot a lot of other men who never did me any personal harm." He sighed. "I've often wondered what it's like to know peace, inside as well as outside."

Mackenzie sent Laura and Tom out of his head.

"Of course," Speyer went on, "the fundamental reason you—and I, for that matter—distrust the Espers is that they do represent something alien to us. Something that may eventually choke out the whole concept of life that we grew up with. You know, a couple weeks back in Sacramento I dropped in at the University research lab to see what was going on. Incredible! The ordinary soldier would swear it was witchwork. It was certainly more weird than... than simply reading minds or moving objects by thinking at them. But to you or me it's a shiny new marvel. We'll wallow in it.

"Now why's that? Because the lab is scientific. Those men work with chemicals, electronics, subviral particles. That fits into the educated American's world-view. But the mystic unity of creation... no, not our cup of tea. The only way we can hope to achieve Oneness is to renounce everything we've ever believed in. At your age or mine, Jimbo, a man is seldom ready to tear down his whole life and start from scratch."

"Maybe so." Mackenzie lost interest. The settlement was quite near now.

He turned around to Captain Hulse, riding a few paces behind. "Here we go," he said. "Give my compliments to Lieutenant Colonel Yamaguchi and tell him he's in charge till we get back. If anything seems suspicious, he's to act at his own discretion."

"Yes, sir." Hulse saluted and wheeled smartly about. There had been no practical need for Mackenzie to repeat what had long been agreed on; but he knew the value of ritual. He clicked his big sorrel gelding into a trot. At his back he heard bugles sound orders and sergeants howl at their platoons.

Speyer kept pace. Mackenzie had insisted on bringing an extra man to the discussion. His own wits were probably no match for a high-level Esper, but Phil's might be.

Not that there's any question of diplomacy or whatever. I hope. To ease himself, he concentrated on what was real and present—hoofbeats, the rise and fall of the saddle beneath him, the horse's muscles rippling between his thighs, the creak and jingle of his saber belt, the clean odor of the animal—and suddenly remembered this was the sort of trick the Espers recommended.

None of their communities was walled, as most towns and every bossman's Station was. The officers turned off the highway and went down a street between colonnaded buildings. Side streets ran off in both directions. The settlement covered no great area though, being composed of groups that lived together, sodalities or superfamilies or whatever you wanted to call them. Some hostility toward the Order and a great many dirty jokes stemmed from that practice. But Speyer, who should know, said there was no more sexual swapping around than in the outside world. The idea was simply to get away from possessiveness, thee versus me, and to raise children as part of a whole rather than an insular clan.

The kids were out, staring round-eyed from the porticoes, hundreds of them. They looked healthy and, underneath a natural fear of the invaders, happy enough. But pretty solemn, Mackenzie thought; and all in the same blue garb. Adults stood among them, expressionless.

Everybody had come in from the fields as the regiment neared. The silence was like barricades. Mackenzie felt sweat begin to trickle down his ribs. When he emerged on the central square, he let out his breath in a near gasp.

A fountain, the basin carved into a lotus, tinkled in the middle of the plaza. Flowering trees stood around it. The square was defined on three sides by massive buildings that must be for storage. On the fourth side rose a smaller temple-like structure with a graceful cupola, obviously headquarters and meeting house. On its lowest step were ranked half a dozen blue-robed men, five of them husky youths. The sixth was middle-aged, the Yang and Yin on his breast. His features, ordinary in themselves, held an implacable calm.

Mackenzie and Speyer drew rein. The colonel flipped a soft salute. "Philosopher Gaines? I'm Mackenzie, here's Major Speyer." He swore at himself for being so awkward about it and wondered what to do with his hands. The young fellows he understood, more or less; they watched him with badly concealed hostility. But he had some trouble meeting Gaines' eyes.

The settlement leader inclined his head. "Welcome, gentlemen. Won't you come in?"

Mackenzie dismounted, hitched his horse to a post and removed his helmet. His worn reddish-brown uniform felt shabbier yet in these surroundings. "Thanks. Uh, I'll have to make this quick."

"To be sure. Follow me, please."

Stiff-backed, the young men trailed their elders through an entry chamber and down a short hall. Speyer looked around at the mosaics. "Why, this is lovely," he murmured.

"Thank you," said Gaines. "Here's my office." He opened a door of superbly grained walnut and gestured the visitors through. When he closed it behind himself, the acolytes waited outside.

The room was austere, whitewashed walls enclosing little more than a desk, a shelf of books, and some backless chairs. A window opened on a garden. Gaines sat down. Mackenzie and Speyer followed suit, uncomfortable on this furniture.

"We'd better get right to business," the colonel blurted.

Gaines said nothing. At last Mackenzie must plow ahead:

"Here's the situation. Our force is to occupy Calistoga, with detachments on either side of the hills. That way we'll control both the Napa Valley and the Valley of the Moon… from the northern ends, at least. The best place to station our eastern wing is here. We plan to establish a fortified camp in the field yonder. I'm sorry about the damage to your crops, but you'll be compensated once the proper government has been restored. And food, medicine—you understand this army has to requisition such items, but we won't let anybody suffer undue hardship and we'll give receipts. Uh, as a precaution, we'll need to quarter a few men in this community, to sort of keep an eye on things. They'll interfere as little as possible. Okay?"

"The charter of the Order guarantees exemption from military requirements," Gaines answered evenly. "In fact, no armed man is supposed to cross the boundary of any land held by an Esper settlement. I cannot be a party to a violation of the law, Colonel."

"If you want to split legal hairs, Philosopher," Speyer said, "then I'll remind you that both Fallon and Judge Brodsky have declared martial law. Ordinary rules are suspended."

Gaines smiled. "Since only one government can be legitimate," he said, "the proclamations of the other are necessarily null and void. To a disinterested observer, it would appear that Judge Fallon's title is the stronger, especially when his side controls a large continuous area rather than some scattered bossdoms."

"Not any more, it doesn't," Mackenzie snapped.

Speyer gestured him back. "Perhaps you haven't followed the developments of the last few weeks, Philosopher," he said. "Allow me to recapitulate. The Sierra Command stole a march on the Fallonites and came down out of the mountains. There was almost nothing left in the middle part of California to oppose us, so we took over rapidly. By occupying Sacramento, we control river and rail traffic. Our bases extend south below Bakersfield, with Yosemite and King's Canyon not far away to provide sites for extremely strong positions. When we've

consolidated this northern end of our gains, the Fallonite forces around
Redding will be trapped between us and the powerful bossmen who still
hold out in the Trinity, Shasta, and Lassen regions. The very fact of our
being here has forced the enemy to evacuate the Columbia Valley, so
that San Francisco may be defended. It's an open question which side
today has the last word in the larger territory."

"What about the army that went into the Sierra against you?" Gaines
inquired shrewdly. "Have you contained them?"

Mackenzie scowled. "No. That's no secret. They got out through
the Mother Lode country and went around us. They're down in Los
Angeles and San Diego now."

"A formidable host. Do you expect to stand them off indefinitely?"

"We're going to make a hell of a good try," Mackenzie said. "Where
we are, we've got the advantage of interior communications. And most
of the freeloaders are glad to slip us word about whatever they observe.
We can concentrate at any point the enemy starts to attack."

"Pity that this rich land must also be torn apart by war."

"Yeah. Isn't it?"

"Our strategic objective is obvious enough," Speyer said. "We have
cut enemy communications across the middle, except by sea, which
is not very satisfactory for troops operating far inland. We deny him
access to a good part of his food and manufactured supplies, and most
especially to the bulk of his fuel alcohol. The backbone of our own
side is the bossdoms, which are almost self-contained economic and
social units. Before long they'll be in better shape than the rootless
army they face. I think Judge Brodsky will be back in San Francisco
before fall."

"If your plans succeed," Gaines said.

"That's our worry." Mackenzie leaned forward, one fist doubled on
his knee. "Okay, Philosopher. I know you'd rather see Fallon come out
on top, but I expect you've got more sense than to sign up in a lost
cause. Will you cooperate with us?"

"The Order takes no part in political affairs, Colonel, except when
its own existence is endangered."

"Oh, pipe down. By 'cooperate' I don't mean anything but keeping out from under our feet."

"I am afraid that would still count as cooperation. We cannot have military establishments on our lands."

Mackenzie stared at Gaines' face, which had set into granite lines, and wondered if he had heard aright. "Are you ordering us off?" a stranger asked with his voice.

"Yes," the Philosopher said.

"With our artillery zeroed in on your town?"

"Would you really shell women and children, Colonel?"

O Nora—"We don't need to. Our men can walk right in."

"Against psi blasts? I beg you not to have those poor boys destroyed." Gaines paused, then: "I might also point out that by losing your regiment, you imperil your whole cause. You are free to march around our holdings and proceed to Calistoga."

Leaving a Fallonite nest at my back, spang across my communications southward. The teeth grated together in Mackenzie's mouth.

Gaines rose. "The discussion is at an end, gentlemen," he said. "You have one hour to get off our lands."

Mackenzie and Speyer stood up too. "We're not done yet," the major said. Sweat studded his forehead and the long nose. "I want to make some further explanations."

Gaines crossed the room and opened the door. "Show these gentlemen out," he said to the five acolytes.

"No, by God!" Mackenzie shouted. He clapped a hand to his sidearm.

"Inform the adepts," Gaines said.

One of the young men turned. Mackenzie heard the slap-slap of his sandals running down the hall. Gaines nodded. "I think you had better go," he said.

Speyer grew rigid. His eyes shut. They flew open and he breathed. "*Inform* the adepts?"

Mackenzie saw the stiffness break in Gaines' countenance. There was no time for more than a second's bewilderment. His body acted for him.   The gun clanked from his holster simultaneously with Speyer's.

"Get that messenger, Jimbo," the major rapped. "I'll keep these birds covered."

As he plunged forward, Mackenzie found himself worrying about the regimental honor. Was it right to open hostilities when you had come on a parley? But Gaines had cut the talk off himself—"Stop him!" Gaines yelled. The four remaining acolytes sprang into motion. Two of them barred the doorway, the other two moved in on either side. "Hold it or I'll shoot!" Speyer cried, and was ignored.

Mackenzie couldn't bring himself to fire on unarmed men. He gave the youngster before him the pistol barrel in his teeth. Bloody-faced, the Esper lurched back. Mackenzie stiff-armed the one coming in from the left. The third tried to fill the doorway. Mackenzie put a foot behind his ankles and pushed. As he went down, Mackenzie kicked him in the temple, hard enough to stun, and jumped over him.

The fourth was on his back. Mackenzie writhed about to face the man. Those arms that hugged him, pinioning his gun, were bear strong. Mackenzie put the butt of his free left hand under the fellow's nose and pushed. The acolyte must let go. Mackenzie gave him a knee in the stomach, whirled, and ran.

There was not much further commotion behind him. Phil must have them under control. Mackenzie pelted along the hall, into the entry chamber. Where had that goddamn runner gone? He looked out the open entrance, onto the square. Sunlight hurt his eyes. His breath came in painful gulps, there was a stitch in his side; yeah, he was getting old.

Blue robes fluttered from a street. Mackenzie recognized the messenger. The youth pointed at this building. A gabble of his words drifted faintly through Mackenzie's pulse. There were seven or eight men with him—older men, nothing to mark their clothes… but Mackenzie knew a high-ranking officer when he saw one. The acolyte was dismissed. Those whom he had summoned crossed the square with long strides.

Terror knotted Mackenzie's bowels. He put it down. A Catamount didn't stampede, even from somebody who could turn him inside out with a look. He could do nothing about the wretchedness that followed though. *If they clobber me, so much the better. I won't have to lie awake nights wondering how Laura is.*

The adepts were almost to the steps. Mackenzie trod forth. He swept his revolver in an arc. "Halt!" His voice sounded tiny in the stillness that brooded over the town.

They jarred to a stop and stood there in a group. He saw them enforce a catlike relaxation, and their faces became blank visors. None spoke. Finally Mackenzie was unable to keep silent.

"This place is hereby occupied under the laws of war," he said. "Go back to your quarters."

"What have you done with our leader?" asked a tall man. His voice was even but deeply resonant.

"Read my mind and find out," Mackenzie gibed. *No, you're being childish.* "He's okay, long's he keeps his nose clean. You too. Beat it."

"We do not wish to pervert psionics to violence," said the tall man. "Please do not force us."

"Your chief sent for you before we'd done anything," Mackenzie retorted. "Looks like violence was what he had in mind. On your way."

The Espers exchanged glances. The tall man nodded. His companions walked slowly off. "I would like to see Philosopher Gaines," the tall man said.

"You will pretty soon."

"Am I to understand that he is being held a prisoner?"

"Understand what you like." The other Espers were rounding the corner of the building. "I don't want to shoot. Go on back before I have to."

"An impasse of sorts," the tall man said. "Neither of us wishes to injure one whom he considers defenseless. Allow me to conduct you off these grounds."

Mackenzie wet his lips. Weather had chapped them rough. "If you can put a hex on me, go ahead," he challenged. "Otherwise scram."

"Well, I shall not hinder you from rejoining your men. It seems the easiest way of getting you to leave. But I most solemnly warn that any armed force that tries to enter will be annihilated."

Guess I had better go get the guys, at that. Phil can't mount guard on those guys forever.

The tall man went over to the hitching post. "Which of these horses is yours?" he asked blandly.

Almighty eager to get rid of me, isn't he—Holy hellfire! There must be a rear door!

Mackenzie spun on his heel. The Esper shouted. Mackenzie dashed back through the entry chamber. His boots threw echoes at him. No, not to the left, there's only the office that way. Right... around this corner—

A long hall stretched before him. A stairway curved from the middle. The other Espers were already on it.

"Halt!" Mackenzie called. "Stop or I'll shoot!"

The two men in the lead sped onward. The rest turned and headed down again, toward him.

He fired with care, to disable rather than kill. The hall reverberated with the explosions. One after another they dropped, a bullet in leg or hip or shoulder. With such small targets, Mackenzie missed some shots. As the tall man, the last of them, closed in from behind, the hammer clicked on an empty chamber.

Mackenzie drew his saber and gave him the flat of it alongside the head. The Esper lurched. Mackenzie got past and bounded up the stair. It wound like something in a nightmare. He thought his heart was going to go to pieces.

At the end, an iron door opened on a landing. One man was fumbling with the lock. The other blue-robe attacked.

Mackenzie stuck his sword between the Esper's legs. As his opponent stumbled, the colonel threw a left hook to the jaw. The man sagged against the wall. Mackenzie grabbed the robe of the other and hurled him to the floor. "Get out," he rattled.

They pulled themselves together and glared at him. He thrust air with his blade. "From now on, I aim to kill," he said.

"Get help, Dave," said the one who had been opening the door. "I'll watch him." The other went unevenly down the stairs. The first man stood out of saber reach. "Do you want to be destroyed?" he asked.

Mackenzie turned the knob at his back, but the door was still locked. "I don't think you can do it," he said. "Not without what's here."

The Esper struggled for self-control. They waited through minutes that stretched. Then a noise began below. The Esper pointed. "We have nothing but agricultural implements," he said, "but you have only that blade. Will you surrender?"

Mackenzie spat on the floor. The Esper went on down.

Presently the attackers came into view. There might be a hundred, judging from the hubbub behind him, but because of the curve, Mackenzie could see no more than ten or fifteen—burly field hands, their robes tucked high and sharp tools aloft. The landing was too wide for defense. He advanced to the stairway, where they could only come at him two at a time.

A couple of sawtoothed hay knives led the assault. Mackenzie parried one blow and chopped. His edge went into meat and struck bone. Blood ran out, impossibly red even in the dim light here. The man fell to all fours with a shriek. Mackenzie dodged a cut from the companion. Metal clashed on metal. The weapons locked. Mackenzie's arm was forced back. He looked into a broad, suntanned face. The side of his hand smote the young man's larynx. The Esper fell against the one behind and they went down together. It took a while to clear the tangle and resume action.

A pitchfork thrust for the colonel's belly. He managed to grab it with his left hand, divert the tines and chop at the fingers on the shaft. A scythe gashed his right side. He saw his own blood but wasn't aware of pain. A flesh wound, no more. He swept his saber back and forth. The forefront retreated from its whistling menace. *But God, my knees are like rubber. I can't hold out another five minutes.*

A bugle sounded. There was a spatter of gunfire. The mob on the staircase congealed. Someone screamed.

Hoofs banged across the ground floor. A voice rasped: "Hold everything, there! Drop those weapons and come on down. First man tries anything gets shot!"

Mackenzie leaned on his saber and fought for air. He hardly noticed the Espers melt away.

When he felt a little better, he went to one of the small windows and looked out. Horsemen were in the plaza. Not yet in sight, but nearing, he heard infantry.

Speyer arrived, followed by a sergeant of engineers and several privates. The major hurried to Mackenzie. "You okay, Jimbo? You been hurt!"

"A scratch," Mackenzie said. He was getting back his strength, though no sense of victory accompanied it, only the knowledge of aloneness. The injury began to sting. "Not worth a fuss. Look."

"Yes, I suppose you'll live. Okay, men, get that door open."

The engineers took forth their tools and assailed the lock with a vigor that must spring half from fear. "How'd you guys show up so soon?" Mackenzie asked.

"I thought there'd be trouble," Speyer said, "so when I heard shots, I jumped through the window and ran around to my horse. That was just before those clodhoppers attacked you; I saw them gathering as I rode out. Our cavalry got in almost at once of course, and the dogfaces weren't far behind."

"Any resistance?"

"No, not after we fired a few rounds in the air." Speyer glanced outside. "We're in full possession now."

Mackenzie regarded the door. "Well," he said, "I feel better about our having pulled guns on them in the office. Looks like their adepts really depend on plain old weapons, huh? And Esper communities aren't supposed to have arms. Their charters say so… That was a damn good guess of yours, Phil. How'd you do it?"

"I sort of wondered why the chief had to send a runner to fetch guys that claim to be telepaths. There we go!"

The lock jingled apart. The sergeant opened the door. Mackenzie and Speyer went into the great room under the dome.

They walked around for a long time, wordless, among shapes of metal and less identifiable substances. Nothing was familiar. Mackenzie paused at last before a helix that projected from a transparent cube. Formless darknesses swirled within the box, sparked as if with tiny stars.

"I figured maybe the Espers had found a cache of old-time stuff, from just before the Hell bombs," he said in a muffled voice. "Ultra-secret weapons that never got a chance to be used. But this doesn't look like it. Think so?"

"No," Speyer said. "It doesn't look to me as if these things were made by human beings at all."

"But do you not understand? They occupied a settlement! That proves to the world that Espers are not invulnerable. And to complete the catastrophe, they seized its arsenal."

"Have no fears about that. No untrained person can activate those instruments. The circuits are locked except in the presence of certain encephalic rhythms that result from conditioning. That same conditioning makes it impossible for the so-called adepts to reveal any of their knowledge to the uninitiated, no matter what may be done to them."

"Yes, I know that much. But it is not what I had in mind. What frightens me is the fact that the revelation will spread. Everyone will know the Esper adepts do not plumb unknown depths of the psyche after all, but merely have access to an advanced physical science. Not only will this lift rebel spirits, but worse, it will cause many, perhaps most, of the Order's members to break away in disillusionment."

"Not at once. News travels slowly under present conditions. Also, Mwyr, you underestimate the ability of the human mind to ignore data that conflict with cherished beliefs."

"But–"

"Well, let us assume the worst. Let us suppose that faith is lost and the Order disintegrates. That will be a serious setback to the plan, but not a fatal one. Psionics was merely one bit of folklore we found potent enough to serve as the motivator of a new orientation toward life. There are others; for example the widespread belief in magic among the less-educated classes. We can begin again on a different basis if we must. The exact form of the creed is not important. It is only scaffolding for the real structure: a communal, antimaterialistic social group to which more and more people will turn for sheer lack of anything else as the coming empire breaks up. In the end, the new culture can and will discard whatever superstitions gave it the initial impetus."

"A hundred-year setback, at least."

"True. It would be much more difficult to introduce a radical alien element now, when the autochthonous society has developed strong institutions of its own, than it was in the past. I merely wish to reassure you that the task is not impossible. I do not actually propose to let matters go that far. The Espers can be salvaged."

"How?"

"We must intervene directly."

"Has that been computed as being unavoidable?"

"Yes. The matrix yields an unambiguous answer. I do not like it any better than you. But direct action occurs oftener than we tell neophytes in the schools. The most elegant procedure would of course be to establish such initial conditions in a society that its evolution along desired lines becomes automatic. Furthermore, that would let us close our minds to the distressing fact of our own blood guilt. Unfortunately, the Great Science does not extend down to the details of day-to-day practicality.

"In the present instance, we shall help to smash the reactionaries. The government will then proceed so harshly against its conquered opponents that many of those who accept the story about what was found at St. Helena will not live to spread the tale. The rest... well, they will be discredited by their own defeat. Admittedly the story will linger for lifetimes, whispered here and there. But what of that? Those who believe in the Way will, as a rule, simply be strengthened in their faith by the very process of denying such ugly rumors. As more and more persons, common citizens as well as Espers, reject materialism, the legend will seem more and more fantastic. It will seem obvious that certain ancients invented the tale to account for a fact that they in their ignorance were unable to comprehend."

"I see..."

"You are not happy here, are you, Mwyr?"

"I cannot quite say. Everything is so distorted."

"Be glad you were not sent to one of the really alien planets."

"I might almost prefer that. There would be a hostile environment to think about. One could forget how far it is to home."

"Three years' travel."

"You say that so glibly. As if three shipboard years were not equal to fifty in cosmic time. As if we could expect a relief vessel daily, not once in a century. And... as if the region that our ships have explored amounts to one chip out of this one galaxy!"

"That region will grow until someday it engulfs the galaxy."

"Yes, yes, yes, I know. Why do you think I chose to become a psychodynamician? Why am I here, learning how to meddle with the destiny of the world where I do not belong? 'To create the union of sentient beings, each member species a step toward life's mastery of the universe.' Brave slogan! But in practice it seems that only a chosen few races are to be allowed the freedom of that universe."

"Not so, Mwyr. Consider these ones with whom we are, as you say, meddling. Consider what use they made of nuclear energy when they had it. At the rate they are going, they will have it again within a century or two. Not long after that they will be building spaceships. Even granted that time lag attenuates the effects of interstellar contact, those effects are cumulative. So do you wish such a band of carnivores turned loose on the galaxy?

"No, let them become inwardly civilized first; then we shall see if they can be trusted. If not, they will at least be happy on their own planet in a mode of life designed for them by the Great Science. Remember, they have an immemorial aspiration toward peace on earth; but that is something they will never achieve by themselves. I do not pretend to be a very good person, Mwyr. Yet this work that we are doing makes me feel not altogether useless in the cosmos."

Promotion was fast that year, casualties being so high. Captain Thomas Danielis was raised to major for his conspicuous part in putting down the revolt of the Los Angeles citymen. Soon after occurred the Battle of Maricopa, when the loyalists failed bloodily to break the stranglehold of the Sierran rebels on the San Joaquin Valley, and he was brevetted lieutenant colonel. The army was ordered northward and moved warily under the coast ranges, half expecting attack from the east. But the Brodskyites seemed too busy consolidating their latest gains. The trouble came from guerrillas and the hedgehog resistance of bossman Stations. After one particularly stiff clash, they stopped near Pinnacles for a breather.

Danielis made his way through camp, where tents stood in tight rows between the guns and men lay about dozing, talking, gambling, staring at the blank blue sky. The air was hot, pungent with cookfire smoke, horses, mules, dung, sweat, boot oil; the green of the hills that lifted around the site was dulling toward summer brown. He was idle until time for the conference the general had called, but restlessness drove him. *By now I'm a father*, he thought, *and I've never seen my kid.*

At that, I'm lucky, he reminded himself. *I've got my life and limbs.* He remembered Jacobsen dying in his arms at Maricopa. You wouldn't have thought the human body could hold so much blood. Though maybe one was no longer human when the pain was so great that one could do nothing but shriek until the darkness came.

And I used to think war was glamorous. Hunger, thirst, exhaustion, terror, mutilation, death, and forever the sameness, boredom grinding you down to an ox... I've had it. I'm going into business after the war. Economic integration as the bossman system breaks up; yes, there'll be a lot of ways for a man to get ahead, but decently, without a weapon in his hand—Danielis realized he was repeating thoughts that were months old. What the hell else was there to think about though?

The large tent where prisoners were interrogated lay near his path. A couple of privates were conducting a man inside. The fellow was blond, burly, and sullen. He wore a sergeant's stripes but otherwise his only item of uniform was the badge of Warden Echevarry, bossman in this part of the coastal mountains. A lumberjack in peacetime, Danielis guessed from the look of him; a soldier in a private army whenever the interests of Echevarry were threatened; captured in yesterday's engagement.

On impulse, Danielis followed. He got into the tent as Captain Lambert, chubby behind a portable desk, finished the preliminaries, and blinked in the sudden gloom.

"Oh." The intelligence officer started to rise. "Yes, sir?"

"At ease," Danielis said. "Just thought I'd listen in."

"Well, I'll try to put on a good show for you." Lambert reseated himself and looked at the prisoner, who stood with hunched shoulders and widespread legs between his guards. "Now, Sergeant, we'd like to know a few things."

"I don't have to say nothing except name, rank, and home town," the man growled. "You got those."

"Um-m-m, that's questionable. You aren't a foreign soldier, you're in rebellion against the government of your own country."

"The hell I am! I'm an Echevarry man."

"So what?"

"So my Judge is whoever Echevarry says. He says Brodsky. That makes you the rebel."

"The law's been changed."

"Your mucking Fallon got no right to change any laws. Especially part of the Constitution. I'm no hillrunner, Captain. I went to school some. And every year our Warden reads his people the Constitution."

"Times have changed since it was drawn," Lambert said. His tone sharpened. "But I'm not going to argue with you. How many riflemen and how many archers in your company?"

Silence.

"We can make things a lot easier for you," Lambert said. "I'm not asking you to do anything treasonable. All I want is to confirm some information I've already got."

The man shook his head angrily.

Lambert gestured. One of the privates stepped behind the captive, took his arm and twisted a little.

"Echevarry wouldn't do that to me," he said through white lips.

"Of course not," Lambert said. "You're his man."

"Think I wanna be just a number on some list in Frisco? Damn right I'm my bossman's man!"

Lambert gestured again. The private twisted harder.

"Hold on, there," Danielis barked. "Stop that!"

The private let go, looking surprised. The prisoner drew a sobbing breath.

"I'm amazed at you, Captain Lambert," Danielis said. He felt his own face reddening. "If this has been your usual practice, there's going to be a court-martial."

"No, sir," Lambert said in a small voice. "Honest. Only... they don't talk. Hardly any of them. What'm I supposed to do?"

"Follow the rules of war."

"With rebels?"

"Take that man away," Danielis ordered. The privates made haste to do so.

"Sorry, sir," Lambert muttered. "I guess... I guess I've lost too many buddies. I hate to lose more simply for lack of information."

"Me too." A compassion rose in Danielis. He sat down on the table edge and began to roll a cigarette. "But you see, we aren't in a regular war. And so, by a curious paradox, we have to follow the conventions more carefully than ever before."

"I don't quite understand, sir."

Danielis finished the cigarette and gave it to Lambert: olive branch or something. He started another for himself. "The rebels aren't rebels by their own lights," he said. "They're being loyal to a tradition that we're trying to curb, eventually to destroy. Let's face it, the average bossman is a fairly good leader. He may be descended from some thug who grabbed power by strong-arm methods during the chaos, but by now his family's integrated itself with the region he rules. He knows it, and its people, inside out. He's there in the flesh, a symbol of the community and its achievements, its folkways and essential independence. If you're in trouble, you don't have to work through some impersonal bureaucracy, you go direct to your bossman. His duties are as clearly defined as your own, and a good deal more demanding, to balance his privileges. He leads you in battle and in the ceremonies that give color and meaning to life. Your fathers and his have worked and played together for two or three hundred years. The land is alive with the memories of them. You and he belong.

"Well, that has to be swept away so that we can go on to a higher level. But we won't reach that level by alienating everyone. We're not a conquering army; we're more like the Householder Guard putting down a riot in some city. The opposition is part and parcel of our own society."

Lambert struck a match for him. He inhaled and finished: "On a practical plane, I might also remind you, Captain, that the federal armed forces, Fallonite and Brodskyite together, are none too large. Little more than a cadre, in fact. We're a bunch of younger sons, countrymen who failed, poor citymen, adventurers, people who look to their regiment for that sense of wholeness they've grown up to expect and can't find in civilian life."

"You're too deep for me, sir, I'm afraid," Lambert said.

"Never mind," Danielis sighed. "Just bear in mind, there are a good many more fighting men outside the opposing armies than in. If the bossmen could establish a unified command, that'd be the end of the Fallon government. Luckily, there's too much provincial pride and too much geography between them for this to happen—unless we outrage them beyond endurance. What we want the ordinary freeholder, and even the ordinary bossman, to think, is: 'Well, those Fallonites aren't such bad guys, and if I keep on the right side of them, I don't stand to lose much and should even be able to gain something at the expense of those who fight them to the finish.' You see?"

"Y-yes. I guess so."

"You're a smart fellow, Lambert. You don't have to beat information out of prisoners. Trick it out."

"I'll try, sir."

"Good." Danielis glanced at the watch that had been given him as per tradition, together with a sidearm, when he was first commissioned. (Such items were much too expensive for the common man. They had not been so in the age of mass production; and perhaps in the coming age—) "I have to go. See you around."

He left the tent feeling somewhat more cheerful than before. *No doubt I am a natural-born preacher*, he admitted, *and I never could quite join in the horseplay at mess, and a lot of jokes go completely by me; but if I can get even a few ideas across where they count, that's pleasure enough.* A strain of music came to him, some men and a banjo under a tree, and he found himself whistling along. It was good that this much morale remained after Maricopa and a northward march whose purpose had not been divulged to anybody.

The conference tent was big enough to be called a pavilion. Two sentries stood at the entrance. Danielis was nearly the last to arrive and found himself at the end of the table, opposite Brigadier General Perez. Smoke hazed the air and there was a muted buzz of conversation, but faces were taut.

When the blue-robed figure with a Yang and Yin on the breast entered, silence fell like a curtain. Danielis was astonished to recognize Philosopher Woodworth. He'd last seen the man in Los Angeles and assumed he would stay at the Esper center there. Must have come here by special conveyance, under special orders...

Perez introduced him. Both remained standing, under the eyes of the officers. "I have some important news for you, gentlemen," Perez said most quietly. "You may consider it an honor to be here. It means that in my judgment you can be trusted, first, to keep absolute silence about what you are going to hear, and second, to execute a vital operation of extreme difficulty." Danielis was made shockingly aware that several men were not present whose rank indicated they should be.

"I repeat," Perez said, "any breach of secrecy and the whole plan is ruined. In that case, the war will drag on for months or years. You know how bad our position is. You also know it will grow still worse as our stocks of those supplies the enemy now denies us are consumed. We could even be beaten. I'm not defeatist to say that, only realistic. We could lose the war. On the other hand, if this new scheme pans out, we may break the enemy's back this very month."

He paused to let that sink in before continuing: "The plan was worked out by GHQ in conjunction with Esper Central in San Francisco some weeks ago. It's the reason we are headed north." He let the gasp subside that ran through the stifling air. "Yes, you know that the Esper Order is neutral in political disputes. But you also know that it defends itself when attacked. And you probably know that an attack was made on it by the rebels. They seized the Napa Valley settlement and have been spreading malicious rumors about the Order since then. Would you like to comment on that, Philosopher Woodworth?"

The man in blue nodded and said coolly: "We've our own ways of findin' out things—intelligence service, you might say—so I can give y'all a report of the facts. St. Helena was assaulted at a time when most of its adepts were away, helpin' a new community get started out in Montana." *How did they travel so fast?* Danielis wondered. *Teleport, or what?* "I don't know, myself, if the enemy knew about that or was just lucky. Anyhow, when the two or three adepts that were left came and warned them off, fightin' broke out and the adepts were killed before they could act." He smiled. "We don't claim to be immortal, except the way every livin' thing is immortal. Nor infallible either. So now St. Helena's occupied. We don't figure to take any immediate steps about that, because a lot of people in the community might get hurt.

"As for the yams the enemy command's been handin' out, well, I reckon I'd do the same if I had a chance like that. Everybody knows an adept can do things that nobody else can. Troops that realize they've done wrong to the Order are goin' to be scared of supernatural revenge. You're educated men here and know there's nothin' supernatural involved, just a way to use the powers latent in most of us. You also know the Order doesn't believe in revenge. But the ordinary foot soldier doesn't think your way. His officers have got to restore his spirit somehow. So they fake some equipment and tell him that's what the adepts were really usin'—an advanced technology, sure, but only a set of machines that can be put out of action if you're brave, same as any other machine. That's what happened.

"Still, it is a threat to the Order; and we can't let an attack on our people go unpunished either. So Esper Central has decided to help out your side. The sooner this war's over, the better for everybody."

A sigh gusted around the table, and a few exultant oaths. The hair stirred on Danielis' neck. Perez lifted a hand. "Not too fast, please," the general said. "The adepts are not going to go around blasting your opponents for you. It was one hell of a tough decision for them to do as much as they agreed to. I, uh, understand that the, uh, personal development of every Esper will be set back many years by this much violence. They're making a big sacrifice. By their charter, they can use psionics to defend an establishment against attack. Okay... an assault on San Francisco will be construed as one on Central, their world headquarters."

The realization of what was to come was blinding to Danielis. He scarcely heard Perez' carefully dry continuation:

"Let's review the strategic picture. By now the enemy holds more than half of California, all of Oregon and Idaho, and a good deal of Washington. We, this army, we're using the last land access to San

Francisco that we've got. The enemy hasn't tried to pinch that off yet, because the troops we pulled out of the north—those that aren't in the field at present—make a strong city garrison that'd sally out. He's collecting too much profit elsewhere to accept the cost. "Nor can he invest the city with any hope of success. We still hold Puget Sound and the southern California ports. Our ships bring in ample food and munitions. His own sea power is much inferior to ours: chiefly schooners donated by coastal bossmen, operating out of Portland. He might overwhelm an occasional convoy, but he hasn't tried that so far because it isn't worth his trouble; there would be others, more heavily escorted. And of course he can't enter the Bay, with artillery and rocket emplacements on both sides of the Golden Gate. No, about all he can do is maintain some water communication with Hawaii and Alaska.

"Nevertheless, his ultimate object is San Francisco. It has to be— the seat of government and industry, the heart of the nation. Well, then, here's the plan. Our army is to engage the Sierra Command and its militia auxiliaries again, striking out of San Jose. That's a perfectly logical maneuver. Successful, it would cut his California forces in two. We know, in fact, that he is already concentrating men in anticipation of precisely such an attempt.

"We aren't going to succeed. We'll give him a good stiff battle and be thrown back. That's the hardest part: to feign a serious defeat, even convincing our own troops, and still maintain good order. We'll have a lot of details to thresh out about that. We'll retreat northward, up the Peninsula toward Frisco. The enemy is bound to pursue. It will look like a God-given chance to destroy us and get to the city walls.

"When he is well into the Peninsula, with the ocean on his left and the Bay on his right, we will outflank him and attack from the rear. The Esper adepts will be there to help. Suddenly he'll be caught between us and the capital's land defenses. What the adepts don't wipe out, we will. Nothing will remain of the Sierra Command but a few garrisons. The rest of the war will be a mopping-up operation.

"It's a brilliant piece of strategy. Like all such, it's damn difficult to execute. Are you prepared to do the job?"

Danielis didn't raise his voice with the others. He was thinking too hard of Laura.

Northward and to the right there was some fighting. Cannon spoke occasionally, or a drumfire of rifles; smoke lay thin over the grass and the wind-gnarled live oaks that covered those hills. But down along the seacoast there was only surf, blowing air, a hiss of sand across the dunes.

Mackenzie rode on the beach, where the footing was easiest and the view widest. Most of his regiment was inland. But that was a wilderness: rough ground, woods, the snags of ancient homes, making travel slow and hard. Once this area had been densely peopled, but the firestorm after the Hellbomb scrubbed it clean and today's reduced population could not make a go on such infertile soil. There didn't even seem to be any foemen near this left wing of the army.

The Rolling Stones had certainly not been given it for that reason. They could have borne the brunt at the center as well as those outfits which actually were there, driving the enemy back toward San Francisco. They had been blooded often enough in this war, when they operated out of Calistoga to help expel the Fallonites from northern California. So thoroughly had that job been done that now only a skeleton force need remain in charge. Nearly the whole Sierra Command had gathered at Modesto, met the northward-moving opposition army that struck at them out of San Jose and sent it in a shooting retreat. Another day or so and the white city should appear before their eyes.

And there the enemy will be sure to make a stand, Mackenzie thought, *with the garrison to reinforce him. And his positions will have to be shelled; maybe we'll have to take the place street by street. Laura, kid, will you be alive at the end?*

Of course, maybe it won't happen that way. Maybe my scheme'll work and we'll win easy—what a horrible word "maybe" is! He slapped his hands together with a pistol sound.

Speyer threw him a glance. The major's people were safe; he'd even been able to visit them at Mount Lassen after the northern campaign was over. "Rough," he said.

"Rough on everybody," Mackenzie said with a thick anger. "This is a filthy war."

Speyer shrugged. "No different from most, except that this time Pacificans are on the receiving as well as the giving end."

"You know damn well I never liked the business, not anyplace."

"What man in his right mind does?"

"When I want a sermon, I'll ask for one."

"Sorry," said Speyer, and meant it.

"I'm sorry too," said Mackenzie, instantly contrite. "Nerves on edge. Damnation! I could almost wish for some action."

"Wouldn't be surprised if we got some. This whole affair smells wrong to me."

Mackenzie looked around. On the right the horizon was bounded by hills beyond which the low but massive San Bruno range lifted. Here and there he spied one of his own squads, afoot or ahorse. Overhead sputtered a plane. But there was plenty of concealment for a redoubt. Hell could erupt at any minute… though necessarily a small hell, quickly reduced by howitzer or bayonet, casualties light. (Huh! Every one of those light casualties was a man dead, with women and children to weep for him, or a man staring at the fragment of his arm, or a man with eyes and face gone in a burst of shot, and what kind of unsoldierly thoughts were these?)

Seeking comfort, Mackenzie glanced left. The ocean rolled greenish-gray, glittering far out, rising and breaking in a roar of white combers closer to land. He smelled salt and kelp. A few gulls mewed above dazzling sands. There was no sail or smoke-puff—only emptiness. The convoys from Puget Sound to San Francisco and the lean swift ships of the coastal bossmen were miles beyond the curve of the world.

Which was as it should be. Maybe things were working out okay on the high waters. One could only try, and hope. And… it had been his suggestion, James Mackenzie speaking at the conference General Cruik-shank held between the battles of Mariposa and San Jose; the same James Mackenzie who had first proposed that the Sierra Command come down out of the mountains, and who had exposed the gigantic fraud of Esperdom, and succeeded in playing down for his men the fact that behind the fraud lay a mystery one hardly dared think about. He would endure in the chronicles, that colonel, they would sing ballads about him for half a thousand years.

Only it didn't feel mat way. James Mackenzie knew he was not much more than average bright under the best of conditions, now dull-minded with weariness and terrified of his daughter's fate. For himself he was haunted by the fear of certain crippling wounds. Often he had to drink himself to sleep. He was shaved, because an officer must maintain appearances, but realized very well that if he hadn't had an orderly to do the job for him, he would be as shaggy as any buck private. His uniform was faded and threadbare, his body stank and itched, his mouth yearned for tobacco but there had been some trouble in the commissariat and they were lucky to eat. His achievements amounted to patchwork jobs carried out in utter confusion, or to slogging like this and wishing only for an end to the whole mess. One day, win or lose, his body would give out on him—he could feel the machinery wearing to pieces, arthritic twinges, shortness of breath, dozing off in the middle of things—and the termination of himself would be as undignified and lonely as that of every other human slob. Hero? What an all-time laugh!

He yanked his mind back to the immediate situation. Behind him a core of the regiment accompanied the artillery along the beach, a thousand men with motorized gun carriages, caissons, mule-drawn wagons, a few trucks, one precious armored car. They were a dun mass topped with helmets, in loose formation, rifles or bows to hand. The sand deadened their footfalls so that only the surf and the wind could be heard. But whenever the wind sank, Mackenzie caught the tune of the hex corps: a dozen leathery older men, mostly Indians, carrying the wands of power and whistling together the Song Against Witches. He took no stock in magic himself, yet when that sound came to him, the skin crawled along his backbone.

Everything's in good order, he insisted. *We're doing fine.*

Then: *But Phil's right. This is a screwball business. The enemy should have fought through to a southward line of retreat, not let themselves be boxed.*

Captain Hulse galloped close. Sand spurted when he checked his horse. "Patrol report, sir."

"Well?" Mackenzie realized he had almost shouted. "Go ahead."

"Considerable activity observed about five miles east. Looks like a troop headed our way."

Mackenzie stiffened. "Haven't you anything more definite than that?"

"Not so far, with the ground so broken."

"Get some aerial reconnaissance there, for Pete's sake!"

"Yes, sir. I'll throw out some more scouts too."

"Carry on here, Phil." Mackenzie headed toward the radio truck. He carried a minicom in his saddlebag, of course, but San Francisco had been continuously jamming on all bands and you needed a powerful set to punch a signal even a few miles. Patrols must communicate by messenger.

He noticed that the firing inland had slacked off. There were decent roads in the interior Peninsula a ways farther north, where some resettlement had taken place. The enemy, still in possession of that area, could use them to effect rapid movements.

If they withdrew their center and hit our flanks, where we're weakest—

A voice from field HQ, barely audible through the squeals and buzzes, took his report and gave back what had been seen elsewhere. Large maneuvers right and left, yes, it did seem as if the Fallonites were going to try a breakthrough. Could be a feint though. The main body of the Sierrans must remain where it was until the situation became clearer. The Rolling Stones must hold out a while on their own.

"Will do." Mackenzie returned to the head of his columns. Speyer nodded grimly at the word.

"Better get prepared, hadn't we?"

"Uh-huh." Mackenzie lost himself in a welter of commands as officer after officer rode to him. The outlying sections were to be pulled in. The beach was to be defended, with the high ground immediately above.

Men scurried, horses neighed, guns trundled about. The scout plane returned, flying low enough to get a transmission through: yes, definitely an attack on the way; hard to tell how big a force, through the damned tree cover and down in the damned arroyos, but it might well be at brigade strength.

Mackenzie established himself on a hilltop with his staff and runners. A line of artillery stretched beneath him, across the strand. Cavalry waited behind them, lances agleam, an infantry company for support. Otherwise the foot soldiers had faded into the landscape. The sea boomed its own cannonade, and gulls began to gather as if they knew there would be meat before long.

"Think we can hold them?" Speyer asked.

"Sure," Mackenzie said. "If they come down the beach, we'll enfilade them, as well as shooting up their front. If they come higher, well, that's a textbook example of defensible terrain. 'Course, if another troop punches through the lines farther inland, we'll be cut off, but that isn't our worry right now."

"They must hope to get around our army and attack our rear."

"Guess so. Not too smart of them though. We can approach Frisco just as easily fighting backwards as forwards."

"Unless the city garrison makes a sally."

"Even then. Total numerical strengths are about equal, and we've got more ammo and alky. Also a lot of bossman militia for auxiliaries, who're used to disorganized warfare in hilly ground."

"If we do whip them–" Speyer shut his lips together.

"Go on," Mackenzie said.

"Nothing."

"The hell it is. You were about to remind me of the next step: how do we take the city without too high a cost to both sides? Well, I happen to know we've got a hole card to play there which might help."

Speyer turned pitying eyes away from Mackenzie. Silence fell on the hilltop.

NO TRUCE WITH KINGS

It was an unconscionably long time before the enemy came in view, first a few outriders far down the dunes, then the body of him, pouring from the ridges and gullies and woods. Reports flickered about Mackenzie—a powerful force, nearly twice as big as ours but with little artillery; by now badly short of fuel, they must depend far more than we on animals to move their equipment. They were evidently going to charge, accept losses in order to get sabers and bayonets among the Rolling Stones' cannon. Mackenzie issued his directions accordingly.

The hostiles formed up, a mile or so distant. Through his field glasses Mackenzie recognized them, red sashes of the Madera Horse, green and gold pennon of the Dagos, fluttering in the iodine wind. He'd campaigned with both outfits in the past. It was treacherous to remember that Ives favored a blunt wedge formation and use the fact against him… One enemy armored car and some fieldpieces, light horse-drawn ones, gleamed wickedly in the sunlight.

Bugles blew shrill. The Fallonite cavalry laid lance in rest and started trotting. They gathered speed as they went, a canter, a gallop, until the earth trembled with them. Then their infantry got going, flanked by its guns. The car rolled along between the first and second line of foot. Oddly, it had no rocket launcher on top or repeater barrels thrust from the fire slits. Those were good troops, Mackenzie thought, advancing in close order with that ripple down the ranks which bespoke veterans. He hated what must happen.

His defense waited immobile on the sand. Fire crackled from the hillsides, where mortar squads and riflemen crouched. A rider toppled, a dogface clutched his belly and went to his knees, their companions behind moved forward to close the lines again. Mackenzie looked to his howitzers. Men stood tensed at sights and lanyards. Let the foe get well in range—There! Yamaguchi, mounted just rearward of the gunners, drew his saber and flashed the blade downward. Cannon bellowed. Fire spurted through smoke, sand gouted up, shrapnel sleeted over the charging force. At once the gun crews fell into the rhythm of reloading, relaying, refiling, the steady three rounds per minute which conserved barrels and broke armies. Horses screamed in then-own tangled red guts. But not many had been hit. The Madera cavalry continued in full gallop. Their lead was so close now that Mackenzie's glasses picked out a face, red, freckled, a ranch boy turned trooper, his mouth stretched out of shape as he yelled.

The archers behind the defending cannon let go. Arrows whistled skyward, flight after flight, curved past the gulls and down again. Flame and smoke ran ragged in the wiry hill grass, out of the ragged-leaved live oak copses. Men pitched to the sand, many still hideously astir, like insects that had been stepped on. The fieldpieces on the enemy's left flank halted, swiveled about and spat return fire. Futile… but God, their officer had courage! Mackenzie saw the advancing lines waver. An attack by his own horse and foot, down the beach, ought to crumple them. "Get ready to move," he said into his minicom. He saw his men poise. The cannon belched anew.

The oncoming armored car slowed to a halt. Something within it chattered, loud enough to hear through the explosions.

A blue-white sheet ran over the nearest hill. Mackenzie shut half-blinded eyes. When he opened them again, he saw a grass fire through the crazy patterns of afterimage. A Rolling Stone burst from cover, howling, his clothes ablaze.

The man hit the sand and rolled over. That part of the beach lifted in one monster wave, crested twenty feet high and smashed across the hill. The burning soldier vanished in the avalanche that buried his comrades.

"Psi blast!" someone screamed, thin and horrible, through chaos and ground shudder. "The Espers—

Unbelievably, a bugle sounded and the Sierran cavalry lunged forward. Past their own guns, on against the scattering opposition… and horses and riders rose into the air, tumbled in a giant's invisible whirligig, crashed bone-breakingly to earth again. The second rank of lancers broke. Mounts reared, pawed the air, wheeled and fled in every direction.

A terrible, deep hum filled the sky. Mackenzie saw the world as if through a haze, as if his brain were being dashed back and forth between the walls of his skull. Another glare ran across the hills, higher this time, burning men alive.

"They'll wipe us out," Speyer called, a dim voice that rose and fell on the air tides. "They'll re-form as we stampede—"

"No!" Mackenzie shouted. "The adepts must be in that car. Come on!"

Most of his horse had recoiled on their own artillery, one squealing, trampling wreck. The infantry stood rigid but about to bolt. A glance thrown to his right showed Mackenzie how the enemy themselves were in confusion; this had been a terrifying surprise to them too, but as soon as they got over the shock, they'd advance and there'd be nothing left to stop them... It was as if another man spurred his mount. The animal fought, foam-flecked with panic. He slugged its head around, brutally, and dug in spurs. They rushed down the hill toward the guns.

He needed all his strength to halt the gelding before the cannon mouths. A man slumped dead by his piece, though there was no mark on him. Mackenzie jumped to the ground. His steed bolted.

He hadn't time to worry about that. Where was help? "Come here!" His yell was lost in the riot. But suddenly another man was beside him, Speyer, snatching up a shell and slamming it into the breach. Mackenzie squinted through the telescope, took a bearing by guess and feel. He could see the Esper car where it squatted among the dead and hurt. At this distance it looked too small to have blackened acres.

Speyer helped him lay the howitzer. He jerked the lanyard. The gun roared and sprang. The shell burst a few yards short of target, sand spurted and metal fragments whined.

Speyer had the next one loaded. Mackenzie aimed and fired. Over-shot this time, but not by much. The car rocked. Concussion might have hurt the Espers inside; at least the psi blasts had stopped. But it was necessary to strike before the foe got organized again.

He ran toward his own regimental car. The door gaped, the crew had fled. He threw himself into the driver's seat. Speyer clanged the door shut and stuck his face in the hood of the rocket-launcher periscope.

Mackenzie raced the machine forward. The banner on its rooftop snapped in the wind.

Speyer aimed the launcher and pressed the firing button. The missile burned across intervening yards and exploded. The other car lurched on its wheels. A hole opened in its side.

If the boys will only rally and advance—if they don't, I'm done for anyway. Mackenzie squealed to a stop, flung open the door and leaped out. Curled, blackened metal framed his entry. He wriggled through, into murk and stenches.

Two Espers lay there. The driver was dead, a chunk of steel through his breast. The other one, the adept, whimpered among his inhuman instruments. His face was hidden by blood. Mackenzie pitched the corpse on its side and pulled off the robe. He snatched a curving tube of metal and tumbled back out.

Speyer was still in the undamaged car, firing repeaters at those hostiles who ventured near. Mackenzie jumped onto the ladder of the disabled machine, climbed to its roof and stood erect. He waved the blue robe in one hand and the weapon he did not understand in the other. "Come on, you sons!" he shouted, tiny against the sea wind. "We've knocked 'em out for you! Want your breakfast in bed too?"

One bullet buzzed past his ear. Nothing else. Most of the enemy, horse and foot, stayed frozen. In that immense stillness he could not tell if he heard surf or the blood in his own veins.

Then a bugle called. The hex corps whistled triumphantly; their tomtoms muttered. A ragged line of his infantry began to move toward him. More followed. The cavalry joined them, man by man and unit by unit, on their flanks. Soldiers ran down the smoking hillsides.

Mackenzie sprang to sand again and into his car. "Let's get back," he told Speyer. "We got a battle to finish."

"Shut up!" Tom Danielis said.

Philosopher Woodworth stared at him. Fog swirled and dripped in the forest, hiding the land and the brigade, gray nothingness through which came a muffled noise of men and horses and wheels, an isolated and infinitely weary sound. The air was cold, and clothing hung heavy on the skin.

"Sir," protested Major Lescarbault. The eyes were wide and shocked in his gaunt face.

"I dare tell a ranking Esper to stop quacking about a subject of which he's totally ignorant?" Danielis answered. "Well, it's past time that somebody did."

Woodworth recovered his poise. "All I said, son, was that we should consolidate our adepts and strike the Brodskyite center," he reproved. "What's wrong with that?"

Danielis clenched his fists. "Nothing," he said, "except it invites a worse disaster than you've brought on us yet."

"A setback or two," Lescarbault argued. "They did rout us on the west, but we turned their flank here by the Bay."

"With the net result that their main body pivoted, attacked, and split us in half," Danielis snapped. "The Espers have been scant use since then… now the rebels know they need vehicles to transport their weapons, and can be killed. Artillery zeroes in on their positions, or bands of woodsmen hit and run, leaving them dead, or the enemy simply goes around any spot where they're known to be. We haven't got enough adepts!"

"That's why I proposed gettin' them in one group too big to withstand," Woodworth said.

"And too cumbersome to be of any value," Danielis replied. He felt more than a little sickened, knowing how the Order had cheated him his whole life; yes, he thought, that was the real bitterness, not the fact that the adepts had failed to defeat the rebels—by failing, essentially, to break their spirit—but the fact that the adepts were only someone else's cat's paws, and every gentle, earnest soul in every Esper community was only someone's dupe.

Wildly he wanted to return to Laura—there'd been no chance thus far to see her—Laura and the kid, the last honest reality this fog-world had left him. He mastered himself and went on more evenly:

"The adepts, what few of them survive, will of course be helpful in defending San Francisco. An army free to move around in the field can deal with them, one way or another, but your... your weapons can repel an assault on the city walls. So that's where I'm going to take them."

Probably the best he could do. There was no word from the northern half of the loyalist army. Doubtless they'd withdrawn to the capital, suffering heavy losses en route. Radio jamming continued, hampering friendly and hostile communications alike. He had to take action, either retreat southward or fight his way through to the city. The latter course seemed wisest. He didn't believe that Laura had much to do with his choice.

"I'm no adept myself," Woodworth said. "I can't call them mind to mind."

"You mean you can't use their equivalent of radio," Danielis said brutally. "Well, you've got an adept in attendance. Have him pass the word."

Woodworth flinched. "I hope," he said, "I hope you understand this came as a surprise to me too."

"Oh, yes, certainly, Philosopher," Lescarbault said unbidden.

Woodworth swallowed. "I still hold with the Way and the Order," he said harshly. "There's nothin' else I can do. Is there? The Grand Seeker has promised a full explanation when this is over." He shook his head. "Okay, son, I'll do what I can."

A certain compassion touched Danielis as the blue robe disappeared into the fog. He rapped his orders the more severely.

Slowly his command got going. He was with the Second Brigade; the rest were strewn over the Peninsula in the fragments into which the rebels had knocked them. He hoped the equally scattered adepts, joining him on his march through the San Bruno range, would guide some of those units to him. But most, wandering demoralized, were sure to surrender to the first rebels they came upon.

He rode near the front, on a muddy road that snaked over the highlands. His helmet was a monstrous weight. The horse stumbled

beneath him, exhausted by—how many days?—of march, counter-
march, battle, skirmish, thin rations or none, heat and cold and fear,
in an empty land. Poor beast, he'd see that it got proper treatment
when they reached the city. That all those beasts behind him did, after
trudging and fighting and trudging again until their eyes were filmed
with fatigue.

*There'll be chance enough for rest in San Francisco. We're impregnable
there, walls and cannon and the Esper machines to landward, the sea that
feeds us at our backs. We can recover our strength, regroup our forces, bring
fresh troops down from Washington and up from the south by water. The
war isn't decided yet... God help us.*

I wonder if it will ever be.

*And then, will Jimbo Mackenzie come to see us, sit by the fire and swap
yarns about what we did? Or talk about something else, anything else? If
not, that's too high a price for victory.*

*Maybe not too high a price for what we've learned though. Strangers on
this planet... what else could have forged those weapons? The adepts will
talk if I myself have to torture them till they do.* But Danielis remembered
tales muttered in the fisher huts of his boyhood, after dark, when ghosts
walked in old men's minds. Before the holocaust there had been legends
about the stars, and the legends lived on. He didn't know if he would
be able to look again at the night sky without a shiver.

This damned fog—

Hoofs thudded. Danielis half drew his sidearm. But the rider was a
scout of his own, who raised a drenched sleeve in salute. "Colonel, an
enemy force about ten miles ahead by road. Big."

So we'll have to fight now. "Do they seem aware of us?"

"No, sir. They're proceeding east along the ridge there."

"Probably figure to occupy the Candlestick Park ruins," Danielis
murmured. His body was too tired for excitement. "Good stronghold,
that. Very well, Corporal." He turned to Lescarbault and issued instructions.

The brigade formed itself in the formlessness. Patrols went out.
Information began to flow back, and Danielis sketched a plan that

ought to work. He didn't want to try for a decisive engagement, only brush the enemy aside and discourage it from pursuit. His men must be spared, as many as possible, for the city defense and the eventual counteroffensi ve.

Lescarbault came back. "Sir! The radio jamming's ended!"

"What?" Danielis blinked, not quite comprehending.

"Yes, sir. I've been using a minicom," Lescarbault lifted the wrist on which his tiny transceiver was strapped, "for very short-range work, passing the battalion commanders their orders. The interference stopped a couple of minutes ago. Clear as daylight."

Danielis pulled the wrist toward his own mouth. "Hello, hello, radio wagon, this is the C.O. You read me?"

"Yes, sir," said the voice.

"They turned off the jammer in the city for a reason. Get me the open military band."

"Yes, sir." Pause, while men mumbled and water runneled unseen in the arroyos. A wraith smoked past Danielis' eyes. Drops coursed off his helmet and down his collar. The horse's mane hung sodden.

Like the scream of an insect:

"–here at once! Every unit in the field, get to San Francisco at once! We're under attack by sea!"

Danielis let go Lescarbault's arm. He stared into emptiness while the voice wailed on and forever on.

"–bombarding Potrero Point. Decks jammed with troops. They must figure to make a landing there—

Danielis' mind raced ahead of the words. It was as if Esp were no lie, as if he scanned the beloved city himself and felt her wounds in his own flesh. There was no fog around the Gate, of course, or so detailed a description could not have been given. Well, probably some streamers of it rolled in under the rusted remnants of the bridge, themselves like snowbanks against blue-green water and brilliant sky. But most of the Bay stood open to the sun. On the opposite shore lifted the Eastbay hills, green with gardens and agleam with villas; and Marin shouldered heavenward across the strait, looking to the roofs and walls and heights that were San Francisco. The convoy had gone between the coast defenses that could have smashed it, an unusually large convoy and not on time: but still the familiar big-bellied hulls, white sails, occasional fuming stacks, that kept the city fed. There had been an explanation about trouble with commerce raiders; and the fleet was passed on into the Bay, where San Francisco had no walls. Then the gun covers were taken off and the holds vomited armed men.

Yes, they did seize a convoy, those piratical schooners. Used radio jamming of their own, together with ours, that choked off any cry of warning. They threw our supplies overboard and embarked the bossman militia. Some spy or traitor gave them the recognition signals. Now the capital lies open to them, her garrison stripped, hardly an adept left in Esper Central, the Sierrans thrusting against her southern gates, and Laura without me.

"We're coming!" Danielis yelled. His brigade groaned into speed behind him. They struck with a desperate ferocity that carried them deep into enemy positions and then stranded them in separated groups. It became knife and saber in the fog. But Danielis, because he led the charge, had already taken a grenade on his breast.

East and south, in the harbor district and at the wreck of the Peninsula wall, there was still some fighting. As he rode higher, Mackenzie saw how those parts were dimmed by smoke, which the wind scattered to show rubble that had been houses. The sound of firing drifted to him. But otherwise the city shone untouched, roofs and white walls in a web of streets, church spires raking the sky like masts, Federal House on Nob Hill and the Watchtower on Telegraph Hill as he remembered them from childhood visits. The Bay glittered insolently beautiful.

But he had no time for admiring the view, nor for wondering where Laura huddled. The attack on Twin Peaks must be swift, for surely Esper Central would defend itself.

On the avenue climbing the opposite side of those great humps, Speyer led half the Rolling Stones. (Yamaguchi lay dead on a pockmarked beach.) Mackenzie himself was taking this side. Horses clopped along Portola, between blankly shuttered mansions; guns trundled and creaked, boots knocked on pavement, moccasins slithered, weapons rattled, men breathed heavily, and the hex corps whistled against unknown demons. But silence overwhelmed the noise, echoes trapped it and let it die. Mackenzie recollected nightmares when he fled down a corridor that had no end. *Even if they don't cut loose at us*, he thought bleakly, *we've got to seize their place before our nerve gives out.*

Twin Peaks Boulevard turned off Portola and wound steeply to the right. The houses ended; wild grasses alone covered the quasi-sacred hills up to the tops, where stood the buildings forbidden to all but adepts. Those two soaring, iridescent, fountainlike skyscrapers had been raised by night, within a matter of weeks. Something like a moan stirred at Mackenzie's back.

"Bugler, sound the advance. On the double!"

A child's jeering, the notes lifted and were lost. Sweat stung Mackenzie's eyes. If he failed and was killed, that didn't matter too much... after everything that had happened... but the regiment, the regiment—

Flame shot across the street, the color of hell. There went a hiss and a roar. The pavement lay trenched, molten, smoking and reeking. Mackenzie wrestled his horse to a standstill. A warning only. But if they had enough adepts to handle us, would they bother trying to scare us off? "Artillery, open fire!"

The field guns bellowed together, not only howitzers but motorized 75s taken along from Alemany Gate's emplacements. Shells went overhead with a locomotive sound. They burst on the walls above and the racket thundered back down the wind.

Mackenzie tensed himself for a Esper blast, but none came. Had they knocked out the final defensive post in their own first barrage? Smoke cleared from the heights and he saw that the colors that played in the tower were dead and that wounds gaped across loveliness, showing unbelievably thin framework. It was like seeing the bones of a woman who had been murdered by his hand.

Quick, though! He issued a string of commands and led the horse and foot on. The battery stayed where it was, firing and firing with hysterical fury. The dry, brown grass started to burn as red-hot fragments scattered across the slope. Through mushroom bursts, Mackenzie saw the building crumble. Whole sheets of facing broke and fell to earth. The skeleton vibrated, took a direct hit and sang in metal agony, slumped and twisted apart.

What was that which stood within?

There were no separate rooms, no floors, nothing but girders, enigmatic machines, here and there a globe still aglow like a minor sun. The structure had enclosed something nearly as tall as itself, a finned and shining column, almost like a rocket shell but impossibly huge and fair.

Their spaceship, Mackenzie thought in the clamor. *Yes, of course, the ancients had begun making spaceships, and we always figured we would again someday. This, though—!*

The archers lifted a tribal speech. The riflemen and cavalry took it up, crazy, jubilant, the howl of a beast of prey. By Satan, we've whipped the stars themselves! As they burst onto the hillcrest, the shelling stopped and their yells overrode the wind. Smoke was as acrid as blood smell in their nostrils.

A few dead blue-robes could be seen in the debris. Some half-dozen survivors milled toward the ship. A bowman let fly. His arrow glanced off the landing gear but brought the Espers to a halt. Troopers poured over the shards to capture them.

Mackenzie reined in. Something that was not human lay crushed near a machine. Its blood was a deep violet color. *When the people have seen this, that's the end of the Order.* He felt no triumph. At St. Helena he had come to appreciate how fundamentally good the believers were.

But this was no moment for regret, or for wondering how harsh the future would be with man taken entirely off the leash. The building on the other peak was still intact. He had to consolidate his position here, then help Phil if need be.

However, the minicom said, "Come on and join me, Jimbo. The fracas is over," before he had completed his task. As he rode alone toward Speyer's place, he saw a Pacific States flag flutter up the mast on that skyscraper's top.

Guards stood awed and nervous at the portal. Mackenzie dismounted and walked inside. The entry chamber was a soaring, shimmering fantasy of colors and arches, through which men moved troll-like. A corporal led him down a hall. Evidently this building had been used for headquarters, offices, storage and less-understandable purposes… There was a room whose door had been blown down with dynamite. The fluid abstract murals were stilled, scarred and sooted. Four ragged troopers pointed guns at the two beings whom Speyer was questioning.

One slumped at something that might answer to a desk. The avian face was buried in seven-fingered hands and the rudimentary wings quivered with sobs. *Are they able to cry, then?* Mackenzie thought, astonished, and had a sudden wish to take the being in his arms and offer what comfort he was able.

The other one stood erect in a robe of woven metal. Great topaz eyes met Speyer's from a seven-foot height, and the voice turned accented English into music.

"—a G-type star some fifty light-years hence. It is barely visible to the naked eye, though not in this hemisphere."

The major's fleshless, bristly countenance jutted forward as if to peck. "When do you expect reinforcements?"

"There will be no other ship for almost a century, and it will bring only personnel. We are isolated by space and time; few can come to work here, to seek to build a bridge of minds across that gulf."

"Yeah," Speyer nodded prosaically. "The light speed limit. I thought so. If you're telling the truth."

The being shuddered. "Nothing is left for us but to speak truth and pray that you will understand and help. Revenge, conquest, any form of mass violence is impossible when so much space and time lies between. Our labor has been done in the mind and heart. It is not too late, even now. The most crucial facts can still be kept hidden—oh, listen to me, for the sake of your unborn!"

Speyer nodded to Mackenzie. "Everything okay?" he said. "We got us a full bag here. About twenty left alive, this fellow the bossman. Seems like they're the only ones on Earth."

"We guessed there couldn't be many," the colonel said. His tone and his feelings were alike ashen. "When we talked it over, you and me, and tried to figure what our clues meant. They'd have to be few, or they'd've operated more openly."

"Listen, listen," the being pleaded. "We came in love. Our dream was to lead you—to make you lead yourselves—toward peace, fulfillment… Oh, yes, we would also gain, gain yet another race with whom we could someday converse as brothers. But there are many races in the universe. It was chiefly for your own tortured sakes that we wished to guide your future."

"That controlled history notion isn't original with you," Speyer grunted. "We've invented it for ourselves now and then on Earth. The last time it led to the Hellbombs. No, thanks!"

"But we know! The Great Science predicts with absolute certainty—"

"Predicted this?" Speyer waved a hand at the blackened room.

"There are fluctuations. We are too few to control so many savages in every detail. But do you not wish an end to war, to all your ancient sufferings? I offer you that for your help today."

"You succeeded in starting a pretty nasty war yourselves," Speyer said.

The being twisted its fingers together. "That was an error. The plan remains, the only way to lead your people toward peace. I, who have traveled between suns, will get down before your boots and beg you—"

"Stay put!" Speyer flung back. "If you'd come openly, like honest folk, you'd have found some to listen to you. Maybe enough, even. But no, your do-gooding had to be subtle and crafty. You knew what was right for us. We weren't entitled to any say in the matter. God in heaven, I've never heard anything so arrogant!"

The being lifted its head. "Do you tell children the whole truth?"

"As much as they're ready for."

"Your child-culture is not ready to hear these truths."

"Who qualified you to call us children—besides yourselves?"

"How do you know you are adult?"

"By trying adult jobs and finding out if I can handle them. Sure, we make some ghastly blunders, we humans. But they're our own. And we learn from them. You're the ones who won't learn, you and that damned psychological science you were bragging about that wants to fit every living mind into the one frame it can understand.

"You wanted to reestablish the centralized state, didn't you? Did you ever stop to think that maybe feudalism is what suits man? Some one place to call our own, and belong to, and be part of; a community with traditions and honor; a chance for the individual to make decisions that count; a bulwark for liberty against the central overlords, who'll always want more and more power; a thousand different ways to live. We've always built supercountries here on Earth, and we've always knocked them apart again. I think maybe the whole idea is wrong. And maybe this time we'll try something better. Why not a world of little states, too well-rooted to dissolve in a nation, too small to do much harm—slowly rising above petty jealousies and spite but keeping their identities—a thousand separate approaches to our problems. Maybe then we can solve a few of them... for ourselves!"

"You will never do so," the being said. "You will be torn in pieces all over again."

"That's what you think. I think otherwise. But whichever is right— and I bet this is too big a universe for either of us to predict—we'll have made a free choice on Earth. I'd rather be dead than domesticated.

"The people are going to learn about you as soon as Judge Brodsky's been reinstated. No, sooner. The regiment will hear today, the city tomorrow, just to make sure no one gets ideas about suppressing the truth again. By the time your next spaceship comes, we'll be ready for it: in our own way, whatever it is."

The being drew a fold of robe about its head. Speyer turned to Mackenzie. His face was wet. "Anything... you want to say... Jimbo?"

"No," Mackenzie mumbled. "Can't think of anything. Let's get our command organized here. I don't expect we'll have to fight any more though. It seems to be about ended down there."

"Sure." Speyer drew an uneven breath. "The enemy troops elsewhere are bound to capitulate. They've got nothing left to fight for. We can start patching up pretty soon."

There was a house with a patio whose wall was covered by roses. The street outside had not yet come back to life, so that silence dwelt here under the yellow sunset. A maidservant showed Mackenzie through the back door and departed. He walked toward Laura, who sat on a bench beneath a willow. She watched him approach but did not rise. One hand rested on a cradle.

He stopped and knew not what to say. How thin she was!

Presently she told him, so low he could scarcely hear: "Tom's dead."

"Oh, no." Darkness came and went before his eyes.

"I learned the day before yesterday, when a few of his men straggled home. He was killed in San Bruno."

Mackenzie did not dare join her, but his legs would not upbear him. He sat down on the flagstones and saw curious patterns in their arrangement. There was nothing else to look at.

Her voice ran on above him, toneless: "Was it worth it? Not only Tom, but so many others, killed for a point of politics?"

"More than that was at stake," he said.

"Yes, I heard on the radio. I still can't understand how it was worth it. I've tried very hard, but I can't."

He had no strength left to defend himself. "Maybe you're right, duck. I wouldn't know."

"I'm not sorry for myself," she said. "I still have Jimmy. But Tom was cheated out of so much."

He realized all at once that there was a baby, and he ought to take his grandchild to him and think thoughts about life going on into the future. But he was too empty.

"Tom wanted him named after you," she said.

Did you, Laura? he wondered. Aloud: "What are you going to do now?"

"I'll find something."

He made himself glance at her. The sunset burned on the willow leaves above and on her face, which was now turned toward the infant he could not see. "Come back to Nakamura," he said.

"No. Anywhere else."

"You always loved the mountains," he groped. "We–"

"No." She met his eyes. "It isn't you, Dad. Never you. But Jimmy is not going to grow up a soldier." She hesitated. "I'm sure some of the Espers will keep going, on a new basis but with the same goals. I think we should join them. He ought to believe in something different from what killed his father and work for it to become real. Don't you agree?"

Mackenzie climbed to his feet against Earth's hard pull. "I don't know," he said. "Never was a thinker... Can I see him?"

"Oh, Dad..."

He went over and looked down at the small sleeping form. "If you marry again," he said, "and have a daughter, would you call her for her mother?" He saw Laura's head bend downward and her hands clench. Quickly he said, "I'll go now. I'd like to visit you some more, tomorrow or sometime, if you'll have me."

Then she came to his arms and wept. He stroked her hair and murmured, as he had done when she was a child. "You do want to return to the mountains, don't you? They're your country too, your people, where you belong."

"Y-you'll never know how much I want to."

"Then why not?" he cried.

His daughter straightened herself. "I can't," she said. "Your war is ended. Mine has just begun."

Because he had trained that will, he could only say, "I hope you win it."

"Perhaps in a thousand years–" She could not continue.

Night had fallen when he left her. Power was still out in the city, so the street lamps were dark and the stars stood forth above all roofs.

The squad that waited to accompany their colonel to barracks looked wolfish by lantern light. They saluted him and rode at his back, rifles ready for trouble; but there was only the iron sound of horseshoes.

CPSIA information can be obtained
at www.ICGtesting.com
Printed in the USA
BVHW070236131021
618791BV00004B/9

9 789527 303184